DATE DUE			
JUN 3 0 1986			
SEP 0 8 1988			
JUL - 8 '92			
APR 12 1994			
MAR 1 8 1998			
FEB 2 5 2004			
MAY 1 4 2008			

ENHANCING SELF-CONCEPT IN EARLY CHILDHOOD

Early Education Series

Child Care: A Comprehensive Guide
Auerbach, S., Ph.D. (Ed.)

Day Care: Problems, Process and Prospects
Peters, D.L., Ph.D., (Ed.)

Day Care and Early Education Magazine

Headstart: A Tragi-Comedy with Epilogue
Payne, J.S., Ed.D., Mercer, C.D., M.S., Payne, R.A. and

Let's Play and Learn
Hartman, H.

Rationale for Child Care - Programs vs Politics
Auerbach, S., Ph.D.

Model Programs and Their Components
Auerbach, S., Ph.D.

Sparks: Activities to Help Children Learn at Home
Belton, S., M.A. and Terbough, C., M.A.

Home Visitor's Kit:
Training and Practitioner Materials for Paraprofessionals in Family Settings
Gotts, E., Ph.D.

Enhancing Self-Concept in Early Childhood: Theory and Practice
Samuels, Shirley, C., Ed.D.

ENHANCING SELF-CONCEPT IN EARLY CHILDHOOD

THEORY AND PRACTICE

Shirley C. Samuels, Ed.D.
Manhattanville College

HUMAN SCIENCES PRESS
72 Fifth Avenue   3 Henrietta Street
NEW YORK, NY 10011 ● LONDON, WC2E 8LU

Library of Congress Catalog Number 76-58348

ISBN: 0-87705-316-2 Hard
ISBN: 0-87705-353-7 Soft

Copyright © 1977 by Human Sciences Press
72 Fifth Avenue, New York, New York 10011

Printed in the United States of America
9 98765432

Library of Congress Cataloging in Publication Data

Samuels, Shirley C
    Enhancing self-concept in early childhood.

    Bibliography:
    Includes index.
    1. Child psychology.   2. Self-perception.
3. Self-respect.   I. Title.
BF723.S28S25   155.4'18   76-58348

Dedicated
with great affection to Stan, Jeff,
Nita and Mark, whose encouragement
and sacrifice enabled this book to
become a reality.

INTRODUCTION

My mother loves me.
  I feel good.
I feel good because she loves me.

I am good because I feel good
I feel good because I am good
My mother loves me because I am good.

My mother does not love me.
  I feel bad.
I feel bad because she does not love me
  I am bad because I feel bad

I feel bad because I am bad
I am bad because she does not love me
She does not love me because I am bad.[1]

[1]R. D. Laing, *Knots.* New York: Pantheon Books (a division of Random House), 1972, p. 9 (Reprinted with permission.)

CONTENTS

PREFACE

Early childhood is a critical period for the development of self-concept. A key goal of parents and teachers of children under the age of six is to enhance children's self-feelings. In order to do so, parents and teachers must have information relating to self-concept theory and the empirical evidence supporting it, so that they can use this knowledge in their day-to-day interaction with children.

In the early years, first parents and then teachers are also the "significant others" who help children develop attitudes relating to their bodies, their social selves, and their cognitive selves. The young child with negative self-feelings has not yet developed rigid defense mechanisms that prevent changes from being effected by constructive intervention. When rigid defense mechanisms develop later on, it is more difficult for the child to be open to new experiences and to allow a change in self-concept to occur as readily as it did during the preschool years. Moreover, in the early years, parents are more available to work with teachers as partners.

Manifest behavior gives us a view of children's perceptions of themselves. This overt behavior allows teachers to infer how children see themselves, since young children are less likely than older ones to defensively hide their feelings. However, individual children reveal their self-feelings differently. These varying patterns are discussed in this book.

This book is intended to help the parent and teacher with the child who is not severely emotionally disturbed, and to recognize that further help is needed for the one who is. The suggestions on classroom techniques focus on ways to work with normal nursery school and kindergarten-aged children.

The importance of the unconscious self is recognized, since unconscious processes are highly significant in controlling behavior and cannot be ignored. By observing the self in action, substantial clues can be revealed of attitudes children have toward themselves that they may not be completely aware of. Parents and teachers are provided with a beginning understanding of these unconscious processes, for there is a clarification of the role of the unconscious in the development of the self.

Much of the book discusses extensively race, sex, and social class and their relationship to self-concept. The attitudes and forces of society relating to these variables begin to affect the child before the child comes into direct contact with others outside of the family. The family indirectly transmits these attitudes to the child by the time the child enters school.

The theoretical and empirical literature that has accumulated within the past few decades has been extensive. Part I (Chapter 1) provides a theoretical perspective for the book. It defines each of the dimensions of the self-concept (body self, social self, cognitive self, and self-esteem) and discusses the predominant self-concept theories: psychoanalytic theory, social psychological theory, phenomenological theory, and reference group theory. The varying points of view regarding consistency and the striving for self-esteem and the general factors, which are significant for the development of identity from birth to age five, are reviewed and discussed in this section.

Part II summarizes and evaluates the empirical literature. The first chapter in this section (Chapter 2) discusses the empirical problems inherent in the measurement of self-concept. This chapter reviews the studies with young children using self-report and observational methods and discusses the effects of maternal self-concept and child rearing practices on child self-concept. Major development of the child's self-concept occurs in the early years within the context of the child's interactions with the family, and particularly with the mother. Evidence for both the "looking glass," and the "modeling theory" are given, supporting the point of view that how parents treat their children and how they feel about themselves both have an effect on their children's self-concepts. Specific child-rearing practices seem less important than parental attitudes toward themselves and their children.

Chapter 3 summarizes the research relating teacher acceptance of themselves with their attitudes toward the children they teach and reviews the studies on the self-fulfilling prophecy. Empirical work on the child's cognitive self and social self are also explored, highlighting the areas of achievement, independence, anxiety, curiosity, and creativity.

Chapter 4 reviews the theories and research on sex-role development, discussing and evaluating the biological and environmental influences acting on each sex starting before birth. It summarizes the research relating to the treatment of teachers toward boys and girls.

Chapter 5 considers the effects of race, social class, and desegregation on child self-concept. Much of the evidence is contradictory, but this book evaluates the results of studies focusing on psychological, historical, and cultural variables.

The theory and research reviewed in the first two parts of the book provide the background for the emphasis in Part III on how teachers of children under six can meaningfully provide experiences to enhance children's self-concepts. Although all the dimensions of self-concept relate to one another, and global self-esteem results from positive feelings in body self, social self, and cognitive self, specific weakness may occur in only one of the dimensions. Therefore, diagnosis should pinpoint specific weaknesses, so that remediation can be offered in that narrow domain. For this reason, most of Part III discusses self-concept in its separate dimensions. It gives curricular suggestions and annotated bibliographies of children's books for each self-concept dimension. The emphasis is on providing the rationale for daily classroom experiences for enhancing self-concept. The list of suggestions is not meant to be exhaustive but is intended to stimulate the teacher's thinking. In that way, teachers can use their own creativity and experience to develop a program to meet the needs of each individual child based on the understandings gained from this book.

Chapter 6 begins with a brief description of observational techniques to enable the teacher to objectively diagnose children's views of themselves and discusses the importance of remediation. It discusses general teacher attitudes and behaviors that can enhance and maintain global self-esteem. It also reviews the factors related to cognitive adequacy such as success experiences, appropriate praise, and the need to teach concepts related to children's cultural experiences.

Chapter 7 is concerned with the body image: physically, kinesthetically, emotionally, racially, and sexually. Curricular ideas, books for children and methods for dealing with feelings relating to separation, physical handicaps, and the birth of a sibling are discussed.

Chapter 8 stresses the need to work with parents who are still the most important "significant others" for their children. Suggestions are made on how to make them feel more adequate as parents. This chapter urges teachers to include curricular materials relating to the family, sex and culture of all the children in their classrooms to enhance their social selves. Suggestions are given for activities and classroom materials and books which are non-sexist and which focus on minority group children. The value of in-service programs for teachers is discussed and techniques are suggested for working with anxious, withdrawn, and aggressive children.

The studies that are quoted throughout the book are summarized. Specifics such as operational definitions, instruments used, and characteristics of the sample population are largely omitted so as not to encumber the reader with methodological details. A complete bibliography is provided to assist those interested in obtaining more complete information.

In the book, "the child" and "the children" are used as much as possible, as are the pronouns "their" and "them." "Teachers" is also pluralized. Masculine and feminine pronouns are used interchangeably.

I thank and acknowledge the following people who kindly read the entire manuscript and generously offered their critical evaluations: Arthur Zelman, M.D., psychiatrist and associate director of the Center for Preventive Psychiatry in White Plains; Thomas Lopez, Ph.D., clinical psychologist and child psychoanalyst; Harriet Schnurr, Ed.D., psychotherapist; Gertrude Weiss, M.A., nursery school teacher and director of the Therapeutic Nursery School at Grasslands Hospital in Valhalla; Stella Chess, M.D., Professor of Child Psychiatry and director of child and adolescent services at New York University Medical Center; Gilbert Kliman, M.D., psychiatrist and director of the Center for Preventive Psychiatry; and Stanley Samuels, Ph.D., Associate Professor of Experimental Neurology at New York University Medical Center. Recognition must also be given to Hope Leichter, Ph.D., Professor of Education at Teacher's College, Columbia University, whose valuable guidance nurtured this work at its conception.

Part I

THEORETICAL PERSPECTIVE

Chapter 1

SELF-CONCEPT DEFINITIONS AND THEORETICAL FOUNDATIONS

Kinch defined the self-concept as being ". . . that organization of qualities that the individual attributes to himself" (Kinch, 1963, p. 481). If the individual reflects on these attributes, that person is referring to the conscious self, and it is that part of the conscious self that the individual is willing to reveal. The problem with this definition is that we do not necessarily get an accurate picture of the individual's self-feelings and perceptions from what we are told.

Defense mechanisms allow people to deceive themselves and others so that enhancement of the self-picture frequently occurs. Hilgard (1949) was one of the first theorists to state that the self should be defined in such a way that unconscious as well as conscious materials are included. Vernon (1964), expanding this idea, postulated that the self has a series of conceptual levels that consist of the social selves, the conscious private self, the insightful self, and the repressed or depth self. According to him, the social or public selves are displayed openly, the conscious private self is perceived and can be verbalized to those close to us: the insightful self can be brought to the surface by looking at behavior and fantasy and may be rationalized and concealed from the conscious level; and the repressed self can be reached as a result of depth therapy.

DIMENSIONS OF SELF-CONCEPT

The important dimensions of self-concept are body self (or body image), cognitive self, social self, and self-esteem (which is the evaluative aspect of the self-concept) (Sarbin, 1952; Smith, 1960; Horrocks & Jackson, 1972). In other words, we put a value on our bodies, our academic ability, and our selves in roles as student, friend, or son or daughter and we use adjectives such as good and bad to describe ourselves in each of these dimensions.

Body Image

Body image, which includes the physical and sexual self, plays a major role in psychological growth. Schilder (1950) theorized about the body image, and his theory was elaborated on by Kolb (1959a, b) and Schonfeld (1963). Body image is a condensed representation of individuals' current, past, and fantasied experiences of their own bodies. It has both conscious and unconscious aspects (Schonfeld, 1963). The internalized mental image we have of ourselves in our minds may or may not closely resemble our actual body structure. If the cognitive construction of self (reality) conflicts with the somatic perception of self, integration of the total self becomes difficult. It is the task of normal development for this integration to occur. Otherwise, maladjustment in the form of neurosis, psychosis, or problem behavior results (Horrocks & Jackson, 1972). Research studies with adults have shown that people who have negative feelings about their bodies are also likely to feel negatively about themselves as total people and vice versa (Secord & Jourand, 1953; Kurtz, 1971).

Schonfeld (1963, p. 846) defined the constellation of psychological components that determine the "structure" of the body image on both the conscious and unconscious levels: "(1) the *actual subjective perception of the body,* both as to appearance and ability to function; (2) the *internalized psychological factors* arising out of the individual's personal and emotional experiences as well as distortions of the body-concept expressed as somatic delusions; (3) the *sociological factors,* namely how parents and society react to the individual; and, (4) the *ideal body* image, formulated by the individual's attitudes toward the body derived from his experiences, perceptions, comparisons, and identifications with the bodies of other persons."

These factors become operative and begin the process of self definition early in life. Kolb (1959) suggested that the organization of body image probably begins before birth when the fetus is exposed to sensory perceptions. Newborns acquire knowledge of their bodies from tactile impressions with progressive growth. In sucking and feeding, the mouth is the first area to be stimulated. Infants' exploratory movements over their bodies, the use of their hands to make contact with their mothers and their mouths, their grasping of objects in space, all provide primary kinesthetic and tactile sensations (Hoffer, 1949, 1950). These experiences provide varying degrees of pleasurable and unpleasurable somatic stimulation by self and others (Kolb, 1959 a, b). They are the processes on which are founded the beginnings of self-awareness, as the child subjectively starts life unable to differentiate self from others (Mahler, 1963; Jacobson, 1964).

In order to develop an effective identity, it is crucial that a sense of separateness be achieved. At first, the mother and infant feel a sharing of body limits and the neophyte cannot separate self from nonself. To the infant ego, somatic (body) pain (such as hunger, which is experienced as pain) represents a signal of danger and is threatening to the body ego, and pleasurable feelings (when a child is well fed) are a signal of body security (Goldfarb, 1963). It is important that confirmation and reinforcement of infants' sensations are accurate so that they can differentiate between disturbances in their biological and emotional experiences and be able to separate self from nonself, rather than feeling that they are under the influence of external forces only. The psychoanalytic viewpoint states that children's dependence on their mothers to alleviate the tensions originating in their physiological processes will lead to the awareness that displeasure, tension, and discomfort are relieved by the mother's appearance. If discomfort is not consistently followed by appropriate response and relief, developing children are deprived of the essential groundwork for the perceptual and conceptual awareness of their own functions (Bruch, 1962). With consistent care, the mother's image gradually becomes differentiated from the rest of the world and the child learns to feel that he is a separate being (Hoffer, 1950; Bruch, 1962; Mahler, 1963; 1975; Jacobson, 1964). The mother also expresses her attitudes and evaluates her child's body by the way she holds, feeds, touches, and cares for the child. When the child is older, the approval is conveyed verbally. With this good care, the child recognizes and accepts separation from the mother in the later part of the first year (Jacobson, 1964; Mahler, 1963, 1975). In a study of children between eight and eighteen months, Lewis and Brooks-Gunn (1972) found that by the age of eight months in the normal infant, the self as differentiated from others is well established and such specific categories as size, sex, or efficacy may also be established.

Marjorie McDonald's (1970) investigation of skin color

and personality development from a psychoanalytic perspective included case examples to support her theory that "skin color anxiety" is a normal, developmental characteristic. She related this anxiety to the Freudian stages of libidinal development (oral, anal, and genital stages) and demonstrated its function in the development of object relationships (relationships with other people). She theorized that in the first year of life, the skin figures prominently in the beginning establishment of psychological identity and that the infant observes skin color differences before the end of the first year, during the period of stranger anxiety. When circumstances in the first year lead to excessive or aggressive skin stimulation or lack of loving stimulation, the child's sense of separateness may be insecure and remain a vulnerable spot in development, resulting in disturbances in body image with corresponding disturbances in representations of self and others. The skin continues to establish body identity throughout life. She theorized that disturbed white and nonwhite children have color anxiety about dark skin because they equate dark skin with dirtiness and with castration anxiety. She stated that it is difficult to find psychoanalytic studies of infants and young children or of adults to confirm or refute the basic skin color anxiety because of its preverbal roots.

Social Self

The social self includes the racial, ethnic, cultural, and religious self. The society in which children live affects their self feelings because that group (family, school, church, and society as a whole) confers status and has expectations that children internalize and strive to live up to. These expectations are conveyed to them by the significant people in their lives. At first, it is the parents who form the link between social structure and personality. Later, teachers and peers help to define the social self. Some theorists have proposed that each social self perception is specific to the expectations of one or another group to which people belong and with which they identify (Brim, 1960; Gergen, 1968; 1969; 1971; Horrocks & Jackson, 1972). According to Horrocks and Jackson (1972), each of us has an almost infinite number of identities that are a combination of self-concepts in various roles, and a system of values that develop over time, the first two decades being the most crucial. Gergen (1965, 1968, 1971) stated that an individual's self-feeling at any one time centers primarily around the social role or status that is of major importance at that time. Those self-feelings may change from situation to situation. However, Gergen (1968) felt that with most social relationships, the person provides a constant stimulus value that is relatively stable and coherent and has constant effects on the behavior of others.

It appears that a basic social self is internalized and predisposes a child to respond in predetermined ways, but the social self can be modified and changed in new social situations later in life. This makes school a significant social institution for those children whose families lack social status in our society, since teachers can provide experiences leading to positive self feelings in school as a new social situation.

Cognitive Self

Cognition is a process by which individuals become aware of and gain meaning from an object or events in their environment. Children's attitudes toward themselves, as well as their knowledge of themselves, result from their increasing cognitive growth and the attitudes of those around them. In effect, children have within themselves certain organized processes that allow them to move toward greater self understanding in interaction with their environment. A cognitively processed experience may not be an exact replication of what occurred. The organism changes it to fit its already existent experiences and needs (Horrocks & Jackson, 1972).

The development of the different cognitive selves in early childhood was discussed by Sarbin (1952). He suggested that, in the interaction with objects and people at different times in maturation and personal growth, various empirical selves or cognitive substructures are organized. First to develop is an individual's conceptions of his body (the somatic self), then his sense organs and musculature (the receptor-effector self), and finally his concept of social behavior (the social self). In Sarbin's theory, the referrant for the "I" in each individual in the present is a cross section in the total cognitive organization that embraces these more or less enduring substructures.

Piaget focused on cognitive development (Piaget & Inhelder, 1969), defining four stages of development: (1) the sensorimotor stage, which begins at birth and lasts to about the age of two, (2) the preoperational stage, which occurs from about ages two to seven, (3) the concrete operations stage, which is present from about seven to eleven, and (4) the formal operations stage, which begins about the age of eleven. Movement time from stage to stage is influenced by four primary factors: (1) maturation, or physical growth, (2) experience, with materials to be manipulated and thought about, (3) social interaction, dependent on other people, and (4) equilibration, the process of building and rebuilding new mental structures that becomes possible as the result of maturation, experience and social interaction. Cognitive development occurs as the child assimilates (integrates new stimulus events into existing patterns of behavior) and accommodates (modifies her behavior so that there is change or upward development of cognitive structures). In other words, a child cannot learn something new until she has developed internal structures that enable her to assimilate new concepts, but when that internal development has occurred, she can accommodate or change her behavior so that growth is facilitated. Assimilation and accommodation go hand in hand to facilitate this process.

Individuals go through six substages during the sensorimotor period (Piaget, 1952; 1954; 1967). They start life primarily utilizing their reflexes. When the newborn baby is stimulated, there is response by the basic reflexes of sucking, grasping, crying, and movement of arms, trunk, and head. Infants don't seem to be able to differentiate between objects. For example, they will suck on anything placed in their mouths. After a few weeks, they begin to accommodate to their environment. They begin to look for a nipple, a behavior that goes beyond the sucking reflex. They still have no concept of objects and are not aware of causality.

The second substage, which starts at about one month and lasts until four months, is characterized by hand-mouth visual and aural coordination and development of the ability to follow visually moving objects. Children may continue to follow the path of an object after it disappears. Substage three, occurring between the fourth and the eighth months, is when eye-hand coordination develops and children can grasp what they see. During this time, children can reproduce a sound that they hear. They are becoming aware of the permanence of objects, as they anticipate the positions where objects will fall by moving their eyes to that place when the objects are dropped.

Substage four behavior (eight to twelve months) is characterized by children's anticipation of actions. Previously, they always depended on the immediate actions in the environment before reacting. Now they can react beforehand. The constancy of size and shape become stabilized as shown by their coordinated movements. They can turn a bottle around to get the nipple because they know that objects do not change in shape when the perspective changes. For the first time, the child begins to search for objects that disappear, while before this if an object was out of sight, it no longer existed for the child.

Substage five (twelve to eighteen months) is characterized by children's new ability to experiment and to develop new ways to solve problems by coordinating new patterns. Previously they combined old patterns to solve new problems. As mentioned, around the age of twelve months (by the beginning of this period) children are aware that objects continue to exist even though they cannot be seen; but at first children search for objects that are hidden in the place that objects are usually hidden, not in the last place that they saw the objects put. For example, if a toy is placed under a pillow where it is usually placed and then taken from there and put in a new place, the child looks for the toy in the familiar place rather than the new place, even though the child witnessed the change. In stage five, the child is able to search for objects in the last displacement area in which the objects were placed. For the first time, objects beyond the self are seen as causes of actions.

Substage six (eighteen to twenty-four months) terminates in children's ability to see objects internally and to be able to solve problems without active experimentation. We know that solutions are arrived at internally when children make mental combinations independent of immediate experience. Now children are able for the first time to find objects that they don't see. They know that objects are permanent. At the end of this period, children are no longer restricted to sensorimotor behaviors to understand cause and effect. They can think things through internally and symbolically and intellectual development is no long dominated by immediate perceptual and motor activities. For example, children can go right to opening up a box or a drawer without trial and error.

The process described above, occurring during the sensorimotor stage from birth to about the age of two, allows children to separate gradually their bodies from the rest of the world; as they do so, they get to know their bodies better. As children develop language and locomotion, they get an increasingly clearer concept of themselves as individuals separate in body and action from objects and other people. Maturation, experience with objects, and social interaction combine to enable children to define themselves cognitively as separate from others and to recognize that things exist even though they are not present.

The preoperational stage, from the age of about two to seven, is a period when children grow in their ability to use language as symbols of objects. Piaget (1926) suggested that children use primarily egocentric speech up until the age of about four or five. The speech is not primarily communicative, but children are having a conversation with themselves in the presence of others. By the age of six or seven, socialized speech is more possible. At this time children listen to one another's communications. During the preoperational stage there is a gradual transition from egocentric to socialized speech. Self-concept enhancement is dependent on the adult's ability to accept children's egocentricity without depreciating them for being "selfish.'

Piaget (1967) stated that thought comes before language and that language development is based on the prior development of sensorimotor operations. However, when verbal behavior develops, it increases the range and speed of thought (Piaget & Inhelder, 1969). Children integrate self-concept by trying on different roles symbolically and vebalizing self-feelings in relation to them. For example, a girl may assume the role of a mother in play, using verbalization to extend her acceptance of self as she identifies with her mother's positive feelings toward her in nurturing activities.

During this stage, children's perceptions dominate their thinking. For example, if one of two equal glasses of water is changed to a wider glass, children will say the wider glass has less water, even though no water was removed. What is seen is less water in this glass than in the other one. Children cannot reason back to what was (equal amounts of water in equal-sized glasses put into a different form). In order for children to reason back to what was, they must continue to have active experiences with real objects; when they are cognitively ready to accommodate they will move on to the next stage of development. If children are forced to memorize the "right" answer before they are cognitively ready to understand it, their cognitive self-concepts would probably be negatively affected. That is, they may be inhibited from finding their own answers in the future, not realizing that *they* can discover solutions to problems.

During the stage of concrete operations, starting at about the age of seven, children can systematically and more flexibly reverse their thinking to what was, although the process still has to be concretely seen and manipulated. They have developed conservation, which allows them to classify, seriate, and reverse actions. When conservation has occurred, children have achieved the idea of constancy. Number, substance, and quantity are seen as permanent. That is, 3 is always 3 whether it looks like $1 + 2$ or $3 + 0$ (number conservation); or, when given the previous water task, they will say that after the water was put in a wider vessel the amount of water is the same in both glasses since no water was added or subtracted (substance conservation); or, when one of two balls of equal amounts of clay is made into a sausage, when asked which has more clay, they will say that the balls are the same (quantity conservation) (Piaget & Inhelder, 1969; Smart & Smart, 1972).

During the formal operations stage, individuals can think and reason in abstract terms and don't have to figure things out concretely. They can think using the scientific method and can use their minds to figure things out logically and objectively.

Self-Esteem

Self-esteem is the evaluative sector of the self-concept. An individual who has high self-esteem respects herself and considers herself worthy (Bibring, 1953; Coopersmith, 1967; Rosenberg, 1968; Felker, 1974), feels competent (White, 1963; Diggory, 1966), and has a sense of belonging (Maslow, 1954; Felker, 1974). If her self-esteem is low, she lacks respect for the self and believes she is incapable, insignificant, unsuccessful, and unworthy (Coopersmith, 1967). Bibring (1953, p. 24) stated that self-esteem is "(1) the wish to be worthy, to be loved, to be appreciated, not to be inferior or unworthy; (2) the wish to be strong, superior, great, secure, not to be weak and insecure; and (3) the wish to be good, to be loving, not to be aggressive, hateful and destructive."

A person may have positive feelings about his body, but consider himself a bad student; or his attitudes may be more global and all-encompassing—ranging from total acceptance to total rejection (Jersild, 1968). Akert (1959) believed that the individual does not accept or reject himself in a total sense, but that all self-concept dimensions correlate positively and significantly with total self-acceptance.

Coopersmith (1967) summarized the following factors considered significant as they relate to self-esteem: the amount of respectful, accepting, and concerned treatment received from significant others, the history of successes and status and position held in the world, the interpretation and modification of experiences that accord with values and aspirations, and the individual's manner of responding to devaluation.

Narcissism (self-love) is a normal developmental process that regulates self-esteem (Kohut, 1971; Kernberg, 1975). The psychoanalytic view states that the individual develops an "ego ideal" to maintain this self-love (Freud, 1925a). It develops from the primary narcissism of the infant when he could not separate self from nonself and felt he was the source of all pleasure. As he begins to see himself as separate, the mother is glorified and becomes part of him. The infant feels he is the admired, omnipotent, and idealized other (Reich, 1960). In normal development, identification with glorified parental figures to maintain self-love changes to a realistic critical conscience or superego (Sandler, et al. 1963). The ego judges itself by these standards, so that its worth is determined by how close it is to the ideal. Jacobson (1964) has discussed clearly the "processes" that transform the magic images of the self and the love objects into a unified ego ideal that has internalized parental prohibitions and demands and establishes self-critical superego functions. Basically, if the child's needs are not met appropriately at each developmental level, the psyche becomes unable to adequately regulate self-esteem by the use of adequate mechanisms. The ego ideal becomes unrealistic and the person becomes fixated at an infantile level that knows only extremes, either perfection or complete destruction (Reich, 1960). To ward off the pain of complete destruction, he develops an unreal, flawless self-image that compensates for the unacceptable real self. The uses of the unreal self interferes with the ability to create and value accurate images and to develop a graduated scale of values for assessing self-worth (De Saussure, 1971). When self-esteem should be relatively stable, it fluctuates widely in this situation. The overriding necessity to feel great and important alternate with feelings of emptiness and being left out, because the person feels worthless underneath.

SELF-CONCEPT AS SELF THEORY

Epstein (1973) stated accurately that no one as yet has succeeded in defining adequately self-concept as a hypothetical construct. Epstein (1973) and Ames (1975) felt that the self-concept is really a self theory. Self theory is better than self-concept because we can assimilate all self views into one theory. The self can be both subject and object, growth is considered, and emotions and cognition both become important. Epstein discussed the body self, which develops first, the inferred inner self (conscious and unconscious), and the moral self (self-evaluation). The most fundamental aspect of the theory is that the individual aims to optimize the pleasure-pain balance over her lifetime, to facilitate the maintenance of self-esteem, and to organize the data of experiences in a manner that can be coped with effectively. It was Epstein's view that a good self theory carries out these functions effectively. We should use emotions to infer postulates and each emotion implies an underlying cognition. Epstein stated that if we know a person's emotional disposition, it should be possible to reconstruct some of her major postulates. The stronger the positive or negative emotion, the more significant is the postulate that is implicated to maintain a function of the individual.

Whether we can accurately perceive it or not, there is no question that the self-concept affects the emotional, physical, social, and cognitive life of the individual. In order to get at a person's view of herself, observers must infer her self-concept from clues she gives us by her behavior, projective test responses, and from what she says about herself. The state of the art is such, that at this time, our methods are far from scientific. Yet, there is merit to sharpening our observations and making inferences that can be verified by further observation. Teachers are in an ideal position for such observation because they have access to material in a natural laboratory over a long period of time.

SUMMARY

Self-concept as defined in this section includes conscious and unconscious feelings about the self. The revelations that we make about ourselves give only partial information regarding individuals' true feelings about themselves. We must also infer these feelings from the person's behavior. The important dimensions of the self-concept are body self, social self, cognitive self, and self-esteem. People's internalized body image start at birth as they begin the process of separation of self from nonself. They need consistent, loving care for this separation to be successful.

As they interact with their environments, individuals evaluate their body based on these interactions. These individuals may have many social selves formed in each significant social situation that they encounter. The cognitive self develops as a result of growth and development as children interact with their environments. Self-esteem is the evaluative sector of the self-concept, which is theorized as being affected by childrens' interaction with "significant others" and their success and failure experiences. Individuals' self-feelings can range from total acceptance to total rejection with variations in between as a result of their differing self-evaluations in each self-concept dimension.

Psychoanalytic Theory

In psychoanalytic theory, self-esteem depends on the nature of the inner image to which we measure ourselves and on the ways at our disposal to live up to this image. Jacobson (1964, p. 22) stated:

> "By a realistic image of the self, we mean first of all, one that correctly mirrors the state and the characteristics, the potentialities and the abilities, the assets and the limits of our bodily and mental self: on the one hand, of our appearance, our anatomy and our physiology; on the other hand, of our ego, our conscious and preconscious feelings and thoughts, wishes, impulses, and attitudes, of our physical and mental function and behavior."

Jacobson also said that the superego must correctly depict our preconscious and conscious ideals and scales of value and be effective in its self-critical function. This process can best be accomplished if the initial sexual object— the mothering person—gratifies the self-preservative instincts by her initial treatment and attitudes toward the infant. As individuals develop, their own ego can take on the energy of the sexual instincts, leading to love for oneself.

Freud (1925a) stated that primary narcissism is present at the earliest stages of life. At this time, newborns are incapable of loving other people and all the energies at the disposal of the love instincts are invested in themselves. It is called the autoerotic stage because newborns do not know yet that others exist separate from themselves who are meeting their needs and they have a sense of self-sufficiency. At the beginning of life, neonates are not able to distinguish sensations of their own body from those of the external world. As children grow they become aware of the mother. She becomes omnipotent and idealized. The love and care of the mother allows the child to transfer this omnipotence and idealization onto himself.

Kohut (1971, 1972) and Kernberg (1970, 1974, 1975) recently have explored the development of narcissism. In the normal development of narcissism, in Kohut's theory, the equilibrium of primary narcissism is disturbed by the unavoidable shortcomings of maternal care. The child replaces the previous perfection by establishing a grandiose and exhibitionistic image of the self, called "the grandiose self," and gives over the previous perfection to an admired, omnipotent transitional self-object, called "the idealized parent image" (Kohut, 1971). In essence, the child feels, "I am perfect. You are perfect, but I am part of you." (Kohut, 1971, p. 27).

There has to be a replacement of the feeling of omnipotence by sound secondary narcissism where the attitudes about the self are realistic. Normal narcissism is shown throughout life by the pride we have in our endeavors and an acceptance and love of ourselves regardless of our shortcomings. Kohut stated (1972, p. 365) that the goal is "—to transform our archaic grandiosity and exhibitionism into realistic self-esteem and into pleasure with ourselves, and our yearning to be at one with the omnipotent self-object into the socially useful, adaptive and joyful capacity to be enthusiastic and to admire the great after whose lives, deeds and personalities we can permit ourselves to model our own."

If the child suffers from inadequate maternal care, the archaic forms remain unaltered, in that the grandiose self does not merge into relevant ego content and retains its grandiose form and the idealized image is not transformed into an introjected (internalized) superego but remains an archaic transitional self-object that maintains narcissistic homeostasis. Mahler (1975) has stated that when children are at the peak of their delusions of omnipotence, which happens at about fifteen months, their narcissism is particularly vulnerable to deflation. At this time, a separate body ego has already occurred and there is differentiation of self from nonself, but intrapsychic autonomy has not yet been achieved; that is, the power of the caretaker is still attributed to the self (Kohut, 1971). Growth occurs as a result of the mother's availability and some—but not too much— frustration for the child.

Kohut (1971) has separated the developmental sequence of narcissism from the developmental sequence of object love (love for others). He suggested that there are separate processes that are involved in narcissistic development and the development of love and hate of others. In other words, feelings and relations with others may or may not be affected when there are narcissistic problems. This is in opposition to Kernberg (1975) and others (Reich, 1960; Jacobson, 1964; Van Der Waals, 1965; Mahler, 1975) who feel that normal narcissism develops simultaneously with normal love for others and that pathological narcissism develops with hate for others. They therefore have suggested that we cannot divorce normal and pathological narcissism from the libidinal (loving) and aggressive drives. They have hypothesized that an imbalance in narcissism results from an imbalance between self-love and love of others and that it does not have an intrapsychic development of its own.

The grandiose self, which is considered normal at a particular point of development by Kohut (1971, 1972), is felt to be pathological by Kernberg (1970, 1974, 1975). According to Kernberg, this pathological self reflects a fusion of some aspects of the real self (the specialness of the child reinforced early in life), the ideal self (the fantasies and self images of power, etc. used as compensation by the young child for the experiences of severe oral frustration, rage, and envy), and the ideal object (the fantasy of an evergiving, everloving, and accepting mother to replace in reality the devalued parent). Pathological narcissism in this theory is not simply fixation to a normal early stage of development, but a defense against an intolerable reality in interpersonal relationships. Tension between the actual self on one hand and the ideal self and the ideal other on the other is eliminated by the development of an inflated self-concept within which the actual self and the ideal self and ideal object are confused. The unacceptable self images are repressed and projected onto others who are devalued.

Jacobson (1964) has suggested that extreme severe frustrations in relationships with significant others, after differentiation has occurred, may bring about the fusion of self and others' images, allowing the individual to escape the need and dread of the other person. In sum, in normal development, love for self and love for others become dependent on each other. In pathological development, an inflated unreal self-image is developed to protect the self from the underlying rage and envy connected to relationships early in life.

The newborn baby is primarily id directed. The id is the seat of instinctual processes. The energy, which is at its disposal, is free, unbound, and operates under the pleasure principle. Its goal is to strive for pleasure and to avoid pain by immediately discharging energy. It acts impulsively and knows no fear. It is unconscious and has direct contact with the external world only through the ego which develops out of it and becomes independent (Freud, 1962).

The ego is the reality-oriented structure. It overlaps with the id and is mostly unconscious, but it integrates the id forces with societal expectations represented by the superego balancing the demands of both (Freud, 1962). Ego psychologists have suggested that the conflicting demands become reconciled as individuals learn to control and direct their responses by using such higher-level processes as thinking and attention (A. Freud, 1946; Hartmann, 1958; Wolman, 1972). The ego psychologists have discussed the progression of adjusted people toward ego autonomy.

The superego develops as a result of the weakness of children's egos to deal with the power of parental prohibitions (Freud, 1921). The fear of punishment by parents and the need for affection and protection force children to accept the parental demands and to internalize them. The actual development of the superego takes place toward the end of the phallic period when the Oedipus complex is at its peak (Freud, 1924). The boy is afraid of being punished by castration by his father because he loves his mother. He is forced to give up his mother as a sexual object and identifies with his father. The girl must abandon the father as her love object under the threat of losing her mother's love. In essence, children identify with their parents' prohibitions and internalize them. If children can live up to these internalized parental standards, their self-esteem will be high.

Lichtenberg (1975) recently presented a psychoanalytic account of the self that expands the theory of self beyond the structural aspect (what is described in terms of id, ego, and superego processes). He distinguished the structural nonexperiential realm from the experiential realm and bridges the abstraction of structural theory with daily experience. His expanded theory allows for an understanding of the experiential self in terms of conscious, preconscious, and unconscious sensing. According to Lichtenberg, this total sensing bridges the abstraction of the structural theory with daily experience. This total sensing is responsible for the quality of the sense of self including its cohesiveness, continuity over time, and sameness in the midst of developmental change. As a result of maturation and experience, the infant becomes able to differentiate self from nonself. Mental precepts of the self and mother become organized as nonexperiential structures in the id, ego, and superego. The experiential self consists of images that reflect these structures. Before self and nonself are separated, the pleasurable or unpleasurable experiences given by the child's caretakers provide the first images of self. After there is considerable development of the underlying supportive structures, the clusters of early self-images become integrated into a cohesively experienced self. Disruptions in the sense of self can occur in its precohesive state or in a more integrated state.

Lichtenberg described the development of these component groups of self-images that must be integrated for cohesiveness to occur. The first is the body self, which early in life is associated with instinctual need satisfaction and leads gradually to the establishment of body boundaries. Freud (1962) felt that body representations are the core of the self (ego), essentially the child "lives in his body."

The second group of images making up the self origi-
nate from the differentiation of the self from others. As
children develop they acquire a growing inner world of
experiential images. As they move away from the mother
with development, children become able to evoke her image at will. When this occurs, the child "begins to 'live' a
bit less in his body and a bit less in exclusive response to
the outer world; he lives a bit more in his mind." (Lichtenberg, p. 461). The self is experienced as discrete from the
mother, but, at the same time, the self is experienced as
having qualities of the mother that reduce the more total
sense of dependency experienced in the earlier stage. This
identification with the mother becomes part of the self.
When maternal care is markedly deficient or where gratification is excessive, the ego's potental for internalization
will not be as fully utilized and the child becomes more
reliant on the mother and has difficulty developing self-
control, confidence, and reliance. Negative identifications
resulting from poor mothering result in difficulty in inte-
grating a cohesive self that is distinct from the mother and
well linked to reality.

A third group of images comprising the self develops
the grandiose perfectionistic images of the self that include
the omnipotent images of the self and the idealized images
of the parents. During early life, the mother has to have
empathetically cued in on her infant's dependent needs so
that their shared omnipotence reaches its fullest intensity;
subsequently, as the child moves away from the mother, the
carrying power of this omnipotence depends on the empa-
thetic support of the mother. The sixteenth to the eigh-
teenth month is the height of this inflated sense of
omnipotence. In the next eighteen months, this state must
become divested of its delusional aspects. This second
eighteen months are a period of vulnerability on the child's
self-esteem. When his disappointments with his parents are

within tolerable limits, he can develop a realistic self-image and modify the grandiose self-image and integrate it with the other self-image components.

These three component self-images must be "blended" together into a cohesive whole that permits change, but at the same time retains the essential feeling of sameness of self. As they are integrated, self-experiences achieve a continuity in time. Lichtenberg places the early integration of these three groups of self-images and the beginning feeling of sense of cohesion at the second half of the third year of life.

When we speak of ego autonomy vis-à-vis the id, we speak of the superego and the external world being at an optimal sense of cohesion at the experiential level. The self is experienced more and more as an active agent capable of giving impetus and direction to the child's expanding functional potentialities, so that repeated fulfillment of conscious and unconscious self-desired goals occur. The alignment between idealized images within the child and the goals and demands of the external world ensures against overly abrupt drops in self-worth.

SELF VERSUS EGO

There is much confusion in the literature as to the distinction between the self and the ego. The issue is an important one because if self-feelings arise in the id as Freud (1962) theorized, then the unconscious determinants of the self-concept would be more powerful than the conscious ones. We know that conscious evaluations of the self do not necessarily agree with unconscious self-feelings. Psychotics may report high self-esteem and relatively normal people frequently hide their true self-feelings. In Freud's definition, the ego mediates between the instincts (the id) and the world of reality. The ego's integrative and defensive mechanisms stabilize the organism and protect the individual from excessive anxiety, conflict, stress, and frustration. Therefore, it is an inner agency that screens the unmanageable impulses deciding what should be kept from consciousness and, if necessary, distorting the true picture of self.

Allport (1937, 1943, 1955) emphasized the importance of the aware self and refers to the ego and the self as synonymous. The proprium (or self) develops with time. According to Allport (1937, 1943, 1955), all the three-year-old has achieved is bodily sense, self-identity, and self-esteem. Allport viewed personality as an intrapsychic organization, while the social psychologists have placed greater emphasis on the relationship between the environment and the self.

Most modern theorists generally have defined the self in two distinctly different ways. The first definition regards the self-as-object, refering to people's attitudes, feelings, perceptions, and evaluations of which they are aware and can report. The second is the self-as-process. These psychological processes (such as thinking, remembering, and perceiving) govern behavior and adjustment. They have unconscious roots that are not necessarily consistent with the conscious evaluations of the self (Hall and Lindzey, 1970). The self-as-process can be thought of as the ego as defined by Freud and his disciples.

Erikson's (1968) theory of identity formation clarified this issue. He postulated a self aspect and an ego aspect. He separated the "I" and the selves from the ego, consigning to the ego the Freudian meaning. He stated (1968, p. 218): "The selves are mostly preconscious, which means they can become conscious when the 'I' makes them so and insofar as the ego agrees to it." In this theoretical distinction between the meanings of "I," "ego," and "self," the "I" is all conscious, the selves are mostly preconscious and can be made conscious by the "I," and the "ego" is mostly unconscious. Erikson felt that we become aware of the ego's work but never of it. Even though he did not underestimate the importance of the unconscious ego, he stated that we should not ignore the conscious "I," which he felt psychoanalytic theory has done. By ignoring it, he believed we delete the core of human awareness that makes self-awareness possible. Both he and Hartmann (1950) preferred to use self identity rather than ego identity when referring to the self-as-object.

The point was also made by White (1963) that psychoanalytic theory has failed to account for the ego's relation to reality.[1] White (1963) stressed the interactive theory in the development of self-esteem. He theorized that a respect for self is essential for self-esteem and self-esteem has an important root in the experience of efficacy (a sense of competence). Our actions and our sense of competence are influenced by the evaluations that proceed from others and influence the way in which we perceive ourselves.

If we are concerned about attaining as accurate a picture of an individual's self-feelings as possible, there must be ways to gain access to the conscious self-evaluations and some insight, albeit limited, to the unconscious evaluations of the self. Sensitive observers can get clues to both aspects of the self, and can infer the self-concept from these clues. It is easier to abstract the unconscious meanings from behavior in the young child. The difficulty arises when we attempt to obtain a scientific and testable definition of the underlying processes. In spite of this difficulty, which makes it hard to get agreement between observers, sensitivity to universal behaviors and background information about children and critical skillful observational techniques can give clues to underlying meanings. We need not throw up our hands in defeat since new insights are possible without complete scientific control. Theory and research to support the theory would elucidate the variables that are significant in evaluating behavior; but meanwhile teachers can become better observers before the variables are completely defined.

SOCIAL PSYCHOLOGICAL THEORY

The social psychological approach takes into account both the psychological and the sociological influences affecting the individual. The social psychological emphasis on the self-concept was initiated by William James (1893). He referred to the "I" as the knower and the "Me" as the known or empirical self. The empirical self is everything that an individual can call hers. In the order of importance, James divided the empirical self into the spiritual self, the material self, the social self, and the bodily self. The spiritual self is the individual's concrete states of consciousness, psychic powers, and dispositions. It is the source of interest, attention, effort, will, and choice. The material self is our property, body, clothes, homes and immediate family. James linked the social self to social interaction. He theorized that there must be not one, but many social selves, and that the social *me* grows out of the recognition that we receive from others. The bodily self is least important to James. He mentioned the need to nourish our bodies and to deck them with clothes and to have a minimum of selfishness in the bodily sense.

The concept of the "looking glass" self was coined by Cooley (1902), who stated that the self is a reflection of what individuals think others' judgements are of them. In Cooley's theory, how a mother perceives and treats her child would result in a favorable or unfavorable self-concept.

Both James and Cooley felt that the individual was consciously aware of the self, although neither of them discussed the process by which the self comes into existence.

Mead (1934, 1956) systematically theorized how the self develops. He hypothesized that infants are born without a self and the self-concept arises as a result of social experience. According to Mead, children take on the attitudes toward themselves of significant others in their world, those on whom they depend and who control them. Mead referred to the social group that gives individuals their unity of self and against which they evaluate themselves as the "generalized other." The self is an object of awareness rather than a system of processes. Mead's point was that the groups to which an individual belongs serve as significant frames of reference.

Adler (1927) emphasized the social determinants of behavior. Unlike Freud, he stressed consciousness as the center of personality (Adler, 1927). He felt that individuals are aware of the reasons for their behavior. Adler was the first to suggest that individuals are as much a product of their culture as of their psychological drives. According to him, a person sets up a life plan to overcome or compensate for fancied or real inferiorities. The tendency to disparage is an overcompensation arising from feelings of inferioirty (Adler, 1930).

Horney (1937, 1939) also thought that the demands of culture were as influential as the instincts in adult conflicts and neurosis. She mentioned the importance of parental love or lack of love for the child's self-conception. Horney wrote (1937, p. 80): "The main reason why a child does not receive enough warmth and affection lies in the parents' inability to give it on account of their own neuroses." She felt that people who do not love themselves are incapable of loving others (Horney, 1939). In an atmosphere of rejection by others, children are likely to acquire an attitude of rejection toward themselves.

Fromm (1939) and Sullivan (1940, 1947, 1953) put

greater stress on sociological factors than did Adler and Horney. In their writings, distorted relationships with people are considered to be significant in the development of the self-concept (Vernon, 1964).

Fromm (1939) argued that the parents transmit to the child from birth onward the spirit prevalent in their society and class. He stated, "The family, thus, is the 'psychic agency' of society" (Fromm, 1939, p. 515). He theorized that people who dislike themselves tend to criticize themselves, feel stupid, unattractive, or attribute to themselves other negative inferiority feelings. Hatred turned against oneself becomes inseparable from hatred directed against others (Fromm, 1939).

Sullivan (1953) considered the self-concept as being central to human personality in his interpersonal theory of personality. He felt that individuals cannot exist apart from their relations with other people, and that the organization of personality consists of interpersonal events, not intrapsychic ones. Sullivan was the first to describe the empathy that exists between the infant and the mother. If mothers provide solicitous care, children will have their tensions relieved and feel secure. The differentiation of the good-me, the me rewarded by a tender, good mother; the bad-me, the me punished by the anxiety-evoking mother; and the not-me, the me overwhelmed by intense anxiety as a result of the reflected appraisals of the mother. Children first learn to differentiate the "good mother" from the "bad mother." Later, they differentiate the "good me" and the "bad me." The early mother-child interactions bring about these differentiations. What is significant in Sullivan's theory is that the behavior and situations involving the self and other people are made before language can accurately define anxiety-provoking situations. He stated, "If these (self-appraisals) were chiefly derogatory ... then the self dynamism will itself be chiefly derogatory. It will ... entertain disparaging and hostile appraisals of itself." (Sullivan,

1940, p. 10). Sullivan (1953) noted that a person's perceptions may be unrealistic and distorted. Sullivan called the learning experiences that are illogical and bad and badly connected with other perceptions parataxic experiences. If a child has had these kinds of unrealistic negative experiences at home, the perceptions are likely to generalize out to school. Sullivan stated that experiences that produce logical order can allow an individual to share more realistic perceptions with others. He called these experiences syntaxic. Therefore, Sullivan's theory supports the concept that children's negative perceptions of self start in infancy.

Erikson's (1950) theoretical model addressed itself to the question of "Who Am I?" His eight stages of man, which are based on psychoanalytic theory, are universal. During each stage, society must meet conditions to fulfill the psychological needs in the striving for identity as defined in each culture. Identity has a self aspect, which is conscious, and an ego aspect, which is unconscious (Erikson, 1968). Failure to develop optimally at one stage can be rectified by success at later stages; but complete failure at a stage can prevent future development. Although one particular task is predominant at each stage, it continues to be important (in a lesser sense) throughout life.

The stages are trust versus mistrust (first year), autonomy versus doubt (second and third years), initiative versus guilt (fourth and fifth years), industry versus inferiority (ages six through eleven), identity versus role confusion (ages twelve through eighteen), intimacy versus isolation (late adolescence to middle age), generativity versus self-absorption (middle age), and identity versus despair (old age).

During the first year, consistent care, where the child is fed and held with love, leads to the basic sense of trust. The sense of autonomy predominant during the second and third year of life is able to develop when infants are helped to feel adequate in their expanding development of independence in controlling their feces and urine, and in language and in locomotion. A sense of initiative is encouraged when parents and teachers allow children to explore their world, encourage curiosity and a healthy pushing out into the world. Our interest in the preschool child encompasses these three stages of development. If the home fails to help children to negotiate these stages optimally, the school's role becomes more important. Erickson's theory recognizes the influential role of the greater society in helping individuals to grow toward a sense of identity.

Maslow (1954, 1968), a humanistic psychologist concerned with normal development, theorized that the highest need that we strive for is "self-actualization." When we are self-actualized, we have become what we have the potential to become. According to Maslow, needs are hierarchically arranged. When the lowest need is satisfied, the next highest need emerges to be satisfied. The lowest needs are the physiological needs; the second level needs are the safety needs; the third level are the love and belonging needs; the fourth are the esteem needs; and the final level are the self-actualization needs. The goal of the educative process should be to facilitate attainment of these needs.

As compared to the Freudians, the social psychologists put greater emphasis on conscious awareness and generally put greater stress on sociological factors than on instinctual ones in the development of the self.

Phenomenological Theory

Combs and Snygg (1959) believed that conscious feelings, cognitions, and perceptions were the predominant aspect of the self-concept. As phenomenologists, they believe that awareness is a cause of behavior and that what individuals think and feel determines what they will do. Those perceptions about self that seem most vital to the individual, and are at the very core of personality, are organized into the self-concept. The self-concept is that part of the phenomenal field that has been differentiated as definite and fairly stable characteristics of the self. They suggested that self report may be distorted, and that inference of the person's perceptions by use of such things as observation, interview, and autobiography may be necessary to determine a person's phenomenological field.

Combs and Snygg (1959) noted that children can only develop perceptions about themselves in terms of their experience and the treatment they have received from those responsible for their development. They stated (p. 136):

> "In his interaction with father, mother, and siblings, the young child begins his differentiations of self as liked or unliked, wanted or unwanted, acceptable or unacceptable, able or unable, worthy or unworthy, adequate or inadequate. These are the kind of perceptions through which the individual is able to symbolize his own degree of self-actualization."

As a proponent of the phenomenological viewpoint, Rogers (1951) stressed that most of our unconscious experiences are capable of becoming conscious when the need arises. He accepted individuals as the best source of information about themselves and elaborated on the interpersonal experiences by which the structure and the evaluation of the self is formed. He stated (1959, p. 225), "He (the child) develops a total gestalt as to the way he is regarded by his mother and each new experience of love or rejection tends to alter the whole gestalt. Consequently, each behavior on his mother's part such as a specific disapproval of a specific behavior tends to be experienced as disapproval in general. . . ." Rogers theorized that children soon tend, quite independently from the mother or others, to view themselves in the same way others have viewed them. As a humanist, Rogers maintained that each individual has a basic tendency to actualize, maintain, and enhance himself (Rogers, 1951).

The plethora of empirical research in the last two decades focusing on the self-concept based on the phenomenological theories of Combs and Snygg and Rogers indicates the influence these men have had in the field. Their view stressed that a person behaves in a manner consistent with his ". . . perceptual field which is his perception of an event at any time."

EXISTENTIALISM

Existentialism's central concern is the need for individuals to develop a sense of personal identity and to build meaningful links with the world. The basic concepts of existentialism stem from the European philosophers Heidegger, Jaspers, Kierkegaard, and Sartre (Coleman, 1972). Heidegger was the bridge to modern existential psychology. He wrote that individuals are beings-in-the-world. They don't exist in relation to the world or interacting with other things making up the world, but being and world are one (Heidegger, 1962; Hall & Lindzey, 1970). The individual strives to become a totality in a purposeful direction (Tiryakian, 1968). Moreover, no one dimension of a person can be understood isolated from his whole existence in the world and individuals must be studied as totalities, not just biologically or behaviorally. Nonbeing (the opposite of being), in its ultimate form, is death. Awareness of this inevitable death leads individuals to worry about leading meaningful lives. To the extent that they fail to realize their potential, they experience existential anxiety (Hall & Lindzey, 1970).

Another significant aspect of existentialism, as expounded by Heidegger and present-day existential psychologists, is its use of phenomenological analysis to understand and describe immediate experience. Only what can be seen or experienced is real and nothing lies behind phenomena (Coleman, 1972). In other words, the self's reality is its conscious experiences and decisions. People are also consciously free by choice to fulfill their potential, but if they don't, they become alienated from themselves (Binswanger, 1963, May 1969b). To choose, people must be open enough so that the possibilities can become reality. This may be difficult in our bureaucratic and dehumanizing society but can be resolved by people either conforming blindly to the group or by striving for self-definition in their own existence. Existentialists have stated that blind conformity is unauthentic and leads to anxiety (May, 1969a, 1969b; Laing, 1967, 1969; Coleman, 1972).

Binswanger (1963), Boss (1963), and Laing (1967, 1969) are three modern-day European existentialist psychological thinkers and May (1969a, 1969b) has been influential in the United States.

Binswanger wrote that the aim of existential analysis is to reconstruct the individual's inner world of experience (Binswanger, 1963; Hall & Lindzey, 1970). Binswanger (1963) and Boss (1963) have stated that there are no cause-effect relationships in human existence; that is, a particular event that happens to a child is not the cause of the child's behavior as an adult. Since individuals' existences are not determined by past experience, they are free and responsible each moment for their existence. They replace the concept of causality by the concept of motivation. The person is said to be "motivated" by the past, but this motivation is predicated by the present being-in-the-world.

May (1969a, 1969b) wrote about the need to look at truth from each person's perspective. Reality lies in the person's present conscious experience of an event (May, 1969a). May stated (1969a, p. 11): "Existence means centering upon the *existing* person and emphasizes the human being as he is *emerging, becoming.*" May (1969b) also felt that we have to confront our schizoid world today. In this world, alienation leads to identity confusion, apathy, powerlessness, and finally to violence. He stated that we have the power to change this. It is our human responsibility to confront the fact of our schizoid world by love and will. In this way, we will become conscious of others and counter the emptiness of our technology. May wrote that love and will are present in every genuine act and by getting in touch with them, we can mold ourselves and our world at the same time. Thus individuals do not have to be controlled by their environment.

Laing (1967, 1969) also stressed the sociocultural factors that lead to abnormal behavior. He wrote that a child's compliance to a schizophrenic social order betrays the self and limits the child's range of experience. Children are crippled to fit into society and this occurs when they are betrayed into surrender of self by love (Laing, 1967). In other words, children are good not out of their own positive desires, but as conformity to others' standards, prompted by fear of withdrawal of love. This love takes the child from permissiveness to discipline and then to acceptance. Acceptance leads to compliance, which is a betrayal of self. Laing stated (1967, p. 58): "By the time a new human being is 15 or so, we are left with a being like ourselves, a half-crazed creature, more or less adjusted to a mad world. This is normality."

A false self, which develops in the child as a result of the compliance with other people's intentions and expectations, leads to avoidance of the discovery of the true self, according to Laing (1967). He sees a psychotic breakdown occurring when the split no longer can be maintained. In essence, the individual tries to recover her wholeness as a human being and to preserve herself from total extinction by showing her "false self." Behind the facade of the schizophrenic person, there is an "inner self"—the real person—that may remain intact. Laing (1969) suggested that treatment should focus on finding a way to this remote and often inaccessible world.

The question is raised by critics of existential psychology (Hall & Lindzey, 1970) and by this writer, as to whether individuals are really free to choose. Environment and biology limit possibilities before a child can make rational choices. Even existentialists agree that individuals have a ground, that is, a destiny or inheritance. Existentialist psychologists have stated that we are free to make of our endowment what we choose, but the question is: What are the limitations of avenues open for choice in our society? For example, children born into poverty, who are malnourished and become brain damaged, may have few choices open, not by their own doing. However, openness to experience can be nurtured by significant others (parents and, later, teachers). This leads to greater control and freedom of choice.

REFERENCE GROUP THEORY

Hyman (1942) first used the term "reference group" to mean the group with which individuals compare themselves. Hyman distinguished between a "membership group" (the group to which an individual belongs), and a "reference group" (the group used to compare himself for self-appraisal). The membership group may or may not be the reference group (Deutsch, 1965). Hyman's statement, "where there is in actuality no mobility and little realistic channel of achieving the higher status, there may be much insecurity," (Hyman, 1942, p. 86), could be relevant to the castelike position that the lower-class individual has in our society. We conclude that people who judge themselves by the standards of a higher status group will be less satisfied with their own status and more prone to negative self-esteem.

Kelly (1952) expanded Hyman's definition by adding to the comparison aspect of the theory the concept that the reference group is in a position to award recognition to the person or to withold it. A reference group can be either positive or negative, according to Newcomb (1950). A person is motivated to be accepted in a positive group and doesn't want to be treated as a member of a negative group. Merton (1968) used evidence from empirical research to strengthen his theory that the greater the prestige that nonmembership groups confer on individuals, as compared to their own membership groups, the more likely will they be to use the former as frames of reference. Sherif and Sherif (1966) believed that reference group standards are internalized in individuals by learning as part of the ego and that they may not be conscious of those standards.

Brim (1960) and Gergen (1968, 1971) theorized that individuals view and appraise their performance in terms of evaluation of their behavior along certain dimensions within specific roles. The individual is a composite of many self-perceptions pertaining to one role or another. These self-perceptions relate to the expectations of one reference group or another (Brim, 1960). Brim stressed that proper study of personality requires that we focus on internalized differences within various roles.

McCarthy and Yancey (1971), in a theoretically and empirically documented article, expressed doubt about the theory that lower self-esteem results from the caste position of the lower-class black American. In effect, they discounted the reference group theory for lower-class Negroes by implying that the members are neither influenced by nor aspire to the values of the dominant group. They stated that lower-class blacks simply withdraw loyalty from conventional structures. They argued that lower-class whites would exhibit lower self-esteem than lower-class blacks because the white population is more vulnerable to the dominant middle class and it is likely that those who are upwardly mobile would be more subject to negative self-feelings.

McCarthy and Yancey suggested that lower-class blacks blame white oppression and caste deprivation for their economic position, but that these blacks do not feel inferior. Blame to the system would not be as likely an option for middle-class blacks whose self-esteem is theorized to be lower than that of middle-class whites. They are more likely to strive for the values of the dominant group.

Yancey et al (1972) found some evidence indicating that other variables (such as place of residence, education and marital stress) may be more significant in determining an individual's self-evaluation than race or social position. They theorized that black and white individuals may be affected differently by these variables. Cummings (1975) reviewed the studies on the self evaluation of black children and suggested that there is a cultural bias when theorists assume black children evaluate themselves negatively. He stated that psychological processes among black children are more complex than suggested in the literature.

Rosenberg (1968, 1972) also suggested that individuals may refuse to accept society's evaluation of their ethnic group as part of their self-image. Based on his studies of adolescents, Rosenberg felt that subcultural norms or other characteristic aspects of experience are more important as determinants of self-esteem. He gave four arguments to support his viewpoint: first, he suggested that members of a lower-prestige group will often rank their own group higher than others rank it. Second, they may tend to react to the disesteem in which they are held as an expression of pathology of the evaluator rather than any inadequacy in themselves. Third, people in low-prestige groups may compare themselves with others in that group over whom they have superiority. Finally, group members living in socially homogeneous neighborhoods are likely to confine their associations to their own group, so that their feelings of self-esteem may be based on relative prestige within that group, rather than between groups. Rosenberg concluded that self-esteem may therefore be more a matter of position within a group than the rank of the group in relation to other groups. Heiss and Owens (1972) feel also that blacks tend to use other black people, rather than white individuals as self-evaluative references.

Nobles (1973) theorized that there is a "we" self that must be taken into account when looking at self-concept. The "African reality" of black people living in America is an example of this "we" self. This existential approach suggests that there is an awareness of a historical reference group that transcends the inferior status of groups being studied in the present. He felt that consistency between the "I," "me," and "we" is of fundamental importance to the individual's conception of self. This suggests that those in lower reference groups who have a "we" feeling, even though they are presently in a lower status group, would not necessarily be self-rejecting. Evidence that supports this view comes from ethnic groups that may be economically deprived, but who still maintain pride in their heritage and themselves. The implication of this theory is that schools can have a positive effect on self-concept by highlighting the "we" (historical contributions) of each group. The culturally different (not deficient) perspective would allow the values of the economically lower status group to be reinforced and should positively affect self-concept.

It is likely that an individual's role in society and his self-evaluations in these roles must have definite sociocultural referents. The family serves as a mediator between the child and the greater community. By its actions and words, it interprets community evaluations of itself and its children. Most theorists have suggested that groups that confer status in our society would negatively affect individuals who are not members of these groups. However, is it inevitable that those in lower status groups aspire to become members of and judge themselves by the standards of the higher status group? We can't deny that the higher reference group is in the position to award or withhold recognition and reward to those with lesser status. Some theorists suggest that the withholding of this recognition and reward does not necessarily result in negative self-concept because of past history and/or present values. Our place in society is one factor that acts in combination with other variables, among which are parental attitudes and expectations, sex-role identification, and peer and teacher expectations.

SUMMARY

The psychoanalytic point of view has stressed the need for a balance of id, ego, and superego forces for an individual to have positive self-feelings. Moreover, positive self-esteem requires a realistic ego ideal whose standards are lived up to. The ego is primarily unconscious and consists of a group of processes that affect behavior and from which self-feelings can be inferred. The self is conscious and pre-conscious, and can be brought to awareness when the need arises.

The social psychologists have asserted strongly that individuals' conceptions of themselves are learned from social interaction. The responses of others to them determine how they perceive themselves. If the individual grows up without love, he will find fault with others and with himself. The phenomenologists have put greater stress on conscious awareness. They have given the self-concept a central position in their theory and have stated that individuals are the best source of information about how they feel toward themselves, although there can be distortion in their response and we may have to infer people's self-concepts from their behavior. The reference groups to which individuals compare themselves may affect their role behavior and self-concept. Children's attitudes toward themselves may be indirectly affected by their parents' position in society.

SELF-CONSISTENCY THEORY

Self-consistency theory hypothesizes that individuals' receptivity of information from other people is strongly affected by their tendency to create and maintain a consistent state in self-evaluation. If there is inconsistency in their relationships with others, they may change their conception of themselves, their own actions, or terminate their relationship with the other person. They may interact only with those whose behavior validates their self-concept or change the actions of the other person who produces the inconsistency (Jones, 1973). The theory proposes that those with high self-evaluations will react more favorably to approval than disapproval, and those with low self-evaluations will react more favorably to disapproval than approval. Therefore, self-consistency theory argues that individuals adjust their cognitions and orient their relationships with others in order to keep their evaluations of themselves consistent with others' evaluations of them.

William James (1893) was among the first to write about the importance of inner consistency of the self. Lewin (1935), viewed the self as a central and relatively permanent organization that gives consistency to the personality. According to Lecky (1945), the organism needs to maintain a unified organization. Stagner (1951) felt that homeostasis, as a general biological law, applies to some extent to the psychology of personality and that the individual seeks to maintain constancy with regard to the perception of self. Hilgard (1949) stated that a unity of self is bound together by a continuity of memories, habits, and motivational patterns.

Rogers' (1951) self-theory held that the self strives for consistency, that the person behaves in ways consistent with the self, and that experiences not consistent with the self are perceived as threats and are either distorted or denied, but the self may change as a result of maturation and learning.

Festinger (1957, p. 260) theorized, "that the human organism tries to establish internal harmony, consistency, or congruity among his opinions, attitudes, knowledge and values. That is, there is drive toward consonance among cognitions." If there is "dissonance"—which occurs when an individual has feelings, ideas, or perceptions that are in opposition to one another—the individual tends to find ways to gain cognitive consistency and to reduce dissonance. Individuals may misperceive evaluations, which are inconsistent to already existent feelings and perceptions, in order to prevent themselves from becoming psychologically uncomfortable as a result of contradictions of conflicting perceptions.

Allport (1961) theorized that behavior has greater consistency when it relates to what is warm, central, and important to us than when this is not so. Allport (1955) used the term proprium to refer to the self. The proprium contributes to a sense of inward unity, allowing for an awareness of a bodily self, a sense of continuity over time, a need for self-esteem (self-enhancement), identification of the self beyond body borders (ego extention), the synthesis of inner needs with outer reality (rational process), the perception and evaluation of the person (self-image), the function of knowing, and the motivation to decrease tension, expand awareness, and seek out challenge.

Combs and Snygg (1959) stated that the stability of the phenomenal self makes change difficult because the self ignores aspects of experience that are inconsistent with it or selects perceptions in such a way as to confirm concepts of self we already possess. They felt that change in perceived self depends on the clarity of experience provided by the new perception, the way the new concepts fit into the existing self-organization and the relationship of the revised concepts to the individual's needs.

Gergen (1968) challenged the concept of self-consistency. He emphasized that the self is altered by specific others and the expressed views of others toward the self in each new situation brings about this alteration. Thus, the level of expressed self-esteem changes, depending on the characteristics of other people in each new situation. To some degree, we perceive consistency because with most social relationships, we provide a constant stimulus value that is relatively stable and coherent and may have constant effects on the other's behavior. Yinger (1963) also theorized that the self-concept is emerging in varying situations, but has continuity because it already has some internal organization before the individual enters a situation.

Ziller (1973) theorized that low self-esteem is associated with short-term adaptation and inconsistency, whereas high self-esteem is associated with long-range adaptation and consistency across tasks. He cited studies that indicated that high self-esteem people assimilate new information to maintain consistency and disregard irrelevant information, but low self-esteem people tend to conform passively to the influence of the persuasive field.

The rapid and significant development of the self-concept in the early years of childhood is widely accepted. It is generally acknowledged that stability of the concept of self begins early in life. Adler (1927) indicated that attitudes, feelings, and apperceptions became fixed at an early age and it becomes difficult for the style of life to change thereafter. Sullivan (1940, p. 10) expresses this point of view when he wrote, ". . . [the self] tends very strongly to maintain the direction and characteristics given to it in infancy and childhood." He hypothesized that since the self system guards the person from anxiety—originally transmitted by the mother—it is resistant to change (Sullivan, 1953). The "core" concepts that lie closest to the center of the personality and are formed earliest are suggested as being most difficult to change (Symonds, 1951). Bloom (1964) reported, in his summary of studies on stability and change in personality, that 40 percent of ego development is reached by about the age of seven.

Felker (1974) viewed the role of the self-concept as threefold. First, self-concept maintains inner consistency, which predisposes people to act in ways consistent with the views they have of themselves; second, individuals interpret new experiences in terms of previous experiences, which make it hard to change; and third, self-concept leads to a set of expectations that create conditions that determine how others will treat us. Children who have been conditioned to think badly of themselves expect to continue to be treated badly and act to get negative reactions. Even when these reactions are not forthcoming, they frequently misinterpret the reactions to meet their expectations. They say they were treated badly whether they were or not and "egg on" new others until they get the expected negative reactions. This makes it difficult for teachers to change self-feelings, and indeed for some children, therapy may be the only answer.

SELF-ESTEEM THEORY

Self-esteem theory postulates that individuals have a need for positive self-esteem, which is satisfied by the approval they receive from others and is frustrated by their disapproval. To the extent that their esteem need is satisfied by others' evaluations, individuals will respond favorably to them (Jones, 1973). This theory assumes that individuals have a need to enhance their self-evaluation and to increase, maintain, or confirm their feelings of worth, effectiveness and self-satisfaction. These feelings may be manifested with respect to a particular aspect of self-evaluation or to global feelings. The difference in this theory from self-consistency theory is that the individual wishes to gain self-esteem rather than to achieve self-consistency. In this case, the person would respond favorably to positive evaluation of self, which is assumed to satisfy esteem needs; and to respond unfavorably to negative evaluations of self, which would frustrate the esteem needs. Therefore, low self-esteem people would respond more favorably to positive evaluations from others; and more unfavorably to negative evaluations as compared to high self-esteem individuals. This is based on the assumption that low self-esteem people have greater needs for esteem enhancement and therefore are more satisfied by the approval of others and more frustrated by disapproval of others, than are high self-esteem people who have enough positive self-esteem to begin with.

If self-esteem needs are met, the low self-esteem person will respond to others. This provides a more optimistic view for teachers. It means that if teachers can provide experiences to enhance self-esteem for those children who lack it, the children will respond and presumably grow toward more positive self-feelings. This is supported by evidence of change we frequently see in people. Horrocks and Jackson (1972) reported that self development is open to positive change over time. They suggested that there exists a dynamic process of cognitive-affective integration and differentiation of meanings of self over time.

Jones (1973) compared the self-consistency theory with the self-esteem theory by critically evaluating studies, that supported both theories. His paper makes a stronger case for the value of the self-esteem theory. In most studies the self-denigrator is happy when praised and unhappy when censured to a greater extent than the self-confident person. Jones extended the self-esteem theory to include interpretations of self-consistency studies. These studies have shown that the anticiapted exposure of people's qualities tends to make them look at themselves more honestly and therefore more self-consistently, in order to avoid eventual disapproval of others. In other words, low-esteem individuals may need to feel high self-esteem, but they are worried that they might be found out if they deny the negative evaluation. To prevent this from occurring, they agree with those who evaluate them negatively and this coincides with their own negative evaluations, although they would prefer to think of themselves in more positive ways. Jones felt that people will forfeit immediate gratification of esteem needs in anticipation of less self-derogatory experiences in the future. Furthermore, Jones cited studies indicating that self-consistency per se is not a general motivational state. These studies suggested that, when individuals like and think they are liked by others, they prefer self-consistent evaluations, but when individuals dislike others and are disliked, inconsistent evaluations are preferred. That is, significant others' attitudes support consistency of the self-picture.

If we agree with Jones that some apparently self-consistent responses can be viewed in terms of people forfeiting immediate gratification of esteem needs in anticipation of more enhancing or less self-derogatory experiences in the future, we can have faith that if experiences are offered to counteract previous negative ones, changes in perception will eventually follow. It may be difficult to do if the person cares about the new significant other, but change is possible with time. For example, a child who comes to school with the feeling that he is stupid or ugly may at first resist attempts of those he likes to change his self-perception and might deny facts that contradict this perception, but the striving for positive self-esteem can enable new significant others to modify the child's self-picture. This is more likely to occur with children under five because rigid defenses have not yet been developed. The added role of concerned educators working with parents can help to create conditions to enhance parental attitudes, so that change can be reinforced positively in the home.

THEORY ON THE EARLY DEVELOPMENT OF THE SELF

The importance of the first five years of life has been continually stressed. Bloom (1964) suggested that growth and development of personality are not equal over time and that the most rapid growth is likely to be in the first five years of life. The basic self is acquired within the family early in life. At the beginning of life, as discussed earlier, the child must become aware that he is distinct and separate from other people. Initially, the infant cannot distinguish between self and nonself (Jacobson, 1964). The baby does not know where his body ends and his environment begins. The development of the self begins by the baby's direct interaction of his organism with incoming stimuli, starting with tactual kinesthetic contacts with the mother. Beginning separation is made easier as the child identifies with the mother and/or other love objects. When the child perceives that gratification or frustration are associated with another, identification begins.

Mahler (1963) conceptualized the genesis of the eventual sense of identity. She regarded the demarcation of the body image of the child from the body of the mother as the core of the process that occurs as a result of the predictable gratification from an available loving mother; and with some limited frustration. The child wants to ascribe to the self what is pleasant, and to the outside world what is unpleasant (Jacobson, 1964). Overgratification or severe frustration may delay the establishment of firm boundaries between the mother and the self, and prevent normal separation from occurring.

Mahler (1963) and Spitz (1957) described the first signs of separation from mother at the end of the third or the beginning of the fourth month. From birth to thirty-six months, according to Mahler (1963, 1975), the child moves from symbiotic union through awareness of separation to a sense of self and object relatedness to the mother. Separation increases through the toddler phase of development. The toddler is unable to cope with the demands of the separation-individuation phase of development unless the proceeding symbiotic phase has been successful (Mahler, 1963). Symbiosis refers to the infant's dependence on the mother and her complementary involvement with the infant when the "I" is not yet differentiated from the "not I."

The experiences during the period of the formation of the self during the first years of life become the prototype of the specific forms of later vulnerability and security in the narcissistic realm. These experiences determine the ups and downs in self-esteem, the need for greater or lesser praise and of other forms of narcissistic sustenance and of self-cohesion (Kohut, 1972). Problems early in life with developing a cohesive self start with a deficiency in adequate "mirroring" from the environment. These "mirroring" responses include admiration and approval. When this is lacking, the child turns to self-stimulation to retain the precarious cohesion of self and the grandiose body-self love remains fixated and the grandiosity and exhibitionism cannot be integrated with the rest of the psychic organization. It becomes split off and repressed, but breaks through later in life (Kohut, 1971, 1972). Other theorists, who have also worked primarily with narcissistic personalities after early childhood, have suggested if a traumatic situation occurs too early and is too overwhelming when the ego cannot develop adequate defenses to ward off this threat and anxiety, interest passes from others to the self (Winnicott, 1958; James, 1960; Reich, 1960; Kernberg, 1970, 1975). Kernberg (1970) stated that it is hard to evaluate whether pathological narcissism is determined by a strong aggressive drive, a constitutional lack of anxiety tolerance relating to aggressive impulses or severe frustration in the first years of life. The mothers of his adult pathologically narcissistic patients seemed to be cold and hostile. The child had to meet the mother's narcissistic needs and any of the child's "specialness" was used to give the mothers admiration and greatness.

Brody and Axelrad (1970) and Mahler (1975) observed children early in life. Brody and Axelrad (1970) suggested that the amount of positive and negative, internal and external stimulation that the infant receives cannot be greater than can be absorbed in a given time span. Small degrees of sensorimotor arousals, which evoke the exercise of the young infant's mental equipment, seem to adequately tap the infant's own narcissism for optimal psychological development. Mahler's studies of the separation-individuation process show how relations with the mother and narcissism develop together. She observed that the relationships with others developed from primary narcissism to secondary narcissism as the separation-individuation process evolves. The mother's sensitivity and care, if it is developmentally appropriate and well timed, allows for the development and maintenance of adequate self-esteem.

Erikson (1950, 1955) described the consistent, loving care of the mother in infancy as being essential for the development of a basic sense of trust in the child. This sense of trust is the foundation for the development of identity. Sense of trust develops in the child the ability to predict the continuity and regularity of satisfaction of basic needs during babyhood. Contact with a caring, loving mother who meets the routine needs of the child with regularity sets the stage for future confidence and trust. This sense of trust must continue to be enhanced later in life, although the critical stage for its development is during the first year of life.

According to Benedek (1959), the self-image is built up by identification as children internalize (or introject) the mother's attitudes. Through each single and interrelated series of identifications, children develop a picture of self as good or bad. If they introject primarily a good mother, they develop a good self (good mother = good self); and if they introject primarily a bad mother, they feel they are bad. Whatever negative experiences children have must be outweighed by positive experiences for them to have an integrated, good self. That is, a minimum of bad experiences can be neutralized by the predominance of positive experiences.

Primitive identification is shown by the child's imitation of the gestures, voice, inflections, and affective behaviors of the love objects. Peller (1965) reported that at about six or seven months, the child, seeing a well-liked adult touch himself, will try to imitate that gesture. A landmark is reached in identification at about the first year, when the child recognizes her image in the mirror (Smiroff, 1971). In a unique study with infants as subjects and the use of a mirror, Dixon (1957) described the child's developing awareness of self as distinct from others. He noted that at about one year of age, the child's behavior begins to suggest true self-recognition.

The prevalence of love in children's relationships with important people in their lives builds up a positive, loving self-image that is necessary in order for children to achieve a unified concept of self and positive self-esteem. Disturbances in identification leave children lacking in confidence, fearing their impulses, and feeling hopeless (McDevitt, 1971).

Murphy (1947) theorized that all the real essentials of the self seem to be well separated by the end of infancy, roughly by the time the child is two years old. He felt that starting in infancy, the child's self-image is based in considerable measure on the mother's self-image (Murphy, 1947). In the second year, the child learns that people exist when out of sight and ascribes a separate existence to others (Piaget, 1954; Mahler, 1963, 1975). This increases the child's self-consciousness as a person separate from others.

The acquisition of language helps children to know who they are. Many theorists stressed the fact that self-awareness accelerates and expands as children acquire a more effective use of language (Mead, 1956; Lynd, 1958; Combs & Snygg, 1959; Peller, 1965; Piaget, 1967). Mead (1956) was one of the first to feel that language was the connecting link between others and the self. Children can verbalize the attitudes of others toward themselves, their vocal behaviors can be observed by themselves and the other people. As children use language in many situations, a concept of "generalized other" develops. According to Mead, others' attitudes become organized and children can become their own object and think in terms of both the "I" and the "me," that is, they see themselves as others see them.

Piaget (1967) discussed how behavior is modified, both affectively and intellectually, as a result of the acquisition of language. He stated (pp. 17–18):

"In addition to all the real or material actions the child learns to master during this period, as he did during the preceding period, he now becomes able, thanks to language, to reconstitute his past actions in the form of recapitulation and to anticipate his future actions through verbal representation. This has three consequences essential to mental development: (1) the possibility of verbal exchange with other persons, which heralds the onset of the socialization of action; (2) the internalization of words, i.e., the appearance of thought itself, supported by internal language and a system of signs; (3) last and most important, the internalization of action as such which from now on, rather than being purely perceptual and motor as it has been heretofore, can represent itself intuitively by means of pictures and 'mental experiments.' From the affective point of view a parallel series of transformations follows: development of interpersonal feelings (sympathies and antipathies, respect, etc.) and of internal affectivity organized in a more stable manner than heretofore."

According to Erikson (1955), from the ages of one to four, the environment must allow the child the gradual and well-guided experience of the autonomy of free choice. The task of the caretaker is to allow the child autonomy with which to cope and not make the child feel ashamed of this assertion. Shaming the child indicates to him that his desires to be independent are wrong. Autonomy must include reasonable limits so that he doesn't become overwhelmed with decisions that are too difficult to handle, creating doubt and hindering positive growth toward autonomy. Erikson stated (1955, p. 203): ". . . the kind and degree of a sense of autonomy which parents are able to grant their small children depends on the dignity and the sense of personal independence which they derive from their own lives." In the Erikson model, at the age of four and five, a sense of initiative is manifested in the child's development. The concept of the self as male or female grows as the child identifies with his same-sexed parent, and he intrusively and vigorously comprehends his future roles in society. Conscience becomes firmly established during this period. Erikson (1955) states that too much guilt at this time may develop in the child a feeling that he is essentially bad. The concept of self in the five-year-old depends on whether or not the parent-child relationship has fulfilled the requirements necessary to develop trust, autonomy, and initiative.

SUMMARY

There is an inner consistency that is needed to maintain constancy. Self-concept begins to stabilize and becomes resistant to change early in life. "Core" concepts that are learned early are central to the individual and are the most resistant to change. However, there is a striving toward positive evaluation of self to meet self-esteem needs, so change is possible. New experiences with new significant others can allow this change to occur.

The early childhood years are significant ones in the development of the "core" self-concepts. The influence of healthy or unhealthy parent-child relationships are reflected in children's attitudes toward themselves and are developed from birth onward. During the first year, consistent, loving care leads to a sense of trust, which is the foundation for the development of identity. The healthy relationship with the caretaker enables children to begin the process of separating themselves from the caretaker. This separation-individuation process, if successful, is ideally completed by the time the child is three years old. The development of language and the ability of the child to move in space helps to accelerate the child's sense of autonomy, which aids in the development toward individuation. The child's sense of initiative must be encouraged during the fourth and fifth year. Positive self-concept in all its dimensions will result if trust, autonomy, and initiative are appropriately encouraged.

NOTES

1. Lichtenberg's new theory (1975), mentioned earlier, expands the psychoanalytic view to include daily reality experiences to get an understanding of the self.

Part II

REVIEW OF THE EMPIRICAL
LITERATURE

Chapter 2

AN ASSESSMENT OF SELF-CONCEPT
IN YOUNG CHILDREN

An attempt to understand the self has been made and written about by philosophers from early times, for we have always tried to understand ourselves. More and more, during the past few decades, psychologists have attempted to define the self scientifically, in order to separate it from its metaphysical base. This requires that it become open to empirical verification. The task has been a difficult one, because self-concept is a nebulous construct. Many diverse intruments have been devised to measure various aspects of the self-concept (Wylie, 1961). Self-report techniques to tap the phenomenological self-concept have been developed widely. Projective techniques have been used to infer unconscious self-feelings. Observation has been frequently employed in an attempt to find a relationship between people's views of themselves and others' views of them (Gordon, 1966).

CHILD SELF-CONCEPT USING SELF-REPORT

In her comprehensive book, Wylie (1961) summarizes and critically evaluates the vast literature that has resulted from the interest in the self as a personality construct. In briefer reports, other investigators also have reviewed the different instruments and problems in self-concept research (Strong & Feder, 1961; Crowne & Stephens, 1961; Zirkel, 1971; McNelly, 1972). These reviews convey the fact that, in many respects, the instrumentation leaves much to be desired, particularly in the area of validity. Furthermore, self-concept is such a complex phenomenon that researchers using different techniques have obtained scores that are unrelated (Viney, 1966; Akert, 1959). Akert (1959) argued that individuals do not accept or reject themselves in a total sense, since the self-concept consists of dimensions that individuals value differently. We have a positive global self-concept if there are more positive dimensions than negative ones. There is a need for replication studies with valid and reliable instruments, measuring the various dimensions and correlating them with one another, in order to see the interrelatedness between them.

Self-concept studies using self-report instruments have been rare for children under six. One reason for a lack of data for young children is that of measurement problems. The use of the verbal report, which is a method used frequently with older children and adults, depends on verbal ability and insight that may be lacking in the younger child. A number of investigators have criticized self-report instruments because denial, social desirability, and other unconscious factors distort responses to questions (Brunswick, 1939; Hilgard, 1949; Smith, 1950; Edwards, 1957; Taylor, 1961). Ozehosky and Clark (1971) indicated that verbal devices such as sentence completion tests appear to have little validity at the kindergarten level. Using a self-concept inventory, a nonverbal test, and teacher ratings, they reported congruence between the teacher's ratings and the nonverbal instrument. Other workers also felt that pictorial techniques may be more suitable for children (Williams, 1968; Perkins & Shannon, 1965). Self-responses to pictorial stimuli may differ from those made to verbal material. Perkins and Shannon (1965) suggested that some clarification of this point may be achieved by studies that equate response categories for both techniques.

The stability of the self-concept of young children has been another limitation on research. Very few studies are available that analyze the data for stability. Most of the data come primarily from test-retest correlations more to demonstrate the reliability of a self-evaluation test than to explore the stability of the self-concept (Bloom, 1964; Heath, 1965). In general, self-concept measures that have been longitudinal have demonstrated moderate stability over time. Engel (1959) measured a group of sixth and eighth graders for self-concept. Two years later, she repeated the measurements. Even though the relative stability of the self-concept after two years was 0.53 (ten-day test-retest reliability was 0.68), the younger children showed as high a level of stability as the older ones. Kelly (1955), in a twenty-year study, found consistency in self-rating to be 0.30, which was a statistically significant, moderate correlation. After twenty years, there appeared to be some change and modification, but nevertheless there was a significant stability in self-rating. Kagan and Moss (1962) studied the stability of selected motive-related behaviors, defensive reactions, and modes of interpersonal interactions from earliest childhood through young adulthood. They found that many of the behaviors exhibited by the child during the period from age six to ten and a few during the three- to six-year-old period were moderately present during early adulthood. One problem with this study in which behavior was observed is that self-report is not comparable to observation, and it may not be measuring the same dimension of personality.

The question of the stability of the self-concept is certainly unanswered at this time. Theoretical formulations to test stability, and the factors related to it, have outpaced methodological techniques. The only conclusion that can be made at this time is that some stability seems evident, but longitudinal research has yet to definitely substantiate this premise. The social forces and experiences that individuals have with more and more significant others must have some effect on the stability of their self-concept. Earlier, we said that there is a striving for self-esteem and the change in varying situations is possible. A basic premise of this book is that the school has a primary role in bringing about this change. Kagan and Moss, in the previously quoted study (1962), found that behavioral stability seems to depend on societal expectations for each sex. That is, passive boys and aggressive girls do not show stability in contrast to aggressive boys and passive girls, underlining the significance of changing environmental expectations to effect change in self-feelings.

Self-report instruments focus on individuals' verbalizations of their self-feelings, ignoring the aspect of self-concept that those individuals are either unwilling or unable to reveal about themselves (Hilgard, 1949; Combs & Soper, 1957; Purkey & Cage, 1973). Although a few investigators studying elementary school children did find that there is a high correlation between observation and self-report (Coopersmith, 1959; Ozehosky & Clark, 1971), defense mechanisms frequently bolster self-esteem unrealistically and, therefore, distort revelation of self-feelings (Hilgard, 1949). According to Hilgard, this occurs because there is a need to maintain or restore self-esteem, since belittlement of the self is to be avoided if the individual feels threatened and anxiety or guilt is to be concealed.

Combs & Soper (1957) listed several factors that may influence an individual's self-report resulting in inaccurate responses: clarity of the person's awareness, availability to the person of adequate symbols of expression (language), willingness to cooperate, feelings of personal adequacy, and freedom from threat and expectations of the person (social expectancy). Combs and his co-workers (Combs & Soper, 1957; Combs & Snygg, 1959; Combs, Soper, & Courson, 1963), who are phenomenologists, put more stress on conscious feelings, cognitions, and perceptions, whereas Hilgard (1949) considered the unconscious to be as important; nevertheless, they all felt that because of verbal distortions in self-report, the self-concept should be inferred from the individual's behavior.

THE INFERRED SELF

Inferring the self-concept in young children by observing their behavior has seemed more realistic in view of the problems discussed (Combs et al., 1971). Parker (1966), in a study of thirty sixth-grade students, indicated that inferred self-concept was a more accurate description of students than self-report at a statistically significant level. The self-concept correlated with school records, whereas self-report did not.

Rogers (1951, 1959) and Chodorkoff (1954) found that relatively well-adjusted people have less need for defensiveness, and for them there will be greater agreement between varying descriptions of self, but for those who are threatened—whether it be consciously or unconsciously—we need other ways to evaluate their feelings about themselves.

A growing body of data has accumulated suggesting that individuals are not able to behave independently of the way they think of themselves (La Benne, 1968). The task then becomes one of inferring the self-concept by observing behavior. For example, chidren who lack confidence in their ability to climb, but have the physical capacity to climb, are also likely to behave in ways that are consistent with this feeling. They either avoid climbing, fall because of their anxiety, or request help going from rung to rung. They may not have been physically capable of climbing at one point, but readiness in itself doesn't guarantee success. When readiness occurred, whether they were overprotected, admonished, or felt fearful because of previous experiences in new situations, they felt they couldn't climb. This negative self-concept prevents success and gives children further evidence to support their negative self-concept. We have a vicious cycle of a feeling of failure leading to further failure (the self-fulfilling prophecy).

Patterns of behavior can be ascertained by informally observing children in many different situations over and over again, or by scientific observation that controls variables, using valid and reliable instruments and specific procedures—the methodology of the research worker. Although the child development researcher gives the teacher valuable information about the variables that are important, and many of the instruments presently available have been developed by scientific methods, the informal observation of the teacher can yield as much useful information about children's feelings relating to self. Teachers are in an ideal position to observe behavior over a long period of time. Observation must focus on children's objective behavior, instead of on subjective evaluation of that behavior (Cohen & Stern, 1958; Almy, 1959; Gardner, 1973). In order to become competent observers of children, teachers must learn to see and describe children's actions objectively. What children do and how they do it, give us clues to their feelings about themselves.

On the other hand, Combs (1965, p. 66) asked observers to "... get the 'feel' of what's going on, to see if they can get inside the skin of the person being observed, to understand how things look from this point of view." There are problems with this approach, for each of us have had different experiences that color our perceptions of others. Nevertheless, experience and our sensitivity to what lurks beneath the behavior is important and can yield valid information about children and can help us form hypotheses that can be verified by further observation. For example, a child may consistently refuse to listen to a group story. The teacher has to see the child's resistance from the child's point of view. Instead of punishing the child for refusing to listen, the teacher has to allow the child to do something else while the story is being read. The teacher understands that the child is not yet able to conform to this pattern. The teacher may not yet know the reason for this reaction, although he may have some hypotheses relating to them. These hypotheses become verifiable or refuted by further objective observation of the child's behavior. In time, after gathering enough information, the teacher will be able to create conditions that would more likely help the child grow and be able to spend more and more time with the group.

Borowitz et al. (1970), in a study of thirty-two four-year-old lower-class children, assessed competence levels to compare ratings from various sources on the child's interactions with toys, examiners, and play situations. They found that the highest correlation occurred between psychiatrists' and teachers' judgments of overall competence, indicating that teachers who objectively focus on the play of young children can agree substantially with the evaluations of psychiatrists who are highly trained, objective observers.

Observational records accumulated over time can reveal recurring patterns. Alterations in the school environment based on these patterns can allow changes to be affected in order to enhance self-concept. For example, if children denigrate their appearance in play, the teacher can provide experiences that focus on enhancing their attitude about their appearance. Some problems that occur when we make assumptions about underlying feelings based on observed behavior are (1) that the same overt behavior in two different children can hide opposite feelings, (2) that opposite actions of two different children can indicate equal self-concepts or (3) that the same child at different times or in different roles can differ in behavior. An example of the same behavior, but opposite self-feelings is when two children fight for a toy. One may be fighting to prove he's not weak, even though he feels weak. The other may be fighting to recover a toy that is rightfully his and he may feel confident about his ability to do so. An example of two children who reveal opposite behaviors, but feel equally negative about themselves can occur when one child denigrates herself and/or others and when a second child exaggerates her abilities. As discussed earlier, if the former acts stupid and tells the teacher about her unwillingness to cope with academic tasks, she is consciously aware of her feelings. On the other hand, the latter may instead call other children "stupid," which is a projection of her attitudes about herself onto others, or she may brag about how smart she is. These negative feelings may not be related to reality; in fact, she may be quite smart for her age.

Observations of contradictory behavior in the same child at two different times and in different situations are common. A child may be a braggart at one time, stating he can climb better than anyone else, and at another time he may cry and say, "I can't do that puzzle" and ask for help. Relaxation of defenses may occur when the child feels more comfortable about revealing true feelings, or he may feel more adequate physically than academically. Because children feel more secure in some roles than in others, a child may be withdrawn in school but outgoing at home. This is sometimes evident with lower-income children in middle-class school environments. They may have low academic self-concepts because their experiences and concepts may be different from their school peers; thus, they may feel incompetent in the role of student but competent about their body image and social role in their families.

Summary

A review of the assessment techniques used to evaluate self-concept has revealed that methodological problems are common. An example is the difficulty of poor instrumentation and procedures that are magnified when using self-report to measure self-concept in young children. As a result, self-report as an assessment technique is rare in early childhood. Longitudinal studies measuring stability of the individual's concept of self are also sparse, although there is evidence that some stability occurs.

Self-concept inferred from behavior seems to be a better method to evaluate young children's self-feelings. Distortions resulting from verbal measures and language problems are eliminated; however, observation requires skill—which demands an objective viewing of behavior. The same behavior can have different meanings, while different behaviors can indicate equally negative self-feelings. Additionally, there is the possibility that a child's self-concept can vary in differing situations. These difficulties are not insurmountable for the teacher who is in an ideal position to evaluate children over extended periods of time in varying situations.

Relationships Between Maternal Self-Concept and Child Self-Concept

Researchers have tried to measure specific parental-child processes that affect self-concept. Several researchers have put considerable emphasis on the "looking-glass theory"

(Cooley, 1902; Gecas et al, 1974) which supports the predominance of reflected appraisals that children receive from significant others. In this theory, how a parent perceives and treats his or her child results in an unfavorable or favorable self-concept. Others have adhered to the "modeling theory" or "social learning" theory (Bandura & Walters, 1963; Bandura & Kupers, 1964; Bandura, 1969), which stresses the imitation of the child of the parents' behavior. This theory suggests that a child's self-concept is positively related to parental self-concept. The psychoanalytical viewpoint (Fenichel, 1953) also supports the correlation of child self-concept with parental self-concept, but this identificatory process is more than conscious imitation. The child introjects (takes within himself) the image of the parents that would be the unconscious standard that he measures himself against and with which he identifies.

The significant others' appraisals operate in both theories. How a mother perceives and then treats her child and how she sees herself (which is incorporated by the child and become his standards and expectations) seem to be inseparable from one another. Additionally, there is a desire by parents that their children be like them and identify with their ideals. This, too, is consciously and unconsciously communicated. Research evidence that acceptance of self is related to acceptance of others is reviewed in Chapter 3. The treatment accorded by parents to their children can be expected to reflect their self-feelings. This behavior theoretically correlates with child self-concept, meaning that parents who accept themselves are likely to accept their child, treat the child warmly, and have a child who then accepts himself, so in essence the "looking glass" and the "modeling" theory are both operative.

To support this argument, Malone (1967), in his study of forty-five urban slum children from multiproblem families, noted that low self-esteem and self-devaluation was evidenced in the mothers and there was a close relationship between maternal self-denigration and the children's poor self-images. The parents' sense of hopelessness regarding their future lot in life and helplessness to deal with personal concerns or environmental forces pervaded family life. Most damaging of all for the children's feeling of self-worth was their mothers' tendency to devalue them.

A review of research relating maternal self-esteem and child rearing will be discussed first, exploring the hypothesis that the treatment accorded by parents to their children reflects their own self-feelings. This is followed by studies relating child self-concept to child rearing and studies relating child self-concept to maternal self-concept.

Maternal Self-Concept and Child Rearing

In their study of working-class and middle-class five-year-old children and their mothers, Sears, Maccoby, and Levin (1957) observed that mothers who felt and expressed warmth toward their children tended to have higher self-esteem than those who didn't feel and express such attitudes. Mothers who spanked frequently even though they thought it less effective were found to have lower self-esteem than the mothers who punished equally often but thought it did some good. Mothers who were found to have comparatively low self-esteem tended not to have wanted their children in the first place. Medinnus and Curtis (1963) reported, in a study of fifty-six mothers in a cooperative nursery school, that mothers who had high self-acceptance, were more approving of their children than mothers with low self-acceptance. In his study of five- and six-year-old children, Swift (1966) noted that parents who expressed less need to control the behavior of their children had a significantly higher level of psychological health than those who exercised more control. Dreyer and Haupt (1966) found that kindergarteners whose mothers fostered autonomy and independence in their children had higher self-esteem than children whose parents were more controlling. In Coopersmith's (1967) investigation, mothers who had high self-esteem were more likely to accept their roles as mothers and carry them out in a realistic and effective manner. Symonds (1939), in a study of four groups of parents who were accepting or rejecting, dominating, or submissive, found that accepting parents were more likely to have had parents who were themselves adjusted and accepting. He also observed that parents were likely to have an attitude toward their children that resembled that of their own parent of the same sex.

Behrens (1954) felt that the mother's integration into the maternal role depends on her perception of herself and her role. In a study of twenty-five urban, lower-middle-class nursery school children and their mothers, she found that the quality of the child's adjustment depended more on the child's total interaction with the mother and, more specifically, to the mother's character structure than on any specific child-rearing technique.

All the above studies have indicated that maternal child-rearing attitudes, and not necessarily any specific technique, are related to how a mother feels about herself. For example, a mother who feels inadequate in the mothering role will communicate these feelings to her child by her verbal and/or nonverbal behavior. It would be difficult for her to be warm and accepting whatever she did.

Child Self-Concept and Child Rearing

Studies showing the relationship between parental rearing practices and child self-concept have included subjects ranging from preschool to high school. In an investigation of middle-class preschool children, using the Sears, Maccoby, and Levin questionnaire, Schwartz (1966) found that children who had high self-concept had mothers who reported affectionate warmth toward their children. Baum-rind (1967), in another study of middle-class preschool children, concluded that parents of the most competent and mature boys and girls were notably firm, loving, de-manding, and understanding. The Dreyer and Haupt (1966) study, relating maternal control and nurturance[1] to kindergarten children's adjustment to the school situation, indicated that children subjected to high maternal control and low maternal nurturance showed less capacity to cope with the demands of a school situation. Sears (1970), in his follow-up study of 159 children studied seven years earlier, noted that high self-concept in the children at age twelve was related to high maternal and paternal warmth as re-ported at the age of five. In addition, coming from a small family and being the oldest child were also found to be related to high self-concept. For boys only, high self-con-cept was associated with good father-mother relations. Carlson (1963) examined the relative role of identification with parents and peers in the development of child self-concept among forty-three sixth-grade children. Those who identified with supportive parents were reported to be consistently more accepting, less dependent on current so-cial relationships, and were more accepted by their peers. Using a self-report instrument, Coopersmith (1967) found that domination and lack of affection, lack of regard for good behavior, and lack of firm rules, as well as severe punishment by mothers of preadolescents, resulted in lower self-esteem for their children. High-self-esteem boys tended to be more emotionally stable, self-reliant, and resilient. The parents in Coopersmith's study tended to have high expectations of the high-esteem children and to give them consistent support and encouragement. These parents seemed to provide a balance between protective-ness and encouragement of autonomy in that the children were not allowed to try more than they were capable of doing. Fathers of high-self-esteem children in this study were seen to take a more active and supportive role in child rearing than did fathers of children with low self-esteem. Katz (1967b) observed that boys who had a propensity for self-devaluation, low achievement, and anxiety perceived that their parents had low interest and acceptance towards them and were punitive. The subjects in his study were fifth- and sixth-grade black children who described the characteristic reactions of their parents in a variety of situations.

Helper (1958), correlating parental acceptance of eighth- and ninth-grade children with the children's self-evaluations, reported a positive relationship between the two measures. Rosenberg's (1965) results indicated that parental positive attention was significantly related to the self-esteem of the adolescents. Cox (1966), in a study of sixth, seventh, and eighth grades, noted that low self-concept correlated with parental rejection and family tension. Sarason, et al. (1960) indicated that mothers of anxious children responded to and evaluated their children in terms of their own standards and needs, rather than the needs of the child. This parental evaluation led to anxiety and a negative self-concept. Sarason et al. (1960) and Katz (1967b) found that the fathers of high-anxiety children were harsher in their parental judgments than the fathers of low-anxiety children. This was not true of the mothers. Fisher and Cleveland (1958), in a cross-cultural study, used the Rorschach test to measure the perception that people have of their body images and reported the relationship of this to child rearing in nine cultural groups. They concluded that a definite, clear, body image was associated with permissive acceptance of impulse release in young children. They theorized that the more a parent inhibits a child, the harder it is to work out a close communication style, and the less definite is the child's body image. Their finding is consistent with psychoanalytic theory.

In summary, the above studies suggest that parental love manifested by warmth, supportive encouragement, consistency, realistic expectation, and a balance between protectiveness and reward rather than punishment is more likely to result in positive child self-concept. Mothers who have positive self-feelings are more likely to utilize the above-mentioned child-rearing practices.

The studies have not been unanimous in showing a correlation between parental behavior and child self-concept. Burchinal (1958) reported no significant relationship between personality characteristics of children and the parents' child-rearing attitudes. Watson (1957) found no clear personality advantage based on parental upbringing. He compared children in kindergarten to grade six from permissive homes to another group of the same age from strictly disciplined homes. The personality differences that emerged were in favor of children brought up in permissive homes.

Ausuble (1952) commented that parental behavior affected the child's ego development only if the child perceived the parents' behavior. Different children may therefore be affected differently by similar treatment. Measurement of accurate perception is another problem. The lack of significant differences in the Burchinal and Watson studies and the small differences found in some of the other investigations may have been actual or only the result of the particular instruments that were used. Observation would have been preferable to the questionnaires that were usually used, since parents may have distorted the responses and answered in terms of that they thought they were expected to have been doing rather than what they actually were doing. This is supported by a study by Brody (1965). She had mothers of preschool children respond to a parent attitude questionnaire. In addition, independent, direct observations on the same dimensions that were in the questionnaire were made of those mothers' behaviors with their children in a play setting. Less than half of the behavioral indices were significantly related to maternal attitude scales. These findings led Brody to conclude that there was no strong correlation between the verbalized child-rearing attitudes and observations of the mother's behavior with her child. Even observational studies can be questioned, since the presence of the investigator can distort the interactions.

Maternal Self-Concept and Child Self-Concept

There are some studies relating maternal self-concept to child self-concept (Davidson, 1959; Adams & Sarason, 1963; Malone, 1967; Tocco & Bridges, 1971). In the Davidson (1959) and Adams and Sarason (1963) studies, mothers of highly anxious children were found to be more defensive, less verbal, and more dependent and anxious. Malone (1967), observed that there was a correlation between maternal self-esteem and the low self-evaluations of their preschool children. These subjects were preschool children and their mothers from multiproblem, urban slum families. In the Tocco and Bridges (1971) study of the self-concepts of 323 lower-income mothers and their children in kindergarten and first grade, it was found that the mothers' self-concepts were positively related to those of their children. The instruments used for mothers and children do not measure similar dimensions of the self-concept, however. This has been a problem in self-concept research when correlating children and adults in the same study. It is difficult to find instruments that are comparable for both age groups. The problem also applies when we try to evaluate different studies, because the results may be due just as much to the varying dimensions being measured as to real similarities or differences between the samples tested.

SUMMARY

This chapter focused on studies that correlate maternal self-concept with child rearing, child self-concept and child rearing, and child self-concept with maternal self-concept. It is suggested that both the "looking-glass theory" and the "modeling theory" are operative in the socialization of the child. Most of these studies seem to indicate that lack of parental attention, lack of affection, lack of firm rules, severe punishment, and family tension have an adverse affect on children's self-feelings. There seems to be a relationship between maternal self-esteem and attitudes of warmth and permissiveness that affect the children's feelings toward themselves. However, there is support for the idea that exactly what we do may be less important than our attitude toward ourselves. Studies reported primarily deal with mother-child relationships. The father's child-rearing attitudes and his interaction with the mother and child also affect child self-concept, but not enough studies have tested this relationship.

NOTES

1. Nurturance is the parent's affectionate care and attention that encourage the child's growth and development.

Chapter 3

THE EFFECT OF TEACHERS AND OTHER SCHOOL EXPERIENCES ON SELF-CONCEPT

There have been theories suggesting that if an individual thinks well of himself, he is likely to think well of others (Adler, 1930; Fromm, 1939; Murphy, 1947; Rogers, 1951). Empirical studies also have supported the concept that those who accept themselves tend to accept others (Sheerer, 1949; Berger, 1952; Omwake, 1954; Trent, 1957; Suinn & Geiger, 1965; Aspy, 1969). Omwake (1954) found that those who accepted themselves perceived others as self-accepting. In his study of 120 third graders, Aspy (1969) concluded that there was a positive relationship between teachers' self-concept and students' cognitive growth.

Combs, et al. (1969) indicated that teachers' attitudes toward themselves may be more important than their techniques, practices, or materials. Purkey (1974) also stated that positive teacher attitudes transcend methods, skills, techniques, performance, and competencies. These positive attitudes are more likely to be present if the teacher is confident and well adjusted. This was substantiated in Spaulding's study (1964), which found that children with higher self-concepts were in classrooms in which teachers were more learner supportive and were calm, acceptant, and facilitative. When teachers were more dominative, sarcastic, grim, and threatening, the children had negative self-feelings. Spaulding's well-executed study, carried out in twenty-one fourth- and sixth-grade classrooms in nine schools, evaluated the relationship between achievement, teacher behavior, and child self-concept.

Teachers are "significant others" in the lives of young children and those who are threatened by feelings of inadequacy are bound to project these feelings onto the children they teach, regardless of how they structure their programs. Their feelings of worthlessness are particularly devastating for those children who already have negative self-concepts and multiproblem home situations. The effect of negative school attitudes tend to be less severe if the home engenders (and continues to engender) positive self-feelings.

The focus in education is to find teachers who primarily feel good about themselves and who can learn appropriate methods and materials to increase their effectiveness as teachers.

SELF-FULFILLING PROPHECY

The self-fulfilling prophecy is based on the assumption that children will behave as others expect them to behave. Since behavior reflects self-feelings, the self-fulfilling prophecy is a description of how our self-concept is affected by significant others; that is, we see ourselves and act as others treat us and expect us to act.

Davidson and Lang (1960) found that children who perceived their teacher's feelings toward them as being favorable saw themselves positively. A number of studies have reported agreement between teachers' perceptions of lower-income students' self-concepts and the students' self-perceptions (Keller, 1963; Howard, 1968; Long & Henderson, 1968). Davidson and Lang (1960) found that the more positively pupils perceived their teachers' feelings toward them the better was their academic achievement and the more desirable their classroom behavior. Brookover, et al. (1964) and Soares and Soares (1970) also described positive relationships between students' achievements and the perception of them by significant others. Rosenthal and Jacobson (1968) presented similar results. In their study, teachers were told that an experimental group of children actually chosen at random, were "spurters." The children so designated were compared to a control group not so labeled and were found to show higher achievement at the end of the year. In reality, there was no difference between the two groups at the beginning of the experiment. It is unfortunate that the processes that mediated between children's behavior and teacher's expectations were not measured. Rosenthal and Jacobson reported that the differences between the experimental and control groups decreased as one moved from the first to the sixth grade. The authors suggested that the difference between younger and older children was due to three possible factors. First, younger children may have been more malleable, less fixed, and more capable of changing. Second, children's reputations may not have been so fixed in the school in the early grades. Third, the teachers in the early grades may have been more effective than those in the later grades. There are theories suggesting that the children's self-concepts become more stable as they get older and they become more resistant to environmental influences. Unfortunately, the study has been subject to question because of statistical problems pointed out by Thorndike (1969). Thorndike questioned the adequacy of the data gathering and data analysis and the appropriateness of the conclusions based on these. He stated that the conclusion that a self-fulfilling prophecy exists may have been correct, but that this study did not substantiate it. Brophy and Good (1972), in their review of studies on the self-fulfilling prophecy, reported that the effects were observable and measureable and were probably strongest early in the year before teachers had had much time to observe the students. These same authors (Brophy & Good, 1971) in a study of first-grade children, found that teachers were more likely to stay with high-achieving children than with low-expected-achievement children after they failed to answer an initial question. With the high-achieving children, the teachers would more likely repeat their question, give a clue, or ask another question. They tended to call on someone else when the low-achieving children failed to answer. There were also differences in teacher feedback. Teachers failed to give feedback more often to low-achievement children than high-achievement students and high-achievement students were more likely to be praised and less likely to be criticized (Brophy & Good, 1970). Rowe (1969) also noted that teachers waited significantly longer for a response after questioning a high-achieving student than a low-achieving one. When teachers were trained to increase the waiting time, students in the low groups were found to speak up more often, sometimes enough to change the teachers' expectations.

Children from lower socioeconomic groups may manifest behaviors that prejudice teachers' attitudes about the children's learning ability, although these children's behaviors have little relationship to the children's cognitive potential. Brown and Cleary (1973) reported that teachers were influenced by the socioeconomic status of the children, in that they judged the children's ability to learn in terms of their social class membership. Davidson and Lang (1960) concluded, in their study of fourth and sixth graders from a wide socioeconomic range, that upper and middle social-class groups perceived their teachers' feelings toward them more favorably than those in the lower social class.

Rist (1970), in a longitudinal study following a group of lower-income black children from kindergarten through grade two, observed that the subjective evaluations that the kindergarten teacher made about the children's academic potential were based on the teacher's determination of success factors that were related to social class expectations, rather than to measured ability. These ideal traits that the teacher considered necessary for success determined where the children were placed by the eighth day of school. The children who were placed in table one were chosen on the basis of their ability to interact with adults well, their verbalizations in standard English, their leadership abilities, how neat and clean they were, their ability to participate in a group, and the education, employment background, and intactness of their family. The teacher paid more attention to the children put at the first table than to those at tables two and three and, by the end of the year, a self-fulfilling prophecy had occurred and the children's objective scores and behavior matched their placement. There were no statistically significant differences in intelligence between the groups earlier in kindergarten. The top group continued to be in the top group through second grade. No child from a lower group moved up and tests indicated that they were behind. This study with a small group of children clearly revealed the operation of the self-fulfilling prophecy in a blatant way. In other situations, the process could operate in more subtle ways by teachers' nonverbal interactions with children and their underuse of reinforcement behavior.

The sex of the child has also been found to be related to expectations. Palardy (1969) reported that when first-grade teachers in his study expected boys to be less successful than girls in reading, the boys were less successful. On the other hand, when teachers saw no differences between the sexes, differences were not found. Palardy compared five classes for each group of expectations. This result seems to indicate that more boys may be capable of reading at an earlier age. With many capable boys, teachers may not be conveying the feeling that reading is expected of them. Some teachers may generalize their expectation of low reading ability to all boys because they know that girls as a group learn to read earlier than boys. This group expectation may not be accurate when focusing on an individual child. To support this point of view, Stanchfield (1973) used a program to develop reading readiness skills in a sequential, developmental order with kindergarten children representing black, Mexican, and white children. She found no significant differences in the reading achievement of boys and girls. Stanchfield concluded that boys will learn to read if instruction is adapted to meet their learning needs and abilities. The same is true of girls. She stated that the factors that contribute to boys' problems, such as greater aggressiveness, higher activity levels, lesser listening verbal skills, and shorter attention span, may have a cultural component. Boys may be less eager to please the teacher and less motivated to conform to expectations. Another study, which controlled for sex and which looked at how teacher expectations affected boys and girls performance differently, was done by Doyle et al. (1971). They asked first-grade teachers to estimate students' intelligence quotients before an IQ test was administered and found that the girls' IQs were generally overestimated and the boys' IQs were generally underestimated. At the end of the year, students who had been overestimated achieved more than their intelligence scores would have predicted, while those who were underestimated achieved less. Again, the varying attitudes of teachers toward boys and girls predisposed them to have different expectations for each sex not based on objective intellectual factors that could affect cognitive behavior. This may be one reason why girls get better grades in school than boys do (Maccoby & Jacklin, 1974). The problem becomes greater if knowledge of a child's intelligence score is available to teachers. It gives them information that may support their attitudes. Although the intelligence score is frequently not an accurate reflection of the child's true ability, it may feed into the self-fulfilling prophecy. Lower-income children are more likely to be discriminated against in verbal tests. Therefore, this problem is a particularly prevalent one for children from minority groups whose experiental background is different from that of the majority group child, the population with which the tests were standardized (Ginsburg, 1972).

The self-fulfilling prophecy could affect peer interactions. The children in the Rist study (1970), who were in the lower groups, were ridiculed and belittled by the other children and had in-group hostility. Sears and Hilgard (1964) found that teachers who liked pupils tended to have pupils who liked each other. Brown and Cleary (1973) reported agreement between teachers' ratings of children and their classmates rating of them. Are teachers forcing these perceptions of others by their own behavior, or are the perceptions of classmates and teachers independent of each other and based on the characteristics of the children being evaluated? Both of these factors could be true because we act as others treat us and expect us to act. If a child feels negatively about himself, his behavior will likely reveal these feelings, whether or not the teacher is treating the child negatively. Cox (1974) found, in a study of sixth- to ninth-grade students, that children's perceptions of parental acceptance or rejection affected peer acceptance or rejection. If the teacher is overtly reinforcing rejection, this will exacerbate the problem. Teachers as models can counter the other experiences of these children and change perceptions of both the children themselves and their peers. Retish (1973) found that teachers could influence pupil acceptance by peers by overt reinforcement techniques. In his study, overt teachers' reinforcement that was instituted for three weeks resulted in significant net gains in the sociometric status of second and fifth graders. The sample consisted of twenty students low in self-esteem who were matched with a control group receiving no reinforcement. Ludwig and Maehr (1967) also found that improvement in self-ratings occurred in their study of sixty-five, twelve- to fourteen-year-olds after approval by significant others. In their study, the evaluation spread from the areas directly approved to other areas of self-appraisal.

The self-fulfilling prophecy is not supported in all research (Fleming & Auttomen, 1971; Brophy & Good, 1970). Brophy and Good (1972), in a review of research on the self-fulfilling prophecy, reviewed studies that showed no correlation between teachers' expectations and students' academic performances, as well as studies that did correlate these two variables. They stated that in studies where experimenters persuaded teachers that children had certain potential (which may not have been based on reality and where teacher differences were not controlled), the self-fulfilling prophecy was not supported. The teachers had to believe that the experimenter's information was accurate.

There is enough evidence from real situations to support the operation of the self-fulfilling prophecy. Most of the studies show that teachers tend to reinforce student's behavior by their overt or less obvious nonverbal behavior. This, no doubt, affects children's self-concepts and could damage self-esteem.

SUMMARY

Teachers' feelings toward themselves have been shown to affect their acceptance of the children in their classrooms.

This acceptance is revealed by warm supportive behavior, which has been related to high child self-concept. The self-fulfilling prophecy can decrease self-concept. If teachers have negative preconceived ideas about children, which are unrelated to the children's abilities, it can be damaging to their academic and social behavior. Minority group children are particularly vulnerable because their values often differ from those of the majority group.

It is suggested that teachers' attitudes and their verbal and nonverbal behaviors transcend techniques and methods. Children who lack positive self-concept to begin with undoubtedly can be more damaged by destructive teacher behaviors since already-existent negative self-feelings would be reinforced.

SELF-CONCEPT AND ACHIEVEMENT

McClelland et al. (1953) did the original research evaluating achievement motivation, as reflected in TAT fantasy material (Thematic Apperception Test). They suggested that the motive to achieve in children involved standards of excellence permitting the children to evaluate their performance positively or negatively. Atkinson (1964) and Atkinson and Feather (1966) proposed that the tendency to succeed or not to succeed resulted from the positive or negative effects of several factors: fear of failure, perceived probability of success, the incentive value of the task goal, and intrinsic positive motives. These studies did not focus on young children and did not correlate self-concept with achievement.

Numerous investigators have observed a positive correlation between self-concept and achievement. Studies done with children after the first grade found that children with learning difficulties tended to see themselves less adequately than those who were doing well (Lecky, 1945; Walsh, 1956; Coopersmith, 1959; Bruck & Bodwin, 1962; Shaw & Alves, 1963; Brookover et al., 1964; Taylor, 1964;

Henderson, Long, & Ziller, 1965; Zimmerman & Allebrand, 1965; Teigland, 1966; McDaniel, 1967; Caplin,
1968; Herbert, 1968; Williams & Cole, 1968; Gill, 1969;
Piers & Harris, 1969; Frerichs, 1970; Purkey, 1970; Sears,
1970; Greene & Zirkel, 1971; Felker, 1972; Trowbridge &
Trowbridge, 1972; Williams, 1973; Kifer, 1975). Some of
the earlier studies did not control for sex, intelligence, or
socioeconomic class. If these variables are not controlled,
they can obfuscate real correlations, since they can affect
achievement independently of self-concept. Some studies
worth mentioning in greater detail will be discussed.

Lecky (1945) was one of the first investigators to relate
self-concept to school achievement. He noted that some
children made the same number of spelling errors on each
page, regardless of the varying difficulties of the words. He
felt that their responses were due to how they felt they
could spell rather than their actual spelling ability. In a
large sample study of 1050 seventh-grade students Brookover et al. (1964) noted a significant relationship between
self-concept of ability and grade point average, even when
measured intelligence was controlled. Walsh (1956), compared two groups of middle-class bright boys in elementary
school classrooms, one a high-achieving group, the other
a low-achieving group. Using boy dolls to assess their self-
feelings, she found that the low achievers consistently portrayed the boy dolls as being restricted in actions, they were
unable to express their feelings appropriately, and they felt
criticized, rejected, or isolated. The teachers agreed with
the results of the experiment in 90 percent of the cases.
Bruck and Bodwin (1962) and Shaw and Alves (1963), in
studies of normal- and high-intelligence children in elementary and secondary school classrooms, also found that
there was a positive relationship between self-concept and
educational problems. In the Bruck and Bodwin (1962)
study, self-concept was defined as self-confidence, freedom
to express appropriate feelings, liking for self, satisfaction

for one's attainment, and having feelings that one was personally appreciated by others. Williams and Cole (1968), in a study of 80 sixth graders, reported significant positive correlations between the children's concepts of school, social status at school, emotional adjustment, mental ability, reading achievement, and mathematical achievement. Wylie (1963), in a study of 823 junior high school children, controlled for intelligence and found that girls, blacks, and children whose fathers were in lower-level occupations tended to have lower self-estimates relating to achievement ability.

Reading, an achievement area that is a significant skill essential for success in our society, has been found to be correlated with self-concept in many recent studies with children in grades one through twelve (Henderson & Long, 1965; Zimmerman & Allebrand, 1965; Williams & Cole, 1968; Hebert, 1968; Sears, 1970; Trowbridge & Trowbridge, 1972; Williams, 1973). Green and Zirkel (1971) and McDaniel (1967), in studies of Spanish-speaking elementary school children, found that self-concept was positively related to verbal skills in both English and Spanish. In most of these studies race, sex, and social class were controlled and the significant correlations between self-concept and achievement held with these variables controlled. A few studies have indicated that defensiveness can mask correlations between achievement and self-concept (Greenberg et al., 1965; Soares & Soares, 1969; Davidson & Greenberg, 1967). Greenberg (1970) reported, in her sample of fourth-grade, urban, lower-class Negro children, that the good achievers assigned more neutral attitudes to themselves on a semantic differential scale, and the poor achievers chose the positive side more. Soares and Soares (1969) found that middle-class boys were more realistic in their aspirations and achievements and lower in self-concept as compared to lower-class boys. Long (1969) suggested that defensiveness of the lower-class boys in the Soares and

Soares study would tend to cause them to reveal inflated self-concepts, thus masking their true negative feelings.

All the above studies were done after the beginning of the kindergarten experience. It is difficult to determine which is cause and which effect, since failure in school could develop negative self-concept instead of the reverse. Studying children before the effects of academic failure are felt might help to find the cause-effect relationships. A few studies of beginning kindergarten children have evaluated the effect of early childhood self-concept on learning (Wattenberg & Clifford, 1964; Ozehosky & Clark, 1970; Flynn, 1974; Bridgeman & Shipman, 1975). Flynn (1974), in a study relating self-concept to school readiness in lower-class Negro children aged 3.9 to 4.9, found that self-concept accounted for a significant percentage of achievement variance for both sexes. Ozehosky and Clark (1970) reported that the self-concept of a sample of 100 children was related to achievement in kindergarten, not only as measured on self-concept tests but also as reported by teachers judging the children's self-concepts. Wattenberg and Clifford (1964) measured beginning kindergarten children's self-concepts in the competence and self-worth dimensions as well as their intelligence. Two-and-a-half years later these same subject's progress in reading was determined and their self-concept measures were repeated. In general, the measured self-concept at the kindergarten level was predictive of reading achievement two-and-a-half years later, but was not significantly related to mental test scores.

Bridgeman and Shipman (1975) investigated the relationship between achievement and self-esteem in a longitudinal study (prekindergarten through third grade) of 467 black children, controlling for sex, preschool experience, social class and geographic area. Self-esteem scores were not predictive of third grade achievement, but children with high self-esteem in the third grade were achieving in reading and mathematics at that time. There is a serious question about the validity of the self-concept test used earlier, so that this study does not provide evidence for any cause–effect theory.

Other researchers evaluating preschool children found positive correlations between various social–emotional characteristics and later school achievement (Armstrong, 1969; Borowitz et al, 1970; Kohn & Rosman, 1974). Kohn and Rosman (1974) evaluated preschool cognitive functioning, preschool social-emotional functioning, and social factors in 209 black and white boys and correlated the results with elementary school achievement. They found that these preschool boys, who are more likely to utilize their cognitive processes productively later on, are active, assertive, curious, well-organized, and task-oriented.

Armstrong (1969) did a study to test the relationship between patterns of intellectual competencies and coping behavior in nursery school children. He found that, regardless of socioeconomic status, children who got low scores on Stanford-Binet Vocabulary Sub-Tests and/ or the Draw-a-Man Test, but average scores on the Black Design Sub-Test of the Wechsler Intelligence Test (the part evaluating primarily perceptual-motor competence) and the Test of Logical Reasoning (an estimate of competence in logical operations), were rated as responding defensively when coping in the Stanford-Binet situation and in a permissive free-play situation. Children with test profiles involving either all-average or all-low test scores received nondefensive coping ratings.

The defensiveness that was manifested in response to the intelligence test and in play in children, who were normal in logical reasoning and perceptual-motor competence, might indicate that these children felt threatened when relating to new materials. This lack of coping ability, which was undoubtedly related to negative feelings about self-performance, could affect later school achievement.

Borowitz et al. (1970) described and evaluated thirty-two four-year-old, lower-class children's play to determine the salient variables that contributed to their competency levels. The competency levels were determined by teachers and psychologists during the child's interactions with the toys, examiners, and the play situation. The variables that were found significant were the degree of organization of play, the age of appropriate developmental level reflected in the psychosexual content of the play,[1] the quality of imaginativeness in the play, and the quality of verbal articulation. These variables are significant for success in school at the four-year-old level. It is important that teachers working with young children provide conditions that further imaginative play and verbalization to enhance emotional growth. It would have been instructive if there were follow-up studies correlating these children's competency ratings with their future cognitive performance.

High-achieving children, who have high self-concepts, seem to evaluate themselves with realistic criticism only. They accept responsibility for intellectual achievement, are less in need of external reinforcement, and get more approval than disapproval from others (Katz, 1967b; Haynes & Kaufer, 1971; Katz et al, 1976). In a study of 150 third- and fourth-grade students, Haynes and Kaufer (1971) found that high achievers tended to be more critical than low achievers, but the former declined in self-criticism over time, supporting the point of view that they are more likely than low achievers to expect increases in success in time. Katz (1967b, 1976) in studies of black elementary school children, observed that academically unsuccessful boys were more critical and less positive in overall self-evaluations than academically successful boys, despite the fact that no apparent differences were found in the quality of their performance in the experiment. There were no differences in the high- and low-achieving girls. This suggests that academic failure is more central to boys' self-evaluations than to girls' self-evaluations. This result is supported by other studies reviewed in Chapter 4. Haynes and Kaufer (1971) reported that there was an internal mechanism of self- evaluation by which academically successful individuals sustained their performance. They found, in their study, that children of low standing needed external reinforcement but that high achievers showed as much change when feedback was absent as when it was present. Ziller (1973) found that persons with high self-esteem had a history of social reinforcement. He also found that when social reinforcement was withheld they reinforced themselves. In his first paper (1967a), reviewing studies of racial differences in intellectual achievement, Katz concluded that underachievement was associated with a lack of internalized standards or with standards that were excessively low. In his later study (1967b), Katz modified this view because he found the self-critical responses of low achievers indicative of rigidly high self-evaluative standards. The low-achieving children were uncertain about how the experimenter would react to their performance. This could arouse anticipatory anxiety. Katz concluded that self-criticism results in reducing this anxiety. In a sense, the child who feels he will not perform adequately has internalized the negative expectations he thinks other have of him. In his 1976 study, Katz used black and white experimenters and found high achievers evaluated by black experimenters were more self-critical, possibly indicating that they were more apprehensive, since these children were not generally in contact with black authority figures.

Felker and Thomas (1971) reported that fourth-grade children with high self-concepts indicated that they made positive statements about themselves while doing schoolwork, while those with low self-concepts did not do so. Felker and Bahlke (1970) and Stanwyck and Felker (1971) observed, in studies of middle-class elementary school children, that children with high self-concepts accepted responsibility for their own school success. Pupils with low self-concepts gradually assumed less responsibility for such success and showed higher anxiety levels.

Approval or disapproval from adults, as determinants of the internalized or private evaluations of achievement, were studied by Crandall et al. (1960a), Katz (1967a,b, 1976), Bilby (1973), and Dion and Miller (1973). Katz (1967b, 1976) found that the greater the extent of the perceived disapproval and the less perceived approval from their parents, the less favorably the children in his study evaluated their products. Bilby (1973), in his study of fifth- and sixth-grade students, also revealed that parents' evaluations were crucial to children's feelings of competence as students. Dion and Miller (1973), in their study of black inner-city boys, found that those subjects receiving disapproval-oriented reinforcement were less self-approving and less favorable overall in evaluating their own performance than those receiving approval-oriented reinforcement, despite the fact that there were no differences in actual past performance. Crandall et al. (1960b) found that mothers of preschool children, who responded positively when their children sought approval for their achievements, had children who exhibited more achievement efforts in free-play situations than those whose children did not receive such approval. Furthermore, those mothers who usually rewarded and praised their children's achievement efforts spontaneously even when their children did not seek such approval, had children who displayed strong achievement behaviors.

Epps (1970) felt that the fear of failure and the perceived probability of success were related to self-esteem, since low self-esteem may be symptomatic of both fear-of-failure tendencies and perceived low probability of success in a valued domain. The fear of failure-oriented person would be afraid of competition and evaluation because failure would be very painful to him. The child with low initial self-esteem would be less self-confident, would approach new tasks cautiously, and would be likely to be less persistent in meeting academic demands. As a result, she would usually receive fewer rewards and her self-confidence would be lowered. Furthermore the lack of self-confidence would usually be associated with anxiety, which could lead to further failure.

The research that is reported in this section suggests that realistic standards of excellence, elimination of excessive failure experiences, creation of conditions that maximize success, and intrinsic motivation all lead to positive self-concept and allow the child to be open to new experiences.

SELF-CONCEPT AND SOCIAL RELATIONSHIPS

Heathers (1955), who studied forty two- to five-year-olds at the Fels Institute, observed that socially competent children engaged more in social play, were more assertive, and sought attention or approval from children more than from adults. McCandless et al. (1961) observed preschool children in a free-play situation. They found that popularity and emotional dependency were negatively related to one another. The popular children were the more independent individuals. Henderson and Long (1971), in a study of ninety-five black lower-class children a year after school entrance, found, in comparing the children's self-social concepts, behavior ratings by teachers, and reading behavior of the children, that the children in the first grade who were reading had a mature independence, while the nonreaders were overdependent and those who were not promoted were socially withdrawn. Coopersmith (1959), Carlson (1963), Williams and Cole (1968), and Richmond and White (1971), all studying fifth- and sixth-grade students, found that children with positive self-concepts were more likely to enjoy high peer status than were low self-concept students. This difference transcended race and social class. Teigland (1966), in a study of fifth-grade students, found that the achievers were better adjusted and chosen more often by their peers in work and play situations. Simon and Bernstein (1971) reported that sixth-grade subjects in his study, who had high self-esteem, were more likely to believe that people whom they liked reciprocated these feelings. Hovland et al. (1953) found that individuals low in self-esteem were more persuasible and more conforming than those with a high level of self-esteem. They felt that the compliance manifested by those of low self-esteem might be defensive behavior that aimed to please everyone. If the low-esteem individuals were lacking in personal adequacy, they might have an exceptionally strong need for approval. This need for approval could inhibit growth in the intellectual and creative capacities of the individual.

The research seems to indicate that a child who feels good about himself tends to be adjusted socially and to be more accepted by his peers. This social acceptance must increase the self-concept. One sees a vicious cycle developing. As the child succeeds with his peers, he feels better about himself and continues interacting with them. The child who is worried about failing because of past experiences of fear feels like a failure, so he doesn't get involved in a group and the more of a failure he perceives himself to be, the more inadequate he feels and the less he gets involved.

INDEPENDENCE

There are other studies that have correlated independence with peer acceptance (Carlson, 1963; Moore & Updegraff, 1964; Heathers, 1955; Teigland, 1966; Williams & Cole,

1968; Coopersmith, 1959; Richmond & White, 1971), with positive feelings toward teachers (White and Bashov, 1971), with reading (Henderson & Long, 1971; Henderson and Long & Ziller, 1965), with conceptual and abstract ability (Wender, et al. 1967), and with child rearing (Dreyer & Haupt, 1966; Baumrind, 1967; Baumrind & Black, 1967; Sigel, 1973).

Parents of independent preschool children tend to be more firm, loving, demanding, understanding, and less restrictive than parents of dependent children. (Baumrind, 1967; Baumrind & Black, 1967; Sigel, 1973). This independence is shown by the stable assertive behavior of the child.

McClelland et al. (1953), in their classic work on achievement, found that the more physical a demonstration of affection and the reward of fulfilling parental demands for independence, the greater the achievement.

Dreyer and Haupt (1966) evaluated thirty-two middle-class kindergarten children's competence. Using a doll play, coping interview, and a teacher rating scale and observation, they found that those children with more autonomous self-evaluations, as compared to those needing reflective appraisals of their competence from others, were more independent, original, and achievement oriented and were more friendly and sharing. The reflective appraisal children needed external confirmation of their capacities and did not have a stable internal frame of reference about their performance. High maternal control and low maternal nurturance were more characteristic of this group. The more autonomous group seemed to develop in homes where mothers supported their attempts to master their environments.

Crandall et al. (1960b) observed thirty nursery school children in free-play situations and in interaction with their mothers. They were rated on the amount of their achievement efforts and on their help seeking, emotional support seeking, and approval seeking from adults. The results indicated that high-achieving children were less dependent on adults for help and emotional support. Neither maternal affection nor independence training were predictive of the children's achievement behavior, but maternal reward of specific achievement efforts and approval seeking of the child were predictive of achievement.

Self-concept was not directly correlated with independence in most of these studies, so that we cannot definitely say that the empirical evidence shows that children who feel good about themselves are independent. However, theory indicates that development of a positive sense of autonomy and initiative would be essential ingredients for the development of a growing sense of identity (Erikson, 1950). In addition, those children who manifested independent social and academic behavior in the studies quoted, seemed to reveal competence, which is an important aspect of self-concept.

In sum, it appears that children who feel good about themselves are more likely to interact with others in an independent, assertive manner and would be accepted by their peers. This independence also seems to be related to achievement. It is likely that parents who allow their children to be appropriately autonomous and to use initiative and who reward their children for achievement behaviors are helping their children to develop a positive sense of identity.

SELF-CONCEPT AND ANXIETY AND CURIOSITY

Wylie's (1961) extensive review of self-concept studies suggested that self-acceptance is related to adjustment. Subsequent studies have strengthened that point of view. (Taylor, 1964; Teigland, 1966; Coopersmith, 1967; Williams & Cole, 1968). Manifest anxiety has been shown to be significantly related to self-concept in additional studies (Lipsitt, 1958; Bledsoe, 1964; Stanwyck & Felker, 1971; McNelly, 1972).

McNelly (1972) cited studies using different rating devices that showed that there is a definite association between anxiety and a discrepancy between how a child actually perceives herself and how she wishes she were; the higher the anxiety, the greater the discrepancy. He felt that children try to protect themselves from anxiety if they have such self-evaluation, by avoiding anxiety-arousing stresses. Felker (1974), stated that anxiety is bound up in the mechanisms that maintain a positive or negative self-concept. These mechanisms influence the manner in which an individual will respond to situations involving achievement or evaluation. Thus, it seems that the use of these mechanisms, whose role it is to protect the person from further stress and anxiety, would constrict children's behavior and exploration and inhibit growth.

Katahn (1966) found that students with high ability perform better when they are anxious, but those with average or below average scores perform worse. This writer agrees with Epps (1970) that it seems particularly important that we avoid producing anxiety in average or below-average students. Mussen (1969) listed the important variables that are related to an increase of anxiety in children: overly severe punishment and restriction, the setting of unrealistically high standards, criticism of the child's behavior, inconsistency in the treatment of the child, and labile mood swings in relation to the child. As reported previously, Sarason et al. (1960) found that mothers of anxious children respond to and evaluate their children in terms of their own standards and needs, rather than the needs of their children. The task of fulfilling these unrealistic parental expectations led to anxiety and negative self-concept. It was further noted that mothers of highly anxious children were more defensive, less verbal, and more dependent and anxious (Davidson, 1959; Adams & Sarason, 1963). Adams and Sarason (1963) found that a positive correlation between the anxiety of parents and children was highest between mothers and daughters. We might assume that these mothers have low self-concepts and that these feelings toward themselves affect their behavior toward their daughters who tend to identify with them. Thus, overt behavior, plus the internal process of identification that is inherent in children's development, perpetuates negative self-feelings in the children of mothers manifesting anxiety, defensiveness, and dependency.

Several studies have reported a positive correlation of self-concept with curiosity (Maw & Maw, 1970; Minuchin, 1971). Maw and Maw (1970) in their study, which was done with fifth-grade boys using teacher and peer judgments and several self-concept instruments, found that high-curiosity boys were self-reliant; had a sense of personal freedom, a feeling of belonging, strong feelings about things, ego strength; and did not withdraw from experiences. Using drawings and mirror games Minuchin (1971), in a pilot study with eighteen four-year-old Negro children in Head Start programs, observed that children who were exploratory tended to have more differentiated self-images and tended to have stronger expectations of support from the environment and greater conceptual mastery. The children, who showed little curiosity of constructive exploratory behavior, had defused images of themselves. Sisk (1972) in a study of sixth-grade students, found that there was a positive correlation between self-concept and the students' level of originality and flexibility. Torrance (1962) suggested that the child must be free to test his own limits through exploration and experimentation. For children who have already experienced rejection or failure in their relationships with their parents, there would be hesitation to explore and experiment in new situations.

Summary

The studies reviewed confirm that there is a positive relationship between self-concept and achievement, self-concept and peer relationships, and self-concept and curiosity and a negative relationship between self-concept and anxiety. Children may actually be good students or have friends, but may perceive themselves as not having a positive academic or social self-concept. It seems more likely that children who perceive themselves negatively, either in the global sense or in the academic or social dimension of self-concept, will be more anxious and will not achieve or be involved in social experiences. The research suggests that realistic self-criticism, acceptance of responsibility for intellectual achievement, approval from others, and rewards that lead to self-reinforcement and independence are variables related to achievement and positive self-feeling. Children who come to school lacking in confidence and who are in reality capable cognitively might reveal their feelings of inadequacy by being defensive, anxious, and unwilling to try new activities. This should be a danger signal to teachers, because these behaviors could lead to academic and social failure, regardless of the true ability of the child.

NOTES

1. The levels were based on Freudian psychosexual themes, which at this age should be phallic intrusive. Some indicators that the children were at this stage of development were their play themes showing interest in adult heterosexual relationships, play themes focusing on genital behaviors, and general classroom activity that was active, vigorous, and exploratory.

Chapter 4

SEX-ROLE IDENTIFICATION

An individual's conscious and unconscious perception and evaluation of his masculinity or femininity is important for self-concept development. Kagen (1964a) stated that the stereotypes that define sex-role behavior may serve as sex-role standards that the culture approves for males and females, and that are internalized by individuals to guide and evaluate their behavior. Sex-role identity is the means by which individuals see themselves as being masculine or feminine. It also includes body acceptance. For healthy psychological development to occur, it is the role of the like-sexed parent that is to be emulated. Theoretically, if that parent feels positive about being a man or a woman, the child, who identifies with him or her, will evaluate that role positively and desire to live by the standards set for that sex. Later on, others besides the family put values on societal sex roles.

THEORIES OF SEX-ROLE DEVELOPMENT

There are three major theories that deal with sex-role development: social learning theory (Bandura, Ross, & Ross 1961; Bandura & Walters, 1963; Bandura, 1969) psychoanalytic theory (Freud, 1924, 1925b, 1931, 1933), and cognitive-developmental theory (Kohlberg, 1966). Identification plays a role in all of the theories, but the processes leading to identification and its importance in the theories vary.

The social learning theory primarily emphasizes teaching, reward and punishment, generalization, and imitation in the development of sex-typed behavior. Sex-role training starts at birth when appropriate sexual responses are rewarded and sex-inappropriate behaviors are punished (Mussen, 1969). Imitation by observational learning, vicarious learning, and modeling have been considered important by the social learning theorists. Bandura and his supporters have shown that after exposure to aggressive models, children imitate what they see (Bandura, Ross, & Ross, 1961; Bandura & Walters, 1963). The assumption is that by imitating the like-sexed parent's behavior, the child will learn sex-typed responses. The social learning theorists maintain that the direct learning with parents generalize out and occur in response to other similar stimuli. For example, if a girl's compliance is rewarded by her mother, it is likely to be generalized in her relationship to other adults. The theory states that, during the course of development, sex differences in the value and acquired meaning of stimuli become more and more independent of external reinforcement (Mischel, 1970).

Observational learning cannot restrict itself to simple reinforcement principles, so that more than imitation is involved in learning. The child's identification with parents is seen as a way to emulate not only their overt behavior but also their more complex subtle behaviors, thoughts, and feelings.

Bandura (1969) used "identification," "imitation," and "observation learning" as synonyms referring to modifications and behavior resulting from exposure to modeling stimuli. When exposed to several models, the child synthesizes the components of their behavior into unique new patterns, rather than copying their exact behavior (Bandura, Ross, & Ross, 1963). The model's ability to reward, nurturance, power and control over resources, and similarity to the child may facilitate the child's tendency to emulate the model (Mussen, 1969; Mischel, 1970). Mussen and Distler (1959, 1960) found that boys whose fathers were affectionate and warm tended to show greater preference for the male role. They were also more similar to their fathers on a personality inventory (Payne & Mussen, 1956). Sears (1953) found that fathers who were more nurturant, had young sons who assumed the father role in doll play. Mussen and Rutherford (1963) found, that the boys whose fathers were seen as both rewarding and punishing, were more likely to behave in sex-appropriate ways. The findings for girls paralleled those for the boys, as more feminine girls described their mothers in doll play as significantly warmer, more nurturant, affectionate, and gratifying than did the other girls. Mothers' self-acceptance, as well as fathers' masculinity in interest and orientation and the fathers' encouragement of their daughters' femininity were also associated with greater femininity in girls. This finding was not observed in the study by Sears et al., (1965), since there was no evidence that the feminine girls' mothers or the masculine boys' fathers were warm.

Mussen (1969) suggested that developmental identification did not seem to be a complete and adequate explanation of sex typing, since the results of studies were so vastly different. Maccoby and Jacklin (1974), who reviewed over 2000 books and articles on sex-role research, also stated that the evidence for the social learning theory is not impressive, particularly early in life. They found in their review that there have been few rigorous and detailed observational studies to support this theory. They did not find that children resemble the same-sex parent in their behavior; that is, a girl's femininity does not correlate with her mother's femininity nor a boy's masculinity with his father's masculinity. Maccoby and Jacklin noted that reinforcement does not seem to play a major role in sex differentiation. They found that large areas of sex-differentiated behavior do not appear to be taught by reinforcement because boys and girls were found to be socialized relatively uniformly.

Within the psychoanalytic theory, the process is a complex intrapsychic one. This viewpoint links sexual identification to the resolution of the Oedipus complex and is called defensive identification. The boy who has loving feelings toward his mother sees his father as his rival and as an object of antagonism, envy, and hostility who stands in the way of his attainment of his mother's love (Freud, 1924). The boy fears that his father will castrate him in retaliation for his envy, hostility, and sexual desire toward his mother and realizes that he can't win the struggle. This leads to the resolution of the Oedipus complex. The boy identifies with the father, instead of competing with him and this reduces his fear. The girl observes that little boys have penises while she does not. She infers she has been castrated and feels resentment and envy. She develops a wish to acquire a penis of her own, which Freud called penis envy. She feels cheated and blames her mother and feels resentment toward her and sees her as a rival. To compensate for her deficiency, the girl develops a wishful fantasy of having a child by and for her father. Once this fantasy is established, the father becomes her primary sexual object, replacing the mother and the mother becomes the chief rival. She reacts to the mother as a love object by identifying with her. (Abraham, 1920; Deutsch, 1944; Freud, 1925b, 1931, 1933). The culturally oriented theorists (Horney, 1937, 1939) hypothesize that the complex stems from nonsexual factors such as family and social reactions to sex rather than being related to having or not having a penis. Whiting (1959, 1960) further expanded Freud's concept of defensive identification. He felt that competition was not merely in the sexual context of the Oedipal situation, but more broadly involved competition of other social and material gratifications that the high-status parent could offer. The child's identification is motivated by the desire to have the envied resources consumed by the parent (Mischel, 1970).

Identification is a more complicated development process for girls than for boys in the psychoanalytic model. The social learning theory suggests that the process is more complex for boys. The nonpsychoanalytic viewpoint maintains that love and affection for the model bring about identification (Mussen, 1969). At first, according to this theory, both boys and girls identify with the mother, since she is the primary source of nurturance and affection for all infants. After the boy becomes aware of sex differences, about the age of three or four, there is a shift to father identification based on affection and love for him.

The third theory of sexual development is the cognitive-developmental theory (Kohlberg, 1966). It is children's conceptions of their bodies and others' bodies that determine their sexual behavior. It is initiated by the labeling of "boy" or "girl" as applied to them by others. What they learn is based on their concrete simplified experience. This self-categorization is of central importance as the organizer of sex-roles attitudes. The label becomes the major organizer and determinant of many of the child's activities, values, and attitudes. Kohlberg (1966) stated that once children have stabilized themselves as to gender, they value positively those objects consistent with this gender and act in accordance with this identity, since there is a need for cognitive consistency. According to this theory, the child's stereotype of masculine and feminine behavior are not derived primarily by reinforcement or identification, but from universal, perceived sex differences in bodily structure and capacities. Kohlberg theorized that gender identity becomes stabilized at about five or six years of age at about the same time the Piaget concept of conservation is attained. The concept of conservation is discussed in Chapter 1. As the child develops cognitively, and begins to conserve, the concepts become more realistic. Cognitive development, plus the child's growing understanding of cultural sex roles, determine his sexual behavior.

Mussen (1969) hypothesized that, for most children, learning, identification, and cognitive organization all contribute to the development of sex typing and sex-role acquisition. He stated that the first components of a sex role are probably learned by reinforcement and imitation and that identification and cognitive growth become more important later on. As mentioned earlier, Maccoby and Jacklin (1974) stated that direct "shaping" by parents in most instances does not account for acquired sexual behavior. Only narrowly defined areas are so reinforced, for example, boys not wearing dresses or playing with dolls. Maccoby and Jacklin (1974) favored a "self-socialization" process that followed the Kohlberg cognitive-developmental theory. This means that children gradually develop concepts of "masculinity" and "femininity" and when they have understood what their own sex is, they attempt to match their own behavior to their conception of others like themselves. The ideas may be obtained only very minimally from observing their parents. Instead, information would be distilled from a wide variety of sources and would become conceptualized as children develop cognitively.

BIOLOGICAL INFLUENCES

Money and Ehrhardt (1973) reported that prenatal hormones have an effect on later behavior in humans. They studied a group of twenty-five girls, who had suffered from the androgenital syndrome, a genetic defect exposing them to an abnormally high amount of male sex hormones (androgens), *in utero*. At birth, these girls exhibited enlarged clitorises and other anomalies of their secondary sex characteristics. For half of them (the more recent cases), these anomalies were corrected early in life. Twenty of twenty five of the girls were described as tomboys. As compared to a control group, they exhibited higher levels of physical energy, were more indifferent and neglectful of dolls (turning instead to toys that were traditionally masculine), and were late in reaching the boyfriend stage of development and in getting married. Although they preferred not to have children and subordinated marriage to career, most of them became competent mothers. Moreover, they were not considered to be aggressive in childhood—a pattern found in boys in all studies. It is difficult to separate the biological from the environmental in this study, for these girls may have been affected by parental treatment. A parent's unsureness of a child's feminine status could alter the behavioral expectations and socialization practices. It is significant that aggression was not shown by the girls who exhibited other so-called masculine behavior, supporting the hypothesis that aggression may be influenced by environment, a conclusion in opposition to Maccoby and Jacklin (1974). Observation of parent-daughter interaction in the Money and Ehrhardt studies would have clarified the issue of genetic versus environmental effects on aggressive behavior, preferences for masculine activity, and the like. The lack of a comparable boys group as a control weakens the study further.

Maccoby and Jacklin (1974) concluded that biological factors have been most clearly implicated in sex differences in aggression. In all studies, boys consistently differ from girls in early childhood beginning at age two to two-and-a-half. These results are based mainly on direct observation and appear to have considerable cross-cultural generality (Whiting, 1963). Maccoby and Jacklin (1974), found no good evidence that adults reinforced boys' aggression more than girls' aggression. In fact, some studies have shown that adults react somewhat more strongly to aggression in boys, on the grounds that they are likely to fight more and therefore must be kept under closer control. Hamburg and Lunde (1966) pointed to the possibility that hormonal "sensitization" during the prenatal period may be contributory to the arousal of sex-appropriate behavior later in life. In their work with primates, they found that the female offspring of monkeys, who were administered male sex hormones during pregnancy, engaged in more rough-and-tumble play and tended not to withdraw from the threats and approaches of others. Offspring of monkeys who did not receive the male hormone did not engage in rough-and-tumble play and tended to withdraw more. Hormonal differences were not measurable between the experimental and the control offspring. The implication is that prenatal endocrine factors may affect later behavior such as aggression, causing differing male and female patterns to arise.

There are other differences between males and females that are manifested early in life and that seem to be clearly genetic. In the neonatal period, males are more susceptible to many diseases (Kravitz, 1965), physically boys grow and mature more slowly than girls (Bayer & Bayley, 1963), and a higher percentage of males are mentally defective (Everhart, 1960). Girls are more sensitive to touch and have a lower pain threshold (Garai & Scheinfeld, 1968). Kagan (1972) found that there is a slight tendency for females to display more fear and anxiety than boys at four months. According to Kagan, this may be due to the greater maturity of females in discerning discrepancies in new situations. Boys may not yet observe discrepancies in the environment, so they do not assimilate or withdraw from fearful stimuli. Another explanation may be that the fear may be due to greater parental anxiety about females. At birth, male infants seem to be soothed by physical stimulation and female infants tend to quiet down more in response to auditory stimulation (Moss, 1967). This too may relate to the lesser maturity of males who cry more and seem to need to be held and soothed.

Although hormones may preset behavioral tendencies prenatally, there is great individual genetic variation. This contributes to a wide spectrum of normal behavior within each sex (Money & Ehrhardt, 1973). If we are concerned about children feeling positive about themselves, we must enable them to develop as individuals within the context of their inherited abilities.

ENVIRONMENTAL DIFFERENCES

There is anthropological evidence indicating that male and female personality and sexual differentiation varies from culture to culture. (Mead, 1935; Linton, 1936; Barry, Bacon, & Child, 1957). Mead (1935) described three New Guinea tribes: the Arapesh, where men and women were cooperative and unaggressive; the Mundugumor, where males and females were ruthless, aggressive, and unresponsive; and the Tchambuli, where the women were dominant, impersonal, and managing and the men were less responsible and emotionally dependent. However, in most cultures, men have been found to be more aggressive and domineering and women have been found to be more emotional and nurturant. Money (1965) and Money and Ehrhardt (1973) have reported work with children who had been misidentified at birth as to their gender and were reared to fit the role of the sex opposite to their genetic characteristics. Therefore, the gender role expected of the child, not the sexual characteristics, determined the behavior. This was established early in life and became firmly reinforced at the time of development of language, at about eighteen months of age.

Once established, the individual's sexual identification appears to be fixed and irreversible (Brown, 1957; Hartley, 1964; Rutter, 1971; Money & Ehrhardt, 1973). Changing a child's sexual designation after the age of two has been known to result in psychological stress (Hampson, 1965; Money & Ehrhardt, 1973). This was found in studies where the sex of children had to be changed because of mistakes in designation at birth. Brown (1956), Kohlberg (1966), and Vener and Snyder (1966) found that the majority of children could label themselves by sex properly by the age of three. Three-year-olds could also distinguish "functional roles" of each sex and describe the concept of mother (Hartley, 1960). Between the ages of three and five the differentiation of male and female roles was found to increase (Biller & Borstelman, 1967; Fagot & Patterson, 1969). By the age of three or four, boys expressed clear-cut preferences for masculine activities. This was generally earlier than when girls chose feminine activities (Brown, 1957), although Vener and Snyder (1966) found that girls were more clear-cut in their sex preferences than boys. However, even in this study, where two-and-a-half to eleven-year-old children were asked to choose items of clothing or other items appropriate for one sex or another, boys preferred masculine items by the age of seven.

Forty-six male and thirty-three female psychologists were asked to describe what characteristics would define a healthy, mature, socially competent adult (sex unspecified), and what characteristics would define a man and a woman. The clinicians gave the same standards for adults as for men, but their concept of health in women differed from those of adults and males. Emotionally healthy women were described as being more submissive, less independent, less adventurous, more easily influenced, less aggressive, and less competitive and more excitable in minor crises. They were also thought to have their feelings more easily hurt, to be more emotional and conceited about their appearance, to be less objective, and to dislike math and science. Thus, in the opinion of these psychologists, for a woman to be considered healthy and adjusted, she must manifest behaviors that are not consistent with mature adulthood. For example, if she grows more aggressive, she doesn't become healthier. Therefore, double standards of emotional health exist for men and for women (Broverman et al., 1970). Rosenkrantz et al. (1968) also found that the traits of an ideal man were rated higher than those of an ideal woman. These studies parallel the sex-role stereotypes prevalent in society that children observe and undoubtedly assimilate cognitively.

At this point, it could be theorized that women (and girls) evaluate themselves negatively, as compared to men (and boys), but that society's attitude about females have not been validated in the studies on self-concept reviewed by Maccoby and Jacklin (1974). There are some qualitative differences in that girls rated themselves higher in the area of social competence, and boys saw themselves more often as strong, powerful, dominant, and "potent." In some studies, girls saw themselves higher in self-concept; in others boys were higher. Maccoby and Jacklin (1974) concluded that girls were more willing than boys to disclose their weaknesses. Boys got higher scores on "lie" and "defensiveness" scales, which measured to what extent the individual disguised his true feelings and presented a more favorable picture of himself (Bogo et al., 1970).

There are some problems that may be peculiar to research focusing on boy-girl differences (Baumrind, 1972; Maccoby & Jacklin, 1974). We cannot assume that the self-concept studies reviewed in the Maccoby and Jacklin book completely reflect reality because of the limitations in data collection that may not even have been conscious. First of all, in sex-role research that focuses on observation, when the observer knows the sex of the child, an automatic adjustment is made that tends to standardize judgments according to that sex. Second, we can't generalize from social class to social class. More recent studies have focused on lower-class and minority group children, but most of the studies in the Maccoby and Jacklin book used white, middle-class subjects. A third problem is that different degrees of maturation of boys versus girls of the same age complicate comparisons between them. Fourth, Maccoby and Jacklin (1974) suggested that "masculinity" and "femininity" are essential self-defining attributes for some people but not for others. If this is so, reported findings in studies comparing the sexes could not be compared to one another, since the relative concentration of people of each type in the subject population would change from study to study. Finally, we have to differentiate between global self-concept and self-concept as it relates to the sexual self. A high global score may mask a negative sexual self-concept. A boy may have a low self-concept of achievement and a high bodily sexual self-concept, and a girl may score in reverse. The total score would indicate there is no difference, when in reality there would be a great difference in that the girl would not be accepting her sexual self. Such differences may not have been reported by researchers who have used varying instruments and statistical procedures. The contradiction seen between studies and lack of self-concept differences may be due to these factors rather than to reality.

ANXIETY—BOY VERSUS GIRL DIFFERENCES

Maccoby and Jacklin (1974) concluded there is too little evidence in studies showing differences between boys and girls in the areas of fear, timidity, and anxiety. Although teacher ratings and self-report usually have found girls to be more timid and anxious, their results suggest that girls may be more willing to verbalize these feelings. Davidson (1959) suggested that girls are permitted to express anxiety but boys are rewarded if they don't express fears. Boys' defensiveness may account for some of these differences as they do in the differences in self-concept reports. Additionally, the test items may be weighted against girls (Maccoby & Jacklin, 1974). Maccoby and Jacklin (1974) gave, as an example, the fact that it may be more realistic for girls to be more anxious about being alone, since they are worried about sexual molestation.

Kaplan and Pokorny (1972) studied 500 adults who reported childhood experiences that were derogatory for them. They found that women were self-derogatory if as children they didn't have positive familial and maternal evaluation and if they did not fulfill requirements that matched the traditional female role. Males manifested high self-derogation scores if as children they were afraid of being laughed at by other children, or if they were afraid of being punished by their parents. These results were interpreted as a failure to display characteristics associated with masculinity, for example, assertiveness and independence from parental standards. Therefore, in this study deviation from societal expectations created discomfort for both sexes.

Hartley (1974) interviewed forty-one middle-class eight- to eleven-year-old males. She found that the degree of anxiety experienced had a direct relationship to the degree of pressure to be "manly," which was expected from the boys, the rigidity of the pattern to which they were pressed to conform, the availability of a good model, and the apparent degree of success that their efforts achieved. The boys who had the least anxiety seemed to be those who were flexible in pursuing activities, regardless of role expectation, while showing clear understanding of differences between male and female roles and the complementary relationship between them. The most rigid boys were hostile to females.

We should be concerned about anxiety whether it be manifest or latent. As reported earlier, there seems to be a correlation between anxiety and self-concept. It is possible that boys and girls are expressing their anxieties in different ways as expected by society: boys by hiding these feelings or by expressing overt hostility to girls, and girls by expressing the anxiety directly. Neither is benefiting if anxiety is caused by unreal expectations of each sex. We must begin to focus on sexual stereotypes that may be causing these anxieties for each sex. Why should we assume that sexual molestation should make girls more anxious than boys? Molestation of boys is in reality just as scary for them as for girls. Allowing anxiety for such a possibility only in girls perpetuates a sexual stereotype that discriminates against both sexes. We can give many examples such as this one of anxieties artificially created for boys or girls that are maladaptive and probably destructive in terms of the development of positive self-feelings. L'Abate (1960), for example, in a study of nine- to thirteen-year-old children, found no sex difference in anxiety between the scores of boys and girls but noted that they had checked different items. In particular, boys checked that they never wanted to get angry, a maladaptive anxiety that is unfortunately perpetuated by society.

SEX AND ACHIEVEMENT

Maccoby and Jacklin (1974) found that boys' achievement motivation appeared to be more responsive to competitive arousal than girls, but no sex differences have been measured insofar as achievement strivings are concerned. Girls do not obtain higher aptitude or achievement test scores, but they do get better grades throughout their school years.

Girls' language development was found to be superior to that of boys starting early in infancy (Maccoby and Jacklin, 1974). This has been generally attributed to biological differences, but Moss (1967) and Goldberg and Lewis (1969) described differential treatment in verbal interaction between boys and girls from birth. Moss (1967) observed infants at three weeks and at three months. It was found that at three weeks, the mothers initiated vocalizations more with girl babies. At three months, they increased their contact with their daughters and spent less time with their sons when the sons were irritable. This occurred in spite of the fact that at birth the males were held more because they slept less and cried more. Moss suggested that the greater maturity of the female would allow her to quiet down whereas the male would be less responsive. The mother might attribute this to masculinity and reinforce independence and assertiveness in the boy. In girls, attachment, dependency, and language development might be strengthened because of greater contact with the mother beginning in infancy (Moss, 1967).

Although there is male superiority on visual-spatial tasks in adolescence and adulthood, this is not so in childhood. The two sexes are similar in the early acquisition of quantitative concepts and in their mastery of arithmetic during the early years. It is later, after twelve to thirteen years that boys' mathematical skills increase. It is suggested that this change is brought about by teachers' and society's expectations that differ for boys and girls.

Felker (1974) suggested that self-concept and achievement were more related in boys than in girls. Garai and Scheinfeld (1968) and Baumrind (1972) found that girls seemed to be less realistic in their self-evaluations of ability than boys were. Girls' self-concepts were found to have little or no relation to their academic success, while boys' self-concepts were more closely related to their intelligence scores and intellectual performance. Maccoby and Jacklin (1974) suggested that women are less in control of their own fate and believe their achievements are often due to factors other than their own skills and hard work. Levy (1972) suggested that the criticism received by boys may be more task-oriented, which helps them to better evaluate their skills. Girls may also be getting more general and personal criticism that may prevent refinement of their perception of their strength and deficits. Terman and Odin (1947) found no relationship between occupational achievement and intelligence for girls, but a substantial relationship for boys. Gifted girls in his study were less likely to reach occupation levels to equal their capabilities. It was found that girls gave few achievement themes in projective measures when responding to a story or a picture about females. These reactions may not have reflected their own motivations, but rather their concepts concerning the usual characteristics of boys and girls (Maccoby & Jacklin, 1974). Horner (1972) suggested that if a girl fails she is not living up to her own performance standards, but if she succeeds she is not living up to societal expectations of her female role. Horner demonstrated with a story completion test measure that there is "fear of success" among college women. The subjects in her study showed poorer performance in a competitive task than when the same task was performed alone. Horner suggests that this fear exists in women, because in anticipating success they also anticipate negative consequences in the form of social rejection or the loss of femininity. Women who feared success tended to have high intellectual ability and a history of high academic success, but aspired to traditional female careers. Those who did not fear success aspired to graduate degrees in scientific areas such as math and science. Horner observed that men who were motivated both to achieve and to be accepted showed a performance "freeze" when asked to compete with other men. Monahan et al. (1974) found that both men and women, in describing successful people in academic settings, reported painful and embarrassing things happening to successful women and good things happening to successful men. It appears probable that, in situations in which competitiveness is expected, boys are more competitive, although Maccoby and Jacklin could not find enough research evidence to support this.

A few studies failed to find fear of success in girls (Monahan et al., 1974; Robbins & Robbins, 1973). Monahan et al., (1974) used the Horner stories with 120 ten- to sixteen-year-olds. The stories were analyzed for positive and negative attributes expressed toward the boy or the girl relating to achievement. Although more subjects responded to the female than to the male cue with negative attitudes, there were no significant sex differences. Robbins and Robbins (1973), presenting each of Horner's stories to both male and female respondents, found no differences between the sexes in fear of success. The authors questioned Horner's statistical evaluation and stated that the differences between men and women might have reflected realistic variations in current life-style and career possibilities, rather than motivational differences between the sexes. They suggested that more broadly conceived data bases be used before general conclusions are reached about motivation and asked for a reevaluation of the concept of success. This study seems to be consistent with the research quoted above on competition and motivation in that motivation for success may not be less for women, but society may make her demeaning reactions realistic in terms of her chances to compete with men. This may partially explain why girls value achievement less. They may perceive that it doesn't necessarily lead to success, while for men achievement is more likely to determine their professional futures.

A few studies support the differences in boys' and girls' perceptions of their roles in society (Looft, 1971; Iglitzin, 1972; Kirchner & Vondracek, 1973). Kirchner and Von-dracek (1973) found that there were differences between 143 male and 139 female, three- to five-year-old, black and white children in vocational aspirations. Boys were more likely to project in terms of an adult role in general, while girls were more likely to project in terms of the specific role of parent. Boys perceived the range of occupations open to them to be wider than did girls, and girls appeared to be more reality bound than boys. Looft (1971) studied 66 first and second graders equally divided by sex, asking them what they wanted to be when they grew up. The girls gave eight responses as opposed to eighteen for the boys. All the girls responses related to sexual stereotype, except for one girl who said she wanted to be a doctor. The children were then asked what they thought they would really be when they grew up. The one girl who initially said she wanted to be a doctor said she would probably have to be something else, maybe a "store lady." A few girls said they would be mothers, but no boys said they would be fathers. Iglitzin (1972) found sex stereotyping to be prevalent too, in a study of fifth-grade students. Even though girls said they would have careers, the careers were as teachers, artists, nurses, and so on. They also emphasized marriage and family much more than boys who saw themselves as job holders in adulthood. Even at four years of age, children are already perceiving the various possibilities for men and women based on the different sexual expectations in society and seem to be determining their future goals based on their perceptions.

In sum, both sexes are at a disadvantage if the quoted studies are reflecting reality. If a boy fails academically, and is not as competitive as society now expects him to be, he is more apt to value himself less. If a girl doesn't accept her achievement strivings, and doesn't aim to become more than a wife and a mother in adulthood, she is more apt to value herself less. It seems that starting in early childhood, we have to provide conditions that optimize success for each individual, regardless of sex.

SEX AND DEPENDENCY

Few major sex differences have been observed in studies of nursery school children in dependency versus independence (Mischel, 1970; Maccoby & Jacklin, 1974). A recent study of infants, which focused on mother-child interactions relating to dependency, noted differences in the treatment of boys and girls as early as the age of six months (Goldberg & Lewis, 1969). The authors observed mother-child interactions with a small sample of boys and girls, and found that mothers of six-month-old children touched, talked to, and handled their daughters more than their sons. At thirteen months, in a free-play situation, the girls were more dependent and showed less exploratory behavior than the boys. The more physical contact the mother made with a boy at six months, the more he touched his mother at thirteen months. Garai and Scheinfeld (1968) found that despite greater maturity and sturdiness of the female infants, parents saw them as more fragile. As a matter of fact, greater maturity in girls would suggest that they be given independence earlier than boys. Kagan and Moss (1962) found that daughters of protective mothers were passive, noncompetitive, and involved in traditional feminine interests, whereas mothers who allowed early autonomy and independence for their daughters had girls who achieved early independence from family in adulthood. Kagan and Moss (1962), who investigated the relationship between childhood and adult characteristics, found that girls high in passivity and dependence in early childhood manifested these characteristics in adulthood, while boys showed stability in aggressiveness. Passive boys and aggressive girls did not show such stability. Behavioral stability seems to depend on societal expectations for each sex. Some children might have to inhibit behavior to adjust to societal expectations. This inhibition could restrict the normal expression of feeling and prevent the individual from feeling good about himself or herself.

BOY VERSUS GIRL SOCIALIZATION BY PARENTS

In reviewing socialization studies in early childhood, Maccoby and Jacklin (1974) found that the two sexes appeared to be treated with equal affection and were equally allowed and encouraged to be independent and discouraged from being dependent and aggressive. Boys were handled and played with somewhat more roughly and they received more physical punishment, more praise, and more criticism in specific sex-typed behaviors. This is especially true of fathers who actively discouraged feminine toys, activities, or attire by their sons. Most of the studies they reviewed were with children beyond infancy and the method of gathering facts was self-report by the mothers. In a recent study of maternal behavior, eleven mothers were individually tape recorded in play with a six-month-old infant. It was found, that although the infant behaved about the same for all mothers, the mothers' treatment of the baby differed according to whether they perceived it as a male or a female (Will et al., 1974). The same baby was dressed in blue pants and introduced as "Adam" to five mothers; then it was dressed in pink and introduced as "Beth" to the other six mothers. The mothers were encouraged to use a small plastic doll, train, and fish that were available to them. The mothers more frequently handed the doll to the "female" and smiled at her more while they handed the train to the "male." In follow-up interviews, the mothers generally reported that they felt they treated infants the same regardless of sex and that they observed no behavioral sex differences at this age. Jacklin, Maccoby, and Dick (1973) did not find a difference in toy selection responses by mothers of thirteen- and fourteen-month-old boys and girls. The only toy preference of the children was that boys preferred robots. It is hard to know whether the mothers were giving the "expected answers" in this study as in the previous one. In the Will et al. study, the mothers were observed in a "blind" experiment and differences in toy selection were found. These differences may not affect children's overt behavior until later in childhood than fourteen months of age.

To recapitulate, in recent limited studies on infants, we see different interactions of mothers with boys and with girls that contradict some of the earlier studies reviewed by Maccoby and Jacklin. The effects of this differing treatment and of other as-yet-unmeasured behaviors are not assessed by maternal report instruments or by observations made later in nursery school, methods and the age group that comprise the bulk of early childhood studies thus far reported. It is conceivable that some maternal behaviors are more favorable for boys and others are more favorable for girls and that we have not as yet isolated the different variables. This, plus the already-mentioned measurement problems, may be masking some real differences between boys and girls.

TEACHER TREATMENT—BOY VERSUS GIRL

In a review of certain studies Brophy and Good (1973a,b) found that boys received more praise, more criticism, and had more contacts with teachers. A few recent studies are worth noting that indicate differing teacher behavior between preschool boys and girls (Joffee, 1974; Lee and

Gropper, 1974; Biber et al., 1972; Serbin et al., 1973). Joffee (1974) found that girls in a nursery school were frequently admired and received more compliments when they did not wear pants while there was more reinforcement of boys who were physically adept. Lee and Gropper (1974) found that boys and girls did not have equal access to classroom materials. Biber et al. (1972), in a study of fourteen classes of four-year-olds, reported that girls received more instructional contact and positive reinforcement than boys, regardless of whether the program was individualized or more group oriented. The only non-difference in this study was that boys and girls received equal positive reinforcement in the Bereiter-Englemann Program, which stressed positive reinforcement. Serbin et al. (1973), in a study of three- to five-year-old children, observed that teachers reacted more when boys rather than girls were aggressive and gave them louder reprimands. They also gave boys more praise, direction, hugging, and extended time for discussion than they gave to girls. Girls received more attention when they were close to the teacher than when they were far away. They found that boys did not comply as readily to directions as girls did.

Brophy and Good (1973b) suggested that the observed differences in the treatment of boys and girls were due to student behavioral differences rather than the negative attitudes of female teachers toward boys.

Davidson and Lang (1960), McNeil (1964), Fagot and Patterson (1969), Sexton (1969), and Smith (1973) have discussed those attitudes that they found to differ for boys and for girls. Sexton (1969) concluded, after an extensive study, that schools tended to be feminine institutions, particularly unsuited to the needs and temperament of the masculine boys. Smith (1973) suggested that as early as kindergarten boys experienced more difficulty in a feminized environment. For example, we know that boys are more impulsive than girls during the preschool years (Maccoby & Jacklin, 1974). We also know that boys are more aggressive.

Serbin et al. (1973) found that in aggressive or destructive behavior of one child toward another in nursery school, teachers were more likely to intervene if the aggressor was a boy. Martin (1972) found, in a study of second-grade children, that boys who were behavior problems, interacted significantly more with their teachers than girls who were behavior problems, or quieter boys and girls. Impulsiveness, plus greater aggression in boys might lead to more pressures being put on them to temper their behavior. On the other hand, the greater status afforded boys undoubtedly puts more pressure on girls. Perhaps if we treated each child as an individual regardless of sex, we would enhance the self-concepts of both sexes.

Kellogg (1969) and Kagan (1964b) found that elementary school children regarded school objects as feminine, suggesting that school may be more oriented toward girls. Maccoby and Jacklin (1974) suggested that it takes greater efforts to motivate boys. They reported that most of the studies showed that girls exhibited more "autonomous achievements" than boys. That is, they were more self-motivated to achieve. This may be due to the feminizing environment or the greater maturity of girls.

Levitin and Chananie (1972) examined forty female primary school teachers' feelings about aggressive and dependent children. These teachers judged the aggressive boy and the dependent girl as being typical. Dependent behavior rated significantly more approval than aggressive behavior, regardless of the child's sex. Additionally, the achieving girl was significantly preferred over the achieving boy. One would assume that their behavior with the children would enforce their stereotypic expectations. Fagot and Patterson (1969) also observed that female teachers consistently reinforced feminine-type behaviors more than masculine behaviors and reinforced boys but not girls when they performed opposite sex behaviors. However, peers mostly reinforced the same-sexed peers behaviors. This study was done with thirty-six three-year-olds. It is interesting to note that the teachers' reinforcement of feminine behaviors did not affect the boys' preference for masculine behaviors. The authors stated that peer reinforcement plus home reinforcement was adequate to maintain masculine behaviors.

McNeil (1964), in a study of seventy-two boys and sixty girls in first grade, found that boys received more negative admonition than girls, were given less opportunity to read, and were identified as having no motivation for reading. Boys who were negatively rated and received little opportunity to read dropped in their reading rank. However, these boys were not inferior to the girls after autoinstructional procedures were used and they were given equal praise and attention that the girls received. Gorelick (1965) also reported that autoinstructional devices were effective in reducing achievement differences between boys and girls. Other studies observed no teacher differences in treatment of boys and girls during reading instruction (Davis & Slobodian, 1967; Brophy & Good, 1971).

Girls may be at just as much of a disadvantage as are boys. They are rewarded for conforming behavior or ignored (Sears & Feldman, 1966). In a study of 240 student teachers, it was found that they perceived most positively, the rigid, conforming girl; second, the rigid, conforming boy; third, the dependent girl, followed by the male of the same personality (Feshbach, 1969). The lowest rating was given to the independent, assertive girl. Therefore, the independent, assertive girl would probably be in trouble with some teachers. Feshbach (1973) suggested that girls may be rejected if they attempt to become assertive with some teachers. This is cruel for girls who are socialized for adult approval. Caplan's study (1973) supported this finding, that girls who were not promoted were the disruptive ones and who did not differ in report card grades from boys who were promoted. Moreover, low-achieving non-disruptive girls in this study, who were promoted, were significantly lower in achievement than those whom the teacher kept back. Clearly, teachers promoted girls partly on the basis of their behavior and not just on their achievement. This study must be taken with caution because of its sample of forty boys and only ten girls in grades one through three in an urban school system.

There have been no studies reported on the effects of sex-typed school materials on the self-concept of girls. It is likely that the materials may be more sexist than what is present in the greater society. Books that continue to portray girls primarily in roles such as housewives, teachers, and nurses are perpetuating unnecessary myths about stereotypic behaviors and could partially account for the narrower aspirations of girls mentioned in studies earlier in this chapter. There have been some recent positive changes and it is hoped that they will continue. This writer agrees with Brophy and Good (1973a) who suggested that we include verbal facility and school achievements among our expectations for boys and greater assertiveness and independence in our expectations for young girls and that we have more individualized programs. Minuchin (1965) found that children, particularly girls from modern middle-class homes and schools where individualized development was stressed, tended to adhere to less conventional sex-role standards than children from more traditional homes and schools.

The research quoted in Chapter 3 indicated that self-reinforcement, realistic self-criticism experiences that lead to success, acceptance of responsibility for intellectual achievement, and approval of others lead to better self-concept. The research quoted, comparing teacher behavior with boys and girls, is mixed as to which sex is better off in terms of treatment in these areas. The conclusion we must

come to is that the negative treatment balances out; sometimes girls are better off, sometimes boys are at an advantage.

SUMMARY

Positive feelings as to one's maleness or femaleness are
essential for development. Generally the research reviewed
here has indicated that sex-role stereotyping discriminates
against both sexes but in different ways. All the theories
have hypothesized that identification with the parent of the
same sex is facilitated if warmth, reward, punishment, and
power are inherent in the relationship with the child. It
seems that imitation is not the only way one's sex-role is
learned, but more complex cognitive and psychological
processes are operative. Methodological problems may
have prevented researchers from seeing substantial self-
concept differences between the sexes. There may be no
differences in actuality or it is possible that the negative
variables for each sex balance out. Differences in sexual
behavior are based on the complex interaction of biological
factors and socialization practices. There is general agreement that environmental influences affect sex-role behavior, but there is less accord regarding the relative
importance of biological factors. If constitutional variables
differentially influence the behavior of boys and girls in
significant ways, the quality of treatment would not wipe
out sexual differences. On the other hand, if genetic factors
play a minimal role in determining personality, equal
socialization practices would substantially reduce dissimi-
larities.

There are individual predispositions creating a range
of personality types at birth for both sexes (Thomas et al.,
1963). Our recognition of individual differences would enable us to utilize appropriate socialization practices that

consider constructive techniques to develop positive sexual self-concept in every child. A strict definition of how a boy or a girl should be treated in the end may prevent the child from having positive self-feelings and from developing to his or her full potential.

Even though endocrinological differences before birth may predispose each sex to different behavior patterns, the malleability and learning of humans should make biological factors less significant than environmental treatment as determinants of later behavior. The interaction between biological and child-rearing factors are too complex and probably impossible to disentangle. Nevertheless, greater equalization of child-rearing and school practices, based more on individual differences, would allow us to begin to extend the behavioral options for each sex and would result in greater self-acceptance of each child. If independence, assertiveness, and serious intellectual commitment are desirable human qualities, then they are desirable for women as well as for men, and parents should be helped to socialize their children from birth to develop these qualities. Sensitivity and tenderness, which are considered feminine characteristics, are other desirable human qualities. A father or teacher who reveals these traits and encourages them in the boys he socializes creates masculine identification with an expanded range of qualities. The suggestion that conflicts are created when there is deviation from societal sex-role standards actually leads to a perpetuation of sex-role stereotypes. Perhaps the focus should be on changing the standards.

Chapter 5

RACE, SOCIAL CLASS, AND CHILD SELF-CONCEPT

Racial identity develops in stages. In the first stage at about two-and-a-half, children learn to make racial distinctions conceptually. At the same time, attitudes are already beginning to develop toward race. Allport (1958) has called this "pregeneralized learning." Children have only vague preferences, and clear-cut evaluations have not yet developed. Their feelings seem to indicate a hierarchy of preference, rather than clear acceptance or rejection. At the second step, which occurs at about the age of five, a "rejection" stage begins. Children become fully aware of racial attitudes and verbally reflect the poorly evaluated status. Immediately afterward "differentiation" comes into play and this allows children to rationalize their prejudices (Allport, 1958). Porter (1971) suggested that when white children become fully aware of the racial differences and the evaluations attached to them, they reject the unfavored status and almost simultaneously begin to rationalize their feelings. Black children become aware of rejection toward

146

them by the dominant culture and they have differentiated reactions of ambivalence and/or positive feelings toward their own race.

RACIAL SELF-CONCEPT STUDIES

Starting with the studies by Clark and Clark (1939, 1940, 1950, 1952), investigators have found that racial conception first appears in the third year of life and rapidly becomes more evident each year thereafter. More recently, Stevenson and Stevenson (1960) observed two- and three-year-old children in a southern nursery school and determined from controlled observation that racial awareness in the majority of these children occurred before the age of three. In their study of three- to seven-year-old Negro children in southern and northern schools, using brown and white dolls, Clark and Clark (1952) found that at all ages there was a preference for the white doll. The children said that the Negro doll "looks bad." A significantly higher percentage of northern children, as compared to southern ones, thought that the brown doll looked bad. In another study, these same investigators found that the Negro children up to the age of seven rejected the brown color by making escapist responses to its presence (Clark & Clark, 1950). They found that a negation of the color brown was associated with a conflict about identifying with this color. A coloring test was given in addition to the "dolls test." Each child was given a sheet of paper with drawings of a leaf, an apple, an orange, a mouse, a boy and girl, and a box of colored crayons. They were first asked to color the objects. It was assumed that the children knew what colors things really were if they responded correctly. Then they were asked to color the boy and the girl the color they would like the child to be. One hundred sixty children between the ages of five and seven seemed consistent enough to be analyzed. All the Negro children who were light and who colored the figure white or yellow were considered accurate as to how they saw their skin color, but 15 percent of the children with medium brown skin and 14 percent of the dark brown children used the yellow or white crayon. This, according to Clark and Clark, was an indication of emotional anxiety and conflict about skin color. When asked to color a child of the opposite sex, 52 percent of these children refused to color them either black or brown, which supported the results of the "dolls test," whereas 60 percent of the children preferred the white doll or rejected the brown doll. A higher percentage of northern children, as in the dolls test, rejected the darker colors. Only 36 percent of the northern children preferred the brown color, whereas 80 percent of the southern children used the brown color. Morland (1958, 1963), studying southern nursery school children, also found racial identification to be significantly higher for white than for Negro children. He noted emotional reactions only by the Negro children. McDonald (1970), in a study of disturbed nursery school children, found that no white child expressed a conflict about why his skin was white. In contrast, all the Negro children were upset about their brown skin. It was only the minority group child, who sensed himself as different, and "different" inevitably meant "inferior."

The problem with the Clark and Clark research was that the dark-skinned dolls may have confused lighter-skinned black children. Greenwald and Oppenheim (1968), in a study of thirty-six Negro and white northern preschool children, found that by adding a doll of intermediate color along with the white and dark brown dolls used in the Clark and Clark studies, the identification of the Negro children was about the same as that of the white children. Unfortunately, they mentioned that the mulatto doll may have been the appropriate choice for the dark-skinned white children and no measure of the white children's skin color preference was obtained. In another recent study, eighty four-through six-year-old Head Start children were evaluated using color slides of three dolls, each set identical except for color and physiognomy. The findings continued to support the existence of racial misidentification among black children (Gitter & Satow, 1969). They found that it occurred not only in terms of color but also in terms of physiognomy. This may be due to escapist responses or to perceptual difficulties.

While the above-mentioned investigators found escapist responses in Negro children as to their color, other researchers found that Negro nursery children differentiated between white and black children more consistently than did white children (Horowitz, 1939; Landreth & Johnson, 1953). Horowitz (1939) noted that children who seemed aware of being a member of a minority group might still choose a picture of a majority group person as being most like themselves. She suggested that group consciousness and identification is an intrinsic aspect of ego development. Goodman (1964) also found that the Negro four-year-old subjects in her study identified their race earlier than the white children and were uneasy about their color, but she didn't find significant personality differences between the members of the two racial groups.

Stevenson and Stewart (1958) reported that in three-to seven-year-old Negro and white children, there was a high frequency of negative attitudes and the use of stereotypic roles by the Negro subjects. Radke, Trager, and Davis (1949, 1950), studying Negro and white kindergarten, first, and second graders, found that the children's responses to race, indicated rejection of Negroes. More Negro children picked white dolls than white children picked Negro dolls. When using pictures of social situations, negative feelings toward self were observed in the Negro children. Coles' study (1967) showed Negro children drawing themselves as small, incomplete people and white as powerful and strong.

They were reluctant to call themselves brown. He did not work directly with preschool children but observed some of them when studying other members of their families. Responding to a picture and insert test, Negro lower-class children in the Landreth and Johnson (1953) study preferred white over black or brown skin and brown over black skin. They also made more comments expressing hostility and preferences for the darker skin color than did the white upper- and lower-class samples with which they were compared. Brown (1966), comparing white middle- and lower-class nursery school children by the use of words describing themselves, found that Negro lower-class subjects tended to see themselves in less positive ways. Long and Henderson (1968), who also didn't separate class from race, observed that Negro lower-class children beginning school had lower self-esteem than middle-class white children. These same investigators found that lower self-esteem was associated with a less realistic concept in relation to color. Williams and Rousseau (1971), in a study of eighty-nine three- to six-year-old lower-income Negro children in North Carolina, used black and white animal pictures to ascertain self-identity. The children gave the white animal pictures a positive evaluation and the black ones a negative one. There were few errors in color misidentification of the animals. The older children misidentified their color less and were more antiblack than were the younger ones. This was independent of intelligence, as was the self-identity measure. Butts (1963) found a significant relationship in nine- to twelve-year-olds between self-esteem and recognition of their color. Thirteen out of fourteen who misperceived showed preference for children who were lighter or white. Sciara (1972), studying fourth-grade black boys in the Midwest, found that they assigned blackness to lower-status occupations. Of course, this is a reflection of reality, but he also found that the boys preferred models nearer in appearance to the majority white group. In a study of a clinic population of Negro six- to ten-year-old boys, many of the Negro boys had significant conflicts involving guilt-laden wishes to be white rather than Negro, Brody (1963). He found that the mothers, like their sons, exhibited conflict about their skin color and status and their role as Negroes. Mussen (1953), using the Thematic Apperception Test (TAT), in the study of 100 nine- to fourteen-year-old black and white boys, found that the Negro boys tended to perceive the world as hostile and threatening, while the white boys viewed the world in a friendly way. In a study he did of fifth- to sixth-grade Negro and white children, Palermo (1959) determined that there was greater anxiety in the Negro than the white children.

Rosenthal (1974) studied the entire Chippewa Indian child population (233 children), aged three to ten, in Lac du Flambeau, Wisconsin. The interview schedule included indirect and projective assessments of attitude, as well as direct questioning. Rosenthal compared his findings with all other cultures previously investigated. The results indicated that Chippewa Indian children evaluated themselves more negatively and deprecated themselves more than any minority-group culture previously studied. At ten years of age, an average of thirty-six percent of the children still asserted that they were white and the children's shade of complexion (light, medium, dark) did not relate to their self-evaluations. Rosenthal felt that the subordinate role of Chippewa parents in white society, as well as the parents' moroseness, apathy, and repressed hostility, are conveyed to the children. The children, in turn, respond with self-hatred, negative feelings toward themselves, apathy, passivity, and ambivalent attitudes towards white people. On the whole, American-Indian families are prevented from attaining status in middle-class America. Few studies have ascertained the effects of the conditions of their lives on the personalities of their children. There is need for replication studies with other Indian subcultures, using Rosenthal's excellent methodology to get a clearer picture of the personality of the American-Indian child.

All of the studies quoted above show that the group to which children belong may determine their concepts of self and that nonwhite children frequently have negative self-feelings that operate from early childhood. The Brody study (1963), in which the mothers as well as the sons exhibited conflicts about their skin color and status, supports the assumption that insecure parents transmit the values of society at large. They seem to project their dissatisfaction on to their children. Coles (1967, p. 337) stated, "At birth the shade of the child's skin may be very important to his parents—so important that it determines in large measure how he is accepted. . . ."

As mentioned above, many of the earlier investigators who compared northern and southern Negro children, found that northern Negro children saw themselves less favorably than southern children. It was suggested that southern Negro children in those days may have found it difficult to verbalize their knowledge of racial differences because of denial or their unwillingness to discuss their feelings (Proshansky & Newton, 1968). A more logical explanation than inability of southern children to verbalize or their unwillingness to talk about their feelings might have been that their contact with whites was minimal or nonexistent so that their reference group was Negro rather than white. The northern sample, on the other hand, would have had contacts with white children and in comparison have seen themselves in a more unfavorable light. Additionally, conditions in urban ghetto areas may be more conducive to producing negative self-feelings. This is somewhat supported by a recent study that found that a group of preschool children in a southern, rural, all-black community had significantly higher self-concepts than those from a northern, urban, integrated community. The southern samples were from the Mississippi Delta and had little contact with whites. The northern samples were from an urban center outside of Detroit (McAdoo, 1970).

The majority of investigators have reported that the tendency for black children to identify with the white group decreases with age. We may ask whether more of them accept their color as they grow older or whether they hide their negative feelings better. There is also the possibility raised by Greenwald and Oppenheim (1968) as to whether the Clark and Clark dolls may have distorted the responses of young light-skinned black children, since the cognitive abilities of very young children do not enable them to discriminate discrete differences. As discussed earlier, a few investigators added a third intermediate-colored doll and differences early in life between white and Negro children were still found in one study (Gitter & Satow, 1969).

A growing body of recent research of children from nursery school age through high school, using varying measures and definitions of self-concept, has indicated that the self-concept of non-white children seems to be increasing. In these studies, there appears to be no significant difference between the self-concepts of black and white children (Gregor & McPherson, 1966; McDill et al., 1966; Wylie & Hutchins, 1967; Baughman & Dahlstrom, 1968; Guggenheim, 1969; Soares & Soares, 1969, 1970; Durrett & Davy, 1970; Hraba & Grant, 1970; White & Richmond, 1970; Harris & Braun, 1971; Zirkel & Moses, 1971; Getsinger, 1972; Guttentag, 1972; Trowbridge, 1972; Ward & Braun, 1972; David, 1973; Fox & Jordan, 1973). In early childhood classrooms using dolls, several studies found no evidence of negative attitudes towards blacks (Gregor & McPherson, 1966; Durrett & Davy, 1970; Hraba & Grant, 1970; Fox & Jordan, 1973). The subjects were from all racial groups (blacks, Chinese, Mexican, and white).

Fox and Jordan (1973) repeated the Clark and Clark doll studies with 1374 black-American, Chinese-American, and white children, five to seven years old, from New York

City. They did not control for social class. The black children identified as readily with their race as the white children did, but the Chinese children identified less so. The black children's preference for their own race was intermediate between the white and the Chinese children. The light-skinned black children manifested less own-race preference and identification than did either medium- or dark-skinned black children.

David (1973) studied the self-concepts of forty-two black and white three- to six-year-old children also without controlling for social class. He used projective tests as well as self-rating scales. There were no statistically significant differences between the races. He did find a positive relationship between the children's self-concepts and their concepts of their mothers, reinforcing the importance of mother-child relationships in early childhood. David suggested that the reactions of greater society had not yet had an impact on these preschool black children. Perhaps the direct impact of society is not as great as with older children, but the effects of society are indirectly communicated by the family. Mothers who are emotionally adequate and feel greater pride in their blackness, partially as a result of recent societal change, have to communicate these feelings to their young children. In comparing human figure drawings made by elementary school black children before 1960 with those made by black children after 1970, Fish and Larr (1972) found that more black racial indicators were present in the recent drawings. They suggested that this change might be a measure of the current emphasis on the positive aspects of being an Afro-American. The recent drawings showed such features as hair on the face, earrings, and peace symbols, but in the discussion of this article, John F. McDermott, Jr., M. D., suggested that the often-appearing profile heads and omitted limbs may reflect a residue of the depreciated and distorted self that used to be and show that black children are still less complete than their white counterparts.

Ward and Braun (1972) compared thirty lower-class and thirty middle-class six- to eight-year-old black children, using a self-concept instrument and an adaptation of the Clark and Clark test. They found that there was a significant relationship between racial preference and self-esteem, but they found that the majority of the black children preferred a black puppet. Guttentag (1972), also using the doll preference technique, found that a group of black preschool children from a community-control experiment showed a stronger liking for the doll of their same race when compared to a group of children not involved in a community-control experiment. This preference was greater for girls than for boys.

Some recent studies of upper-grade black students indicated that they have higher self-concepts than white students (McDill et al., 1966; Baughman & Dahlstrom, 1968; Guggenheim, 1969; Soares & Soares, 1969; Zirkel & Moses, 1971; Trowbridge, 1972; Powell, 1973). All of these studies had white students in the samples. Guggenheim (1969) reported discrepancies between aspiration achievement levels of the Negro children and high levels of self-esteem. He suggested that the Negro children's school problems centered around low achievement and not low self-esteem. Soares and Soares (1969) measured *generalized* self-concept rather than self-concept of achievement in children in grades four to eight in a lower-income urban school (mostly Negro and Puerto Rican) and a middle-class suburban segregated school and found that the lower-income students had higher generalized self-concepts. Baughman and Dahlstrom (1968), in interviews with Negro and white eighth graders in a rural southern community, found that their statements about themselves in an interview were markedly positive. The Negro children more often reported themselves as being popular than did the white children in their sample. They also said more often that they were very satisfied being the kind of people that they were and described their home lives as being happier than the average child. Furthermore, they seemed optimistic about realizing their educational and vocation aspirations.

Powell (1973) studied the self-concepts of black and white, twelve to fifteen year old children in northern and southern areas. She found that the black students living in the southern part of the country scored higher than the white students. There were no statistically significant differences between the two groups in the northern cities. Powell felt that the higher scores of the black students may indicate that there is a more cohesive black community in the southern part of the country. As suggested earlier, the problems in urban northern ghettos undoubtedly have a negative effect on self-concept.

There is question about the use of self-report as evidence for positive self-feelings. Long (1969) suggested that the higher self-ratings in the Soares and Soares scores of lower socioeconomic children could have been the result of a response set by which the lower-class children responded at the extreme end of the measurement scale; that is, they may have overrated themselves to hide negative feelings about themselves. Therefore, this response may have indicated defensiveness rather than a true self-picture.

Gibby and Gabler (1967) supported the defensiveness point of view. They tested fifty-six black and fifty-nine white sixth graders using three measures of self-concept and analysed the results by race, sex, and intelligence. The results indicated that the Negro children had greater discrepancies than the white children between their intelligence test scores and their self-ratings on intelligence. This suggested that the white children tended to see themselves more realistically, while the black children tended to overrate their intellectual abilities. On the other hand, some evidence has been accumulating with older children and young adults suggesting that participation in various groups, which are actually working to change the status of the black person, can lead to the development of positive self-attitudes (Johnson, 1966; Roth, 1970; Halpern, 1970; Bunton & Weissback, 1974). Recent emphasis to develop pride in the "we" self (group pride), a significant aspect of self-concept, has been suggested by Nobles (1973) and could be a factor responsible for the increasing feelings of self-esteem in the Negro. McCarthy and Yancey (1971) questioned whether Negro Americans experience a "crisis of identity" and exhibit low self-esteem. They criticized social scientists who have provided scientific credibility for many white-held stereotypes of the Negro. They refused to endorse the idea that Negroes are damaged as a result of the lack of respectful, accepting, or concerned treatment from the majority group. The lower-class Negroes' development of life-styles that reflect autonomous and cohesive subcultures presumably give them positive feelings. They felt that Negroes do not necessarily use white evaluations to self evaluate and as a result, the process of self-identity development within the black community would not differ from the process within the white community. One response to failure would result in negative self-evaluation; the other would result in the withdrawal of loyalty from conventional structures and would have no apparent effect on self-esteem. They argued that the second reaction was more characteristic of Negroes who would blame white oppression and past deprivation for their failure and not a sense of inferiority. McCarthy and Yancey refuted the argument that the majority white group was a "significant other" who provided standards for appraisal that was internalized by the lower-income Negro. It seems impossible for blacks of any social class to be totally unaffected by the majority white group, although the recent emphasis on black pride may have decreased the damage in racial self-esteem.

The history of successes and status positions held in the world has been considered by some theorists to be another important aspect of self-esteem. McCarthy and Yancey refuted this as an important variable for lower-class blacks; they stated that lower-class blacks withdraw loyalty from conventional structures, so that status and success is not considered important. We certainly see that lower-income black children frequently become emotionally detached from the middle-class teacher and school and maintain loyalty to their peer group (Labov, 1973). Unfortunately, this too frequently leads to academic failure, and ultimately the children drop out from school. McCarthy and Yancey implied that Negroes who fail do not aspire to white structures and values. These Negroes withdraw loyalty from conventional structures and develop cohesive subcultures and other values. Again, these other values have unfortunately not led to upward mobility and power in our society. According to McCarthy and Yancey, when they withdraw loyalty from the conventional structures, they blame white oppression and past deprivation for their position. Middle-class blacks would be less able to do this and would presumably have lower self-esteem.

McCarthy and Yancey hypothesized that the Negro's manner of responding to evaluation by a facade of accommodation (Uncle Tom behavior) does not indicate a lack of acceptance of self or an impairment of identity. It suggests instead that Negroes play a role to protect themselves from the greater society.

We could hypothesize that if lower-income black children go from their subculture into middle-class society where new "significant others" values and aspirations become a part of their experience, their self-esteem would be affected negatively. Coleman (1966) and St. John (1975) did find that, in desegregated schools, lower-income children's self-concepts were lower than those in segregated schools. Later in this chapter, other empirical research will be presented exploring this possibility further.

There seems no question that membership in a stigmatized group can be countered by a foundation of positive self-esteem in the home. Many lower-income black children come to school having positive self-feelings. It is incumbent on teachers to be concerned about maintaining and increasing the self-esteem of these children. The school has to develop trust in children who lack a positive global self-concept and are defensive by structuring the learning situation so that success experiences predominate, resulting in less defensiveness and openness to psychological and cognitive growth.

CLASS AND PERSONALITY STUDIES

Many of the studies on children's racial attitudes toward themselves mentioned earlier in this chapter have not controlled for social class as well as for race. We might conclude that some of the results may be entirely due to the effects of poverty and the low social status of the Negro. Indeed, it has been suggested occasionally that the self-concept of the Negro is determined in part by factors inherent in poverty, and to some extent these same processes operate in the white lower classes as well (Ausuble & Ausuble, 1963; Rainwater, 1966). However, the Negro has to contend with the reality of his color. In a study of 400 fourth-, fifth- and sixth-grade white and Negro lower-class children, Deutsch (1963) found that even though a relatively high proportion of white lower-class children had negative self-concepts, there were not nearly as many as in the Negro group. Keller (1963) evaluated the self-concepts of forty-six, first- and fifth-grade black and white lower-class children. The black children exhibited more negative self-evaluations than did the white children and the unfavorable responses increased from first to fifth grade. More than half of the Negro children were judged to have little motivation for schoolwork, to be sad and preoccupied, and to be working below capacity. The decrease from first to fifth grade would suggest that as lower-income black children increase in age, negative evaluations by society, which are not countered by significant others in school or at home, have an effect on self-evaluations and achievement.

In studies comparing lower-class, preschool, black and white children, Raymer (1969) and Stabler and Johnson (1972) found that white and black children preferred the white race. Stabler and Johnson (1972) asked the children to guess which objects they liked or disliked that were hidden in black and white boxes. Black and white children both guessed more often that positively evaluated objects were in white boxes, but the black children did so with less consistency, which suggests some conflict about their color. Even though tape-recorded statements were the same in the black boxes as in the white boxes, the statements in the black boxes were considered more negative by the children. Additionally, the children often deposited trash in the black boxes and when told to smash small black or white boxes or bobo dolls, white children tended to hit the black targets first and black children tended to hit the white targets first, indicating rejection and hostility toward each other's race.

The color problem is not limited to the lower-class Negro. The middle-class Negro may still live in a culture where "black" is a word loaded with derogatory implications (Kardiner & Oversy, 1951; Poussaint, 1966, Grier & Cobbs, 1968). Frazier (1957, p. 213) in discussing the black bourgeoisie stated that " . . . their feeling of inferiority and insecurity are revealed in their pathological struggle for status within the isolated Negro world and craving for recognition in the white world." However, if one is to agree with Goff (1962, p. 125) that "the esteem in which the individual holds himself is directly proportional to his feelings of mastery of circumstances, power over events and prestige in acceptance over men," the middle-class Negro is perhaps better off than the lower-class Negro by virtue of his greater mastery, power, and acceptance.

A few empirical studies have been done on the Negro middle class. Sutherland's (1942) early studies of sixteen- to twenty-four-year-olds showed that some of the effects of castelike status are apparent in almost every Negro personality. He stated, however, that caste position is not as character forming as are family relationships and class membership. Kardiner and Oversy (1951) found that among Negroes both the lower and middle class are characterized by low self-esteem due to familial and social rejection. In a psychoanalytic study of personality, they described the mask of oppression theme of the Negro. They proposed that low self-esteem leads to self-hatred because the introjected white ideal is their model. In addition, they stressed that black rage is present and is kept under control by guilt, submission, and depression. They and Liebow (1967) concluded that the upper- and middle-class Negro is not subject to all the disastrous effects on personality that strike the lower-class Negro. Nevertheless, Kardiner and Oversy felt that the dominant conflicts of the Negro are created by the caste situation and that conflict of class is secondary. This was supported by the responses of their black subjects, which could be traced back to a racist motive, even though they appeared to be unrelated to race. Grier and Cobbs (1968) stated that black people are taught to hate themselves as they psychologically identify with the oppressor. They agreed with Kardiner and Oversy, that black persons' defenses are adaptations to their blackness, but they stressed that not all the adaptations to the Negro role are negative or pathological. Stabler, Johnson, and Jordan (1971), in a study of middle-class preschool black

and white children, did find that the black children reported hearing more negative statements originating from
a white box than from a black box. The white children
reported more positive statements coming from the white
box. Actually, the statements "I am good" and "I am bad"
were equally broadcast from both speakers.

There have been a few studies that measured the self-
concept of children using black and white and lower- and
middle-class subjects, so that there was control for both
race and social class (Asher & Allen, 1969; Porter, 1971).
Asher and Allen (1969) comparing three- to eight-year-old
middle- and lower-class black children, that a majority of
them showed a preference for white skin color. They also
found that black males were more white oriented than black
females. Could this be partly due to the greater difficulty
black males have in "making it" in society than black
females and their feeling more disadvantaged and desirous
of being white as a result? Porter (1971) measured the
self-concepts of 400 preschool white and black lower- and
middle-class children in desegregated and segregated
schools in racial and personal self-esteem. Personal self-
esteem was measured by self-portraits and stories related
to them. Racial self-esteem was ascertained by the children's evaluations of black and white dolls. Porter found
that, in the personal dimension of self-esteem, class was a
more significant variable than race. The higher the social
status within each race, the higher was the personal self-
esteem; but within each class, the white child felt more
positively about himself than did the black child of equal
social status. However, there were no racial self-esteem
differences between children based on class differences.
That is, racial self-esteem was lower in all the black children, as compared to all the white children and it varied
among the subgroups of black children. Middle-class black
children rejected their racial status more than either the
working class or the children whose mothers were on wel-

fare. The ADC group (Aid to Dependent Children) had lower self-esteem than the working-class children. Black girls evaluated their body selves (personal appearance) undesirably and showed a high rate of racial rejection. Porter suggested that middle-class black children, and especially the girls, have lower racial and body self-esteem because each of these subgroups compared themselves unfavorably with the more successful white children. This contradicts the Asher and Allen study (1969) previously reported, which found boys to be at a greater disadvantage. The disparity could be due to variations between the studies in the dimensions measured.

This study seems to support the theory that the racial dimension of self-concept is likely to be more negative in black children than in white children regardless of class, and that middle-class blacks suffer more than working-class or lower-class blacks. Perhaps middle-class black children are affected more negatively than lower- and working-class children because of their parents' greater desire for greater recognition from the majority group and their frustration at not receiving it. This was suggested by Frazier (1957), Brennan (1953), Kleiner and Parker (1964), Merton (1968), and McCarthy and Yancey (1971). Working-class black children may be less affected by this problem because they are less likely to have contact with the upper-middle-class group and have the advantage of being better off economically than lower-class black individuals. Hyman theorized that the middle-class black family would more likely compare itself for self-appraisal to the white middle-class group (reference group theory, Hyman, 1942). On the other hand, the personal dimension of self-concept seems to be more class related. It was found to be higher for white than black children of equal class since personal self-esteem can't be completely separated from racial self-esteem. The powerlessness due to *greater* economic and familial instability of the working- and lower-class family would be expected to make class a more potent factor than race in the personal self-concept factors not related directly to racial evaluation.

A few studies have compared Negro, white, and other nonwhite children (Coleman, 1966; Anderson & Safar, 1967; Moses, Zirkel, and Greene, 1973; Chang, 1975; Leonetti & Miller, 1976). Leonetti and Miller (1976), in a study of the self-concepts of low-income Anglo and Mexican-American children, in kindergarten through grade four, found that they differed significantly in kindergarten, in that the Anglo students felt more positive about themselves. The differences disappeared later on when the Spanish-surnamed children's self-concepts increased. Chang (1975) studied the self-concepts of Black-American and Korean-American middle-class children in the intermediate grades. The Korean-American children had higher total self-concepts, but self-concept decreased for both groups as they progressed from grades three to grade six. Using self-report instruments, Moses, Zirkel, and Greene (1973), in studies of elementary school pupils, found that lower-income Puerto Rican students had lower self-concepts than either Negro or white students of equal class. These differences were not seen when teachers used an observer's report instrument to evaluate the children. The differing results may have been due to a language problem inherent in self-report instruments, rather than a self-concept difference. Anderson and Safar (1967) and Coleman (1966) found that Mexican-American and Indian children had lower self-concepts than Negro or white children of equal class. Here again, we have to evaluate the results critically because of possible language problems.

A few studies have found, that there were no within-class differences when children of both white and nonwhite groups were compared, supporting the view that class is a more important variable in affecting self-concept than race (Spurlock, 1969; Linton, 1972; Samuels, 1973). Samuels

(1973), in a study of lower- and middle-class black and white kindergarten-aged children on two self-concept measures, found that the middle-class groups of each race had higher self-concepts than the lower-class groups and that there was no significant difference between middle-class white and black children. The instruments used—the Brown test (1966) and the Clark U test (1967)—did not focus on racial self-concept but measured generalized self-concept. Linton (1972), compared white and Mexican-American students and found that the higher socioeconomic subjects in both ethnic groups saw themselves more positively. Measurement focused on both academic and global self-concept in his study. Mexican-Americans have the same problems as Negroes in our society. Spurlock (1969) studied a small number of four- to nine-year-old black children, using a doll and picture test to ascertain their racial identity and preference. She found that her sample of middle-class children felt comfortable about their identity and preference.

To summarize, studies controlling for race and social class generally seem to indicate that class is a more significant factor in determining self-concept than race and this seems to be particularly so in the personal and academic dimensions of the self-concept. There is some evidence that racial self-esteem may be lower for black middle-class children than that of white children in general and possibly also lower than that of lower-class black children. More research must be done focusing on the racial dimension of self-esteem before this conclusion can be fully supported.

Social class as the only variable relating to self-concept has been evaluated in a few studies. Race was not mentioned and it is assumed that most of the children were white. Burchinal, Gardner, and Hawkes (1958), on a sample of rural and small-town fifth graders, found that children from the higher social classes showed fewer indications of maladjustment, although children whose fa-

thers had some postgraduate education showed greater
indications of personality maladjustment, as compared to
children coming from homes where the fathers were not as
well educated. Sewell and Haller (1965), in a large sample
study of elementary school children, found consistently
better adjustment in the children from the higher socioeconomic classes. The differences were small between the
classes, but a large area of concern of the children from the
lower socioeconomic class was related to status and
achievement, rejection of family, and nervous symptoms.
Tuta and Baker (1973) compared 434 middle- and lower-
class kindergarten children from ten public schools on pictorial self-concept tests. The scores for the disadvantaged
group were lower than those for the advantaged group and
the girls' scores were higher than those of the boys.
Caliguri (1966) gave open-ended questions to tap the self-
concept of 425 intermediate grade lower-income children.
These students indicated a highly noticeable sensitivity toward their physical features—an item that counted for over
one-half of the total responses. Only a few pupils identified
with their ethnic group. Rosenberg (1965, 1972), in his
study of adolescents mentioned previously, reported that
social class was weakly related to self-esteem, with the
lower class being at the greater disadvantage. These studies seem to continue to support the theory that some variance in childhood personality can be explained by the
social status of the child and that the lower class is generally
at a disadvantage.

It would be fallacious to assume that every lower class
or black individual has low self-esteem. Sewell (1961),
found in each social status level that there were many children who made favorable and some who made unfavorable
scores. Taylor (1965) observed in an urban renewal area
that there was less psychopathology than had been expected. He noted that it is easy to forget that the majority
of the poor are able to function adequately.

There have recently been a spate of studies showing that the self-concept of lower-income children, regardless of race, do not differ from those of middle-income-class children (Carter, 1968; Carpenter & Busse, 1969; Soares & Soares, 1969, 1970, Harris & Braun, 1971; Trowbridge & Trowbridge, 1972; Trowbridge 1972). Carter's (1968) study reported a lack of evidence that seventh- to ninth-grade lower-class Mexican-American students had negative self-perceptions. Carpenter and Busse (1969), in a study of fatherless black and white children of welfare mothers, found that the white children's self-concepts became more negative from first to fifth grade, although the white children's self-concepts were slightly higher in the first grade. This supports McCarthy and Yancey's (1971) theory that lower-class blacks would have higher self-esteem than lower-class whites because lower-class whites should be more vulnerable to white middle-class definitions. The Soares and Soares (1969) and the Trowbridge (1972) studies, which have already been discussed in relation to black self-concept, have indicated that disadvantaged white and Puerto Rican students also surpass the white middle-class group in self-concept. Trowbridge and Trowbridge (1972) found, in their study of 3789 mostly white third to eighth graders separated by class, race, and sex, that the children in the lower socioeconomic group seemed to have more positive self-concepts on test items relating to general self, social self, peers, and school, while the middle-income socioeconomic groups scored higher on items relating to home and parents. It seems significant that the lower-class children expected less of themselves and felt that significant others expected less of them. They also perceived school as a failure, although unlike the middle-class children they did not internalize the failure as their own.

It appears that academic self-concept is of more central importance to middle-class children, perhaps because of the greater control teachers and parents have over the school performance of middle-class children than of lower-class children. In a sense, discrimination and powerlessness allows the lower-class black or white child to externalize his failure. Indeed, the teacher's attitude could be subjective and prejudicial and could add to this powerlessness. This feeling might also be supported by the parents, peers, and community of the lower-class child. If a middle-class child does poorly academically, his failure is less likely to be supported by his parents, peers, and community, and this would likely increase his negative cognitive self-concept. Although there were not many middle-class blacks in the studies just mentioned (Soares & Soares, 1969; Trowbridge, 1972; Trowbridge & Trowbridge, 1972), the lower-class children scored higher than those in the middle class, possibly giving support to this suggestion. These studies, however, have to be accepted with caution in view of the possible defensiveness of the lower-class children that might have inflated their scores.

SELF-CONCEPT AND DESEGREGATION

St. John (1975), in her review of the effects of segregation on self-concept, summarized the history of desegregation from forty studies that had been done in this area. She stated that the negative psychological effects of segregation had been stressed by social scientists and their arguments to desegregate schools were a strong force behind the Supreme Court's decision of Brown versus the Board of Education on May 17, 1954. She summarized the arguments that have been given opposing desegregation and that have suggested that self-concept would be negatively affected by desegregation. These arguments are:

> (1) The view that differing intelligence or learning styles of blacks would lead to both races suffering from mixed

schools; (2) That black children would have psychic tensions emanating from desegregation, and; (3) The black power advocates' argument that the elimination of the ghetto would result in loss of black identity and any chance for political effectiveness.

She reviewed the social scientists' answers to these criticisms. Most social scientists deny that there are differences in learning style; they state that psychological hazards have been grossly exaggerated, that stress would be less severe under desegregation than under continued segregation, and that desegregation is needed to eradicate the southern caste system and the northern ghetto.

St. John found, in her review of research, that there are massive weaknesses in definition, instruments, and design and that the evidence from these studies, overall, indicated that the effect of school desegregation on the general or academic self-concepts of minority group children tends to be negative or mixed more often than positive. However, the studies on adults, who were studied to see the effects of desegregation on their self-feelings, showed enhanced self-esteem. Her conclusion was that, in the short run, there tended to be lower self-esteem due to many individual and situational factors; in the long run, however, desegregation was usually found to be associated with higher self-esteem.

The conclusion that desegregation does not automatically and immediately raise black self-esteem seems obvious. Theory would suggest that classroom interactions, including attitudes of teachers and majority group peers, would be important variables affecting self-esteem. Enforced segregation is a symbol of inferior status, but forced desegregation without concomitant attitudinal change couldn't quickly erase the feelings of inferiority that minority group children might feel. As a matter of fact, the new white "significant others" could engender negative feelings. Desegregation per se is not enough; there must be reeducation leading to acceptance of minority group children by the people who will come in contact with them in the schools.

MEASUREMENT PROBLEMS

All the problems that exist in the measurement of self-concept with white middle-class subjects are compounded with minority and/or lower-income groups. Some of the problem areas have already been discussed, but they will be reviewed because their import cannot be underestimated. Middle-class bias is present in language and concepts in most of the standard instruments that exist (Proshansky and Newton, 1968). Zirkel (1971) reviewed other problems that are prevalent when we attempt to ascertain self-concept in minority group children. He suggested, and this author concurs, that with disadvantaged children we must differentiate between generalized self-concept, where the disadvantaged might do well, and self-concept in the area of achievement, where there might be more of a problem. There is also some evidence that we must differentiate between racial self-esteem and global personal self-esteem. Of further concern is the problem that minority group children may respond defensively high because they want to present favorable pictures of themselves (Long, 1969), or they may respond in accordance with expectations.

Katz (1964, 1967a, 1967b, 1968) felt that the experimenter's ethnic group may influence the result. Trent (1954), Katz (1976) and Little and Ramirez (1976) found, in studies of children ranging from first to eighth grade, that nonwhite and white children's responses differed depending on whether the experimenter was white or not. Trent (1954) found that responses on a measure related to personality, given to six year old Negro children by Negro investigators, were significantly more favorable to Negroes than those given by the same subjects to white examiners. Katz (1976) found that academically successful fourth to sixth grade black and white academically successful boys were more self-critical with black experimenters than with white experimenters. Little and Ramirez (1976) discovered, in a study of fifth to eighth grade Chicano and white students, that both the white and Chicano students had more positive self-esteem scores with an Anglo than with a Chicano tester. Others, however, found no such difference between examiners whose race differed from the subjects (Raymer, 1969; Hraba & Grant, 1970). In any case, the race of the tester is a variable that might have affected the results of some of the reviewed studies.

SUMMARY

Racial recognition and evaluation occurs before the fifth year of life and becomes more stable with time. Parents' positions in society, and their feelings in regard to that status, may indirectly affect their child. If the parent is a member of a minority group, their self-feelings may be negative. In the earlier studies that have been conducted on this issue, many of the investigators did not control for class and they found that Negro children had negative self-feelings as compared to white children. Many recent studies controlling for class have suggested that Negro children's self-feelings may not be different from that of white children of equal class. It may be that as a group they really do not have depressed self-concepts, that defensive behavior may distort responses, or that only low academic and/or racial self-concept exists (not social or global personal self-concept). More likely, a combination of these factors are present. It has been suggested that the lower-class black individual's family has its own subculture and has values that give unity and pride to individuals who do not need to identify themselves in terms of middle-class white society. The fact that self-concept seems to decrease as children come in contact with middle-class society, which has been shown (1) by desegregation studies, (2) by research that has compared isolated, southern black children to black children who have had more contacts with white society, and, (3) by studies that have shown middle-class blacks to have lower racial self-esteem, supports the theory that as children are exposed to new "significant others," they tend to evaluate themselves in comparison to these groups. We must not lose sight of the diversity within a class or race, which is undoubtedly accounted for by family stability, racial pride, child rearing, and other factors as yet untested.

Part III

IMPLICATIONS OF RESEARCH
FINDINGS FOR TEACHERS

Chapter 6

OBSERVATION AND CLASSROOM
CLIMATE TO ENHANCE GLOBAL
AND COGNITIVE SELF-CONCEPT

Combs and Snygg (1959) and Combs (1962) stressed that in order to be really effective, education's primary goal must be to help students develop positive views of themselves, to identify with others, and to be open to experience and acceptance by others. It is fortunate if children come to school already on the road to such goals as a result of their early life with a warm, loving family. The school's responsibility becomes that of continuing the process begun in the home, by helping the children as they mature to expand their positive feelings about their body self, their social self, and their cognitive self. A sense of competence and worth, which high-self-concept children seem to have, is related to higher achievement, curiosity, creativity and greater independence. This has been seen in studies discussed earlier in this book. Children who come to school from homes that have engendered these feelings can continue to grow in school. For children who have not had experiences that foster adequate feelings of competence and worth, the school becomes more critical as another important socialization agency. What is somewhat lacking in one place can be compensated for in other circumstances (Erikson, 1950); that is, children who do not feel completely adequate because of experiences at home can be helped to have success experiences at school. Those children, who are most in need of support, are the ones who usually show problems and are difficult for teachers to cope with. It is precisely these children who need the most individual help in our schools. This writer is optimistic for such children in classrooms where self-concept enhancement is a primary goal. The feeling is based on Maslow's theory (1962) that each individual has an urge to grow toward self-actualization and a quest toward finding one's identity. It is this principle, in fact, that makes education possible.

OBSERVATION

Within the classroom all teachers must collect information about children's self-concept, so that they can recognize and deal with symptomatic behavior and treat them in a manner that would help them to develop a more positive self-picture. Skillful observation of behavior over a long period of time, recorded at frequent intervals, yields the information necessary for fairly accurate hypotheses to be made about children's self-concepts. After diagnosing each child over a period of time, each one's weak areas can be pinpointed and remediation can be provided focused on those weak areas. For example, a teacher may find after many observations that a particular child feels negatively about his size. The teacher would consciously plan to use the curriculum and skills to help the child in that area. This is consistent with Akert's (1959) finding, and a basic premise of this book, that individuals don't necessarily accept or reject themselves totally. The task of diagnosis and remediation for self-concept enhancement doesn't differ from a teacher's intervention for diagnosing and remediating any weakness found in school. With children who are found to have an overall positive self-concept, there would be a continued fostering of positive self-feelings, just as with children who read well there are more and more challenging books given them to read. The key to any behavioral change, whether it be in the cognitive or in the affective domain, is to diagnose children's specific weaknesses or strengths and then to use appropriate procedures to move them to more adequate levels of functioning. It happens too frequently that children go through school with the same problems with which they entered because the shot-in-the-dark procedures that teachers sometimes employ miss these weak areas. Diagnosing weaknesses in self-concept is particularly important because it is such a nebulous construct.

Children who seem to feel grossly negative about themselves should be referred to a specialist such as a psychologist, psychiatrist, or social worker. A projective test would give more information about their self-feelings and such a test can only be administered by a psychologist.

Clues are gained not only from observation of children within the setting of the school, but also from the information form and interview that should be obtained from the parents and from the observation of parent-child interactions and the teacher's own interactions with the parents. Things that should be noted are any derogatory or rejecting remarks parents make toward or about the child, whether they be in jest or in seriousness. Parents sometimes disguise their feelings about a child's size or sex by statements such as, "isn't he a tough one for his size," or "he's as sensitive as a girl."

Two types of objective accounts of a child's total behavior, which the teacher can utilize, are a diary or running record, focusing on behavior for a specific period of time; or an anecdotal record, focusing on a completed event in the child's environmental interaction, not based on a particular unit of time (Gardner, 1973). Running records are usually taken over a ten- to twenty-minute period of time and everything a child says and does is objectively recorded. An example of a ten-minute running record follows: The child's name is Edward and he is four years, four months of age. The time of day is first thing in the morning of September 30. The children engage in free play at this time.

9:00—Edward is running across the room with a broad smile on his face. Richard joins him and says, "Let's play with blocks." They move to the block corner with large running steps. Edward has an intense look on his face and says, "I want to build a big house." Richard is distracted by John who has just arrived. Edward continues alone, placing four large blocks side by side in a square. Richard and John return and look at his beginning building for a few seconds. Edward sits back on his heels and looks at John intently and says, "Do you want to play with me?" John turns away and starts his own project. Edward looks at John, screws up his face and goes back to his building. He piles one large rectangular block on top of another, each of the same size as the one under it, and he makes sure the whole edifice is lined up on all sides. Jimmy runs through the block area and brushes against Edward's building and it falls with a loud bang. Edward hits Jimmy in the stomach with a full arm swing and his face reddens as he does so. His mouth is tight and his eyes are partly closed. A teacher comes up to help Jimmy who is screaming. Edward says, "He broke my building," and runs away from the teacher to the other side of the block corner, with his head bowed and his body stiff. When the teacher leaves with Jimmy to another part of the room, Edward resumes his play alone, rebuilding, so that it is again as it had been previously, four piles of blocks piled on top of one another in a square. As he jumps up and down, he says to a passing adult, "See my house". He then screams at the top of his lungs to the teacher at the other end of the room, "Can I leave my house up," and before she responds he runs at top speed to the shelf where the construction paper is kept. He pulls the top sheet out, knocking a few sheets to the floor and runs to the teacher saying, "Write 'Edward's Building.'" He jumps up and down in one spot and every part of his body is being exercised in the process.

The interpretation of this record is as follows:

> Edward seems to be an intense child who is energetic, determined, and assertive. He is satisfied with his work, which shows excellent coordination and concentration. He seemed a little anxious about the teacher's reaction to his hitting Jimmy. He may have difficulty with impulse control, as he hit Jimmy quite hard. This has to be observed more in the future. With further observation of his emotional responses, the teacher can determine patterns of behavior and provide means to help Edward in particular areas of difficulty.

It is difficult for a teacher who is alone with a group of children to do frequent timed recordings. This writer has found anecdotal records to be more realistic in view of this problem. The teacher should have a card for each child or a pad in a pocket all the time. This would allow her to record situations that occur spontaneously during the day.

An example of an anecdotal record would be one of a child who never approached another child before, but the teacher noted that she was making tentative overtures to another child. She decided to note the interaction to get an objective view of it and to have a record of it.

> Amy went to the table where Joan was sitting. She watched Joan do the bear puzzle and when Joan finished it, she asked her for it. She sat down next to Joan, doing this puzzle slowly while Joan did another one. She stopped frequently to glance at Joan's activity.

This was the first time the teacher had observed any social interaction by Amy. There has been concern about her low social self-esteem. The teacher had noted previously that she had to find one child who would help Amy move toward group interaction. Now that she has noted this interaction with Joan the teacher can encourage this relationship. Joan is a good child to begin the process, because she is accepting and popular with the other children. The teacher will create an opportunity for these children to be involved in the same activity again.

In addition to the spontaneous anecdotal records, a teacher will decide in advance to focus her observational recording on one child or another. With any kind of record, she notes everything a child does or says. Date, time of day, setting, and activity should be noted. At the end of each day, the teacher should flip through the cards of every child in the classroom and add any significant things that occurred that she had not recorded earlier. Interpretations are tentatively made and are subject to change, but they are made after enough evidence is accumulated to give clues to a child's self-feelings. More information about the specifics of taking observational records are available in Cohen and Stern (1958) and Almy (1959).

One of the problems inherent in inferring self-concept is that the same action could mean different things for different children. For example, two children may cling to a teacher early in the school experience: one may be an only child who has had limited school experience and is realistically reluctant and just needs to get her bearings and a little experience before venturing out to join the group; while the other may have had many negative social experiences with siblings and peers and may feel anxious and fearful. Over time, as the teacher looks at the behavior of these two children in many activities and situations, he should be able to differentiate between them and act accordingly.

Making Inferences About Self-feelings

The inferences that we make are based, first of all, on children's verbalizations about themselves. They may denigrate themselves by statements like "I can't do that," when they really are physically, socially, cognitively capable of performing the task, or they may brag and say "I can do anything," indicating a defensiveness and a covering up of feelings of inadequacy. The stories that they write or tell give good indications of how they see themselves. A good assignment for very young children to talk about and older ones to write is, "If I had a wish (or a number of wishes), it (they) would be—." The younger the child, the more likely will true feelings be expressed. The voice quality as well as the specific content should be noted. Outside of verbalization, we can infer feelings about self by child's behavior in varying school situations; particularly in dramatic play, art, and movement. In free play, the teacher should observe the roles the child takes. If a child persistently assumes a specific role, such as always being the baby, we have to assume that this relates to negative self-image. There may also be negative feelings in the child about sex or social self. There should be a search for clues to further expand the diagnosis. A child's drawings should be evaluated. For example, if the child constantly portrays violence, blood, death, and the like or if only a small part of a large page is consistently used, it frequently indicates that there are self-concept problems. How children move their posture, as well as the way they use their bodies in day-to-day activities and in rhythmic activities during music time gives us additional information on how they see themselves in space (body self-concept).

Generalized Self-concept Indicators

Various behaviors typify children with global positive self-concept that have been defined by a number of researchers. Purkey and Cage (1973) developed "The Florida Key" to allow classroom teachers to infer self-concept. They identified four factors to account for 92 percent of the common variance in self-concept, using a sample of 1000 elementary school children in Florida and Oklahoma. The four factors are how a child relates (Factor I, Relating), how he asserts himself (Factor II, Asserting), his investment in school (Factor III, Investing), and his coping abilities (Factor IV, Coping). Survant (1972) described the "typical" kindergarten child with a positive global self-concept: (1) He is unafraid of a new situation. (2) He makes friends with other children easily. (3) He experiments easily with new materials. (4) He trusts his teacher even though she is a stranger to him. (5) He is cooperative and can usually follow reasonable rules. (6) He is largely responsible for controlling his own behavior. (7) He is creative, imaginative, and has ideas of his own. (8) He talks freely and may have difficulty listening to others because of his eagerness to share his experiences. (9) He is independent and needs only a minimum amount of help or direction from his teacher. (10) He seems for the most part to be a happy individual.

A child with low global self-concept is characterized as follows by Survant (1972): (1) He seldom shows initiative. (2) He relies on others for direction. (3) He asks permission to do anything. (4) He seldom shows spontaneity. (5) He seldom enters new activities. (6) He isolates himself. (7) He talks very little. (8) He is possessive of objects. (9) He

Table 6.1 Example of a Self-Concept Profile

Child's Name: John B.   Birth Date: 12–13–72
                                                          Sex: M

Date	Evidence	Self-concept area	Area of concern	Remediation[a] suggestion
9/20	Stayed near the teacher for 20 minutes on arrival	Social self	Social self	
9/22	Did puzzle quickly	Cognitive self		
	Named the peg colors accurately			
	Summarized the main ideas of the story			
9/28	Played alone at puzzle; withdrew when Johnny approached him	Social self	Social self	
	Identified his picture on cubby proudly said, "I'm a boy and I have blue eyes and blond hair." (accurate)	Body self (physical and sexual)		
10/5	Withdrew when David took a puzzle piece away from him	Social self	Social self	Find one child who would likely accept him and have them both help the teacher do something; the teacher would stay nearby to encourage the relationship between them. Observe to see if there is a child he seems to watch and/or ask his mother about what he says about the children at school. A particular child so identified would be a good choice to pair with him if the child is accepting. The teacher would encourage home visits between these children by suggesting the possibility to each mother.
	During story time he responded to his name when called up to the front	Body self		
	While doing rhythms his movements were rhythmic and coordinated, but he would not take a partner with whom to run	Body self (kinesthetic self)	Social self	
10/12	Read the words on the walls	Cognitive self		

[a] After a few observations, the teacher would make a decision about what intervention strategies might help the child to enhance his self-feelings in areas found to be weak.

183

makes excessive demands. (10) He withdraws or aggresses. (11) He reacts with signs of frustration.

Self-concept Profile

The assets and liabilities vary in intensity and in kind with children falling on a continuum in self-concept, some having problems in all areas and some in a few. From observation we have to focus on the specific dimensions for each child and develop a profile for him or her. (see Table 6.1)

The child in this example (Table 6.1) has high self-concept in the cognitive self and the body self (sexual, physical and kinesthetic) dimensions, so the teacher's task is to continue to help him feel good about himself in these areas. Her remediation will have to focus on building up his social self.

CLASSROOM CLIMATE TO ENHANCE GENERALIZED SELF-CONCEPT

If generalized self-esteem is to be enhanced and maintained, children need teachers who are accepting, who make them feel secure, who have realistic clear behavioral expectations, and who encourage independence and responsibility. Children in school need a supportive environment where they feel that the tasks that they are given to do are appropriate and will lead to success. They also have to feel free to make mistakes without penalty. Although previous successes and failures will determine their expectations for those young children who have lacked positive treatment by significant others, the need to grow toward more positive self-esteem would allow change to be effected with new significant others in school. The teacher's reactions would give feedback on the appropriateness of behavior in a different situation. As a significant other, the teacher is a model to the children he teaches. By what he says, how he says it and by his facial expressions, the teacher conveys his feelings about a child. He teaches the child by his behavior how the child should perceive herself. He also teaches an entire class how they should perceive individual children. A teacher's interactions are therefore quite significant in that if a child perceives herself negatively and this is reinforced by the teacher, the child's peers will more likely model his behavior and also treat the child negatively. Kagan (1971) stated that as a potential model the teacher's power to create values has been underestimated. He is first a model and then a dispenser of knowledge.

Acceptance comes by the way the teacher talks to a child, how important he makes her feel, how attentively he listens to her, and how he respects the child's sex, race, and individuality. Spaulding (1964) found that there were significantly positive self-concepts in children whose teachers were calm, acceptant, supportive, and facilitative. When the teachers were dominative, threatening, grim, and sarcastic, there were negative self-feelings. Security is fostered by teachers who are secure themselves, who know the developmental expectations for the children they teach, and who set appropriate limits and controls based on these expectations. One cannot expect a normal three-year-old to sit quietly for an hour cutting paper, but one can expect a normal three-year-old not to cut another child with the scissors he is using. Without denigrating the child who physically attacks another child in such a way, the teacher must protect others from the attacks and help the child to develop self-control. Security cannot be fostered if a teacher is not capable of keeping children from physically hurting one another. They must know that adults are strong enough to protect them from danger. This does not mean that the expression of verbal anger should be discouraged. Feelings and emotions that are denied affect behavior in subtle destructive ways. The child should learn not only when to control anger, but also when and how to express it. Verbal attacks that denigrate others are better than physical attacks in terms of danger, but our ultimate goal is to have children express the emotions they are feeling, rather than to use language to attack other children. For example, when one child is angry at another, it is less mature for the first child to call the second child stupid, although this is better than hitting. The ultimate goal is to have the first child tell the second child of the anger felt and why. It takes time to reach such a goal of expressing anger by saying "you make me angry because—". We can be models for such expression and to begin the process toward maturity.

The research reviewed earlier indicated the positive relationship between independence and self-concept. Independence is encouraged when a sense of responsibility is developed by giving children choices and tasks that are challenging, interesting, and developmentally appropriate. However, what is challenging, interesting, and appropriate varies from child to child. This demands that there be continuous diagnosis of cognitive as well as affective development. A firm knowledge of both child development and curriculum are essential so that a "match" (Hunt, 1964) can be made between the internal structure of the child and the materials available for the child's use. In discussing the "problem of the match" Hunt (1964) focused on its meaning in terms of motivation. Success in accomplishment and pleasure are dependent on the amount of "incongruity" the individual meets in new situations. Hunt defines incongruity as the gap between expectations and abilities and the tasks with which one must cope in a particular situation. If the gap is too large, the individual may become apathetic or fearful or may withdraw. If there is no gap, the person lacks the motivation to become involved in learning. At some point between these two extremes, which Hunt called "optimum incongruity," a task has to become sufficiently challenging so that constructive responses and positive affect result. This optimum incongruity provides the motivation for continuous cognitive growth and solves the "problem of the match." Hunt felt that the Montessori materials provide the personal freedom to allow the correct match to occur. Any materials used that stimulate curiosity and a desire to find out would culminate in cognitive and affective growth, especially if the teacher provides the stimulus and direction to allow children to discover their own answers and to control their own learning.

If children are to be motivated to learn at their appropriate level, negative comparison with other children is undesirable and potentially destructive. Santrock and Ross (1975) found, in a study of ninety-six four and five year olds, that children who were compared negatively to others while attempting to solve a difficult problem, were less confident in their expectation of success than a control group of children who received a reward. The negatively compared children persisted longer at the task than the rewarded children, but they worked less efficiently.

Verbal reinforcement that focuses on specific areas of success help children move toward the goal of accepting responsibility for their work. Research has shown that children who accept responsibility for intellectual achievement do better in school (Epps, 1970; Crandall et al., 1962). Children must be helped to see that their own efforts cause their successes and failures. These findings support Rotter's (1966) work with adults. He hypothesized that people who feel they can control their destiny are more alert to aspects of the environment that give them useful information for future behavior. They take steps to improve their environmental conditions and place greater value on achievement rewards. They are more concerned with their ability and are more sensitive to subtle attempts to influence them. Young children can be helped to learn that they are responsible for their acts so that this sense of control becomes internalized.

Friend and Neale (1972) gave fifth graders different types of feedback on a reading task, in an attempt to determine whether ability and effort expended were seen to be more influential in determining results than task difficulty or chance. Black children saw chance and task difficulty as being the more significant variables, while white children were more likely to see ability and their effort as being more important. Coleman et al. (1966) found that feelings of sense of control by high school students was the single most important variable affecting academic success. They found that middle-class students had higher scores than lower-class students and that white adolescents had higher scores than Negroes. As the proportion of middle-class and white students increased in the school, the Negro children's sense of internal control increased, but their self-concepts declined. Crandall et al. (1965b), in a study of 923 children from third to twelfth grade, found that self-responsibility was already established by third grade. In his study, self-responsibility was inconsistently related to self-concept and there were no social class relationships. A feeling of sense of internal control, which gives a child faith that he can control his fate, does not necessarily lead to positive self-concept, but it is suggested that as a child improves academically and feels success in individual endeavors, self-confidence should be enhanced.

The research reported in Chapter 3 indicated that teachers are less likely to give positive feedback to low-achieving students. Low-achieving students' self-concepts are more likely to be low so that it is essential that they particularly receive more positive reinforcement. Katz (1967b) felt that, in the absence of clear external clues, the low-achieving boys in his elementary school study had difficulty accepting their own performance as adequate and internalized an effective mechanism for self-discouragement. Additionally, inward-directed hostility expressed itself as self-criticism that he hypothesized reduced anxiety. He concluded that a child's capacity for sustained academic effort depends heavily on an internalized mechanism of affect-mediating self-evaluations and that this is a core motivational process. In an earlier paper (1967a), Katz stated that internalization does not take place until external reinforced behaviors are developed. The goal would be for self-reinforcement, which is realistic, but young children first need overt, positive, realistic reinforcement. This writer agrees with Gordon (1971) that a positive self-concept, as well as a desire for learning and achievement motivation, needs continual bolstering in order to be sustained. Crandall (1960a) suggested that some children need approval from significant others to define for them how competently they are performing, while other children evaluate their achievement efforts primarily on the basis of their own subjective standards. According to Leeds (1971), Sloan found that kindergarten children made more pronounced self-esteem gains when teachers gave them appropriate and prompt verbal feedback.

Crandall et al. (1963), using experimentally manipulated reinforcements with junior high school students, found that negative adult reactions regarding achievement produced a significantly greater decrease in the pupil's expectations of success than positive reactions increased them. In other words, criticism produced a negative behavior change greater than the positive change effected by praise. This is supported by a study of David and White with would reinforce the child's negative self-feelings about achievement and make him less likely to respond to praise. This is supported by a study of Davids and White (1958), who compared the achievement expectations of normal and emotionally disturbed elementary school boys. Following failure experiences, the disturbed boys decreased their expectations of success more than the normal boys. However, the disturbed boys' success expectations also increased following successful performance. Although the increase was not as high as that of the normal children, it did occur.

The self-consistency theory might explain the differences between the normal and maladjusted boys in their expectations, but it also seems that change leading to positive performance and enhanced self-esteem is possible. As hypothesized by Jones (1973) low-self-esteem boys may be more cautious in reacting to positive experiences, since the fear of being found out always looms in their minds, but the striving for enhancement of self-esteem can be fulfilled through success experiences. The studies have supported the importance of minimizing failure experiences in vulnerable children. They have indicated that performance and self-feeling improve as realistic, positive statements about the students' work are given and as they develop the ability to reinforce themselves. Ultimately, self-reinforcement is to be preferred; as studies reviewed in Chapter 3 have shown those who are overdependent on others for evaluation are lacking in positive self-feeling. If we bolster children's feelings with realistic evaluations, they should develop more intrinsic satisfaction and self-evaluative mechanisms. As they feel satisfaction from performance, there should be less and less of a need for external reinforcement.

Felker (1974) stated that self-reinforcement is important in that children can give themselves verbal feedback relating to their performance. He felt that children with a negative self-concept have probably learned to give themselves negative verbal feedback or have not learned to "talk to themselves" and do not give themselves much feedback at all. He cited studies to substantiate his theory that lack of self-reinforcement can explain both low achievement and low self-concept. Felker described an action program for teachers based on the premise that self-praise leads to more positive self-concept. There are five keys in his program. First, adults should praise themselves in frònt of other people; second, they should help children to evaluate themselves realistically, not based on perfection but on past accomplishments and they should be specific; third, children should be helped to set reasonable goals that are not too distant; fourth, children should be helped to praise themselves by teaching them a new set of self-referent ideas; and finally, they should be encouraged to praise others. His program is based on the premise that children learn by imitation in addition to direct learning. There is certainly merit for this point of view and the research that has been quoted in this book supports Felker's program.

A teacher has to provide an environment for young children that includes material with which the children can identify and that allows them to enact creatively their experiences and to expand their awareness of their physical, social, emotional, and cognitive world. Of particular importance for self-concept growth are puppets, marionettes, dolls, mirrors and other props. Play for young children serves the purpose of allowing them to develop their general self-concept. Singer (1973) suggested that by make-believe play the child develops a more differentiated self-concept. He stated (page 206): "It seems very likely that one consequence of make-believe play for the child is an increasingly differentiated self-concept or awareness of self. In effect, by practicing a variety of make-believe selves in roles, a child gradually differentiates himself from the field around him and sees many options within himself that are not automatically called for by the external situation."

SUMMARY

This section stressed the need to observe children objectively, to record these observations, and to make diagnoses of each child, focusing on areas of strength and weakness based on this information. Those children who feel generally positive about themselves will be able to continue to enhance their self-feelings as the teacher challenges them with appropriate techniques and materials and furthers these positive feelings. Those who have generalized self-esteem problems or evaluate themselves negatively only within certain dimensions of self-concept, need help in those areas. The teacher consciously plans specific individual experiences and structures the environment to help each child with his difficulties. The studies reviewed earlier in this book have shown that acceptance of responsibility for intellectual achievement, realistic self-criticism, and approval from others are necessary for self-concept development. Results don't occur by telling children they are worthy but by the establishment of an atmosphere that fosters security, acceptance, independence, and responsibility and where warmth, praise, and appropriate limits are ever present. It has been suggested that teachers can teach children to reinforce themselves positively by specific procedures. What is taught is less important than how it is taught, since teacher attitudes permeate every aspect of curriculum.

COGNITIVE SELF-CONCEPT

A successful member of society is required to develop the skills to be an adequate worker and problem solver. One of the roles of the school has always been to prepare children to be functional members of society. Many children have had sufficiently good experiences so that they feel positive about their bodies and their social relationships but fail in developing a sense of adequacy in the cognitive domain after they enter school. This may occur because of inadequate cognitive stimulation at home or because of preconceived teacher attitudes.

The self-fulfilling prophecy is particularly destructive for lower-class and nonwhite children. The teacher must believe that children can learn and must challenge them up to their potential. The teacher has to provide children with an appropriate environment in which to learn and help to get other children to accept them. The language and cultural patterns of these children, who may differ from that of the majority group, makes them particularly vulnerable to feeling academically inadequate, even without negative self-feelings. It is for this reason that children's ethnic backgrounds, including their histories and cultures must be included as a major part of the classroom experience. It has been found that increased emphasis on events and needs relevant to black elementary school children improved their self-concepts and reading scores (Carlton & Moore, 1966). This result is logical in view of the inevitable sense of pride that a child would feel as a result of having his culture considered important in school.

Our cognitive growth allows for more objective self-understanding, as well as for greater academic growth. The affective and the cognitive are interrelated and their interaction determines performance. That is, the child who has negative experiences in early childhood, whether or not they relate to learning, will be less likely to grow academically. Some children are not stimulated at all, others are emotionally abused, and still others are pushed beyond their cognitive capabilities. A child who has experienced any of these problems before entering school will probably have lowered cognitive self-esteem. An understanding of the stages of cognitive development and the capabilities of young children is essential for teachers, so that children can be given materials that are appropriate for their emotional and intellectual developmental levels. As children succeed they will more likely feel better about themselves and this will lead to further success.

During the preoperational stage, the stage that most

prekindergarten and kindergarten children are in, children have to be actively involved with the materials they use and must see the results of their learning. Therefore, firsthand experiences with a variety of materials should be the primary method of learning. It is essential that teachers provide such an environment with many materials and with positive social experiences so that the children will move to the stage of concrete operations when they are ready. According to Piaget, it is impossible to force that movement until the child is ready. However, during a transition period, experience helps that movement to proceed. Lavatelli (1970) and Kamaii (1973) have translated Piaget's theory into practical curricular implementation at the early childhood level.

Some children come to school from homes where memorization of material and the "correct" answer has been stressed. These children might be fearful of making mistakes, so their self-confidence has to be raised. Others might begin school with little previous cognitive stimulation and may feel overwhelmed by the sudden inundation of stimulation. The teacher has to pace teaching so that this does not occur.

A child who comes to school with low cognitive self-concept frequently doesn't actively allow herself to become involved with new learning tasks. Such a child needs to have small success experiences with tasks with which she experiences mastery, but which also challenge her within her developmental range. Sears (1940) evaluated the relationship between the level of aspiration and self-concept. She found that when children achieved near their expected level, their future performance and expectations were realistic. Children who had poor records were either overcautious and set goals below their present achievement or were extravagantly high, setting goals beyond possible accomplishment. This study indicated the need for parents and teachers to help children set reasonable expectations, so that they would more readily succeed and gain confidence as a result of their success. Proper assessment and acceptance of children's levels of performance and styles of learning is required in order to allow them to start where they are and to move from there. As stated earlier, this allows for a match between the environment and the child's cognitive level. Diggory (1966), in a series of studies with high school and college students and adults, found that estimates of probability of success were higher when the rate of improvement was high, when the average distance between performance and goal was small, when the deadline was vague, when the rate of performance was irregular, and when reaching the goal was important for the subject. It is likely that these criteria are just as important for young children and teachers should structure learning tasks for them that follow these guidelines. Furthermore, it is best to measure children against their own goals rather than to compare them to others. Comparison between children does not lead to competence, particularly with children who have low cognitive self-feelings as a result of previous failure experiences.

Individualized teaching and freedom to explore utilizing the strategies listed above have been found to improve the academic self-concepts of elementary school children as reported in a series of recent studies (Purkey & Graves, 1970; Ainsworth & Alford, 1972; Sears, 1972; Howard, 1974). Howard (1974) improved the academic self-concepts of second-through fifth-grade children by designing an individualized learning program for them in which they charted their own success and were rewarded for growth. Sears (1972), reported on a small sample of six third-grade classrooms in a lower-income area. She found that individualized teaching significantly increased the students verbal achievements. This style appeared to be especially effective with those children having a relatively positive self-concept to begin with. Sears stated that the development of a positive self-concept and a belief in their ability to control the type of reinforcement they received in school appears to be more likely among children who are well regarded socially by teachers and peers. Utilizing an individualized responsive environment program for three- to five-year-old Hispanic high-risk children, Ainsworth and Alford (1972) noted a significant increase in cognitive growth and self-concept, Continued observation indicated increases in the children's self-concepts.

Purkey and Graves (1970) evaluated the impact on self-esteem of an experimental nongraded school for eight- to twelve-year-old children, which stressed success experiences, eliminated detention, and allowed maximum freedom for exploration. They found that students in this school, as compared to those in a conventional neighboring school, evidenced greater self-esteem. As reported in Chapter 3, teachers give more praise to high-achieving than to low-achieving students, but realistic praise is particularly essential for low-self-concept children. Teachers are sometimes not aware of the varying reinforcement behaviors they manifest towards different children. It is vital that teachers become aware of their interactions with each student, so that change can be effected in their behavior in the classroom.

SUMMARY

Positive cognitive self-concept in early childhood is essential for children to achieve in reading, a skill that is essential for children to have future success and to reach their full potential. The foundations of self as a student are laid in prekindergarten and kindergarten. Academic competence can be fostered by teachers who personalize instruction to meet each child's developmental level so that goals are attainable, success is experienced, and expectations are based on each child's academic potential, rather than on preconceived ideas about children's abilities based on misconceptions relating to race, sex, or social class.

Chapter 7

BODY SELF

Children must view their bodies as being attractive, efficient, and worthwhile for them to see themselves positively and as separate unique individuals. Our goals should be to develop pride in each child for his physical, sexual, and racial characteristics. In order to feel separate and good about body self, a child has to have had good mothering experiences from birth, as discussed in Chapters 1 and 2. Feelings of inadequacy are minimal if most of the child's experiences have been positive. By contrast, they are massive in the schizophrenic child who lacks differentiation of self from nonself. Most children fall at the high end of this continuum.

Teachers have an important role in helping children to accept their bodies more positively. The severely emotionally handicapped child may need more than a regular classroom teacher can offer him. A physically handicapped child may or may not have high self-esteem. Most physically handicapped children should be in classes for normal children, since it benefits both them and the normal children. The close contact between the normal child and the handicapped child enables them to get to know each other while the teacher helps them cope with the fears and problems that arise. The normal children learn not to fear handicapped people and the children with handicaps learn to utilize their strengths in the real world. The feelings of failure of a physically handicapped child are potentially more destructive than the difficulty itself. A child with a handicap, who has been loved and helped to cope with her handicap at home, can continue to cope if her teacher does not allow himself to be frightened or overwhelmed by the handicap or to become too protective or solicitous of the child. There is need for teachers to accept the handicap, to be able to talk about it openly and honestly with the child and his peers, and to structure the environment so that the child can succeed within the limits of her handicap. Open discussions with the other children is essential, because the other children in the classroom may feel threatened by physical malformations. They may believe that when a person has a physical abnormality, that person has done something wrong. They are threatened by the belief that their own negative deeds and thoughts might result in their becoming handicapped. Honest age-appropriate explanations about the abnormality is needed to assuage some of these fears. The problem of a handicapped child in a classroom should be discussed with the parents of the other children in the class. Sometimes the parents' own infantile fears about body malformations make it difficult for them to confront the problem with their children. This adds to their children's anxiety. With the support of informed teachers, parents can be helped to face their own anxieties and to look squarely at the issue with their children.

For all children, a realistic body image can be developed in school by helping them to focus on and appreciate their body parts and to control the movements of their bodies in space (the kinesthetic self). The recognition and appreciation of one's face, hands, feet, and so on, can be fostered by explicit classroom activities and the use of music and rhythms, which gives children excellent opportunities to enhance their kinesthetic sense of self (Grossman, 1971). As infants, children learn to distinguish themselves from the world outside of themselves. As they grow and develop they find out what their bodies can do. By using their bodies, they discover their body parts and they learn different ways of using their bodies. Body movement allows for growth in other self-concept dimensions as well. As children interact with a group, they develop a positive sense of communal identity (Rowen, 1972; Adkins et al., 1971), and as they observe their environment, their cognitive abilities expand.

CURRICULAR SUGGESTIONS

Body Image

1. Greet individual children by name every day and use their names whenever addressing them directly.

2. Use songs and games with the children's names in them. Examples of songs are:

(a) "Where Is (name of child to the tune of Frère Jacques. (Song to be found in Winn, 1966, p. 186).

(b) Mary Wore A Red Dress (Landreth, 1950, p. 12).

(c) "Pau, Pau Patch" (Landreth, 1950, p. 116).

(d) "Get On Board Little Children" (Berg, 1966, p. 122).

3. Identify possessions by each child's name.

4. Use name tags whenever an opportunity comes up to do so (parties, trips, etc.).

5. Put individual children's photographs and names on their lockers; call attention to them as often as possible.

6. Have a central bulletin board where there is a picture of the children and a place near it for them to put their drawings.

7. Take a group picture and discuss it.

8. Have children paste photographs of themselves in a book and dictate (or write) a few sentences about themselves.

9. Have children bring in baby pictures and compare them with pictures of themselves at the present time.

10. Have a small bathroom-size scale to weigh children and to compare the weight at different times of the year, so growth can be observed.

11. Have a yardstick on the wall to use in the same way.

12. Trace around their bodies on large-size paper and have them fill in their skin color, body parts, and clothes.

13. Have a full-length mirror in every dress-up corner; time should be taken to admire and to focus on the body parts and facial expression of the children as they look at themselves in the mirror; a small hand mirror for closer inspection of the face should be used in the same way.

14. Compare children's faces, sizes, hair color, and so on,—always accepting each and stressing the value of individuality.

15. Use the game "Simon Says" to identify body parts.

16. Record their voices and have them listen to them individually; later in the year, play them in a group and have each child pick out her or his own.

17. Have a birthdate chart prominently displayed with each child's birthday on it.

18. Something special should be done for the children on their birthdays. (birthday cards from all, birthday hat, etc.).

19. Make a hand cast in plaster of each child's hands and leave them out to be examined and compared.

20. On warm days make footprints with bare feet on the pavement; in winter do the same with boots in the snow; observe size, shape, and other characteristics.

21. Have cutout parts of the parts of the body and have the children assemble various sizes and shapes of people on a flannel board.

22. Use a movie camera to take pictures of the children in action and reshow them for discussion.

23. Talk about and discuss when and how to brush teeth.

24. Discuss hands, face, and the like while washing.

25. Talk about the need for safety rules when crossing the street and playing on the playground.

26. Discuss foods we eat and the reasons for eating them in terms of growth and development.

27. Make picture book on such topics as:
    (a) "Foods I like."
    (b) "All about me."
    (c) "What I like to do."
    (d) "When I was a baby."

The Kinesthetic Self

A. Freedom of Body Movement

1. Move parts of the body in all directions.

2. Move parts of the body in all directions putting the body at different levels (high, low, etc.).

3. Move freely to music at any tempo.

4. Move strongly or lightly letting the body flow.

5. Let the body take various shapes (twisted, curled, etc.).

6. Run, walk, crawl, roll, and so on.

7. Make the body sway, fly, twist, curl.

8. Throw balls, beanbags, hoops, and the like.

9. Do a combination of movements mentioned above.

10. Close eyes and move to music.

11. Use gym mats for somersaults, rolling, and so on.

Most of the above movements can be done to music indoors. A new dimension is added when these free movements are done outdoors.

B. Control of Body

1. Play the game of "statues."

2. Change the direction of the body to music at a signal (upright, on back, etc.).

3. Move one part of the body at a time.

4. Change from slow to fast in movement, first using the whole body and later with one part of the body or another.

5. Tense up body like an iron figure.

6. Pop up suddenly to "Pop Goes the Weasel"; or jump up at a signal like "Jack in the Box."

7. Mirror a partner's movements.

Children's Books on the Physical Self

Adorjan, C. M. *Someone I know.* New York: Random House, 1968. This book depicts young children's recognition of what they can and cannot do.

Aliki. *My hands.* New York: Thomas Y. Crowell, 1962. Excellent illustrations and text accurately and sensitively help children to become aware of an important part of their bodies, their hands, and to understand what the hands can do.

Aliki. *My five senses.* New York: Thomas Y. Crowell, 1972. This book teaches about the importance of one's senses and how they help the child to discover the outside world.

Baer, E. *Wonder of hands.* New York: Parents', 1970. Excellent photographs and poetic text depict the many uses of our hands.

Barrett, J. *I hate to take a bath.* New York: Four Winds, 1975. A humorous story shows the good and bad aspects of taking a bath.

Birnbaum, A. *Green eyes.* Racine, Wis.: Golden, 1973. A story about a cat's first year of life. The book discusses growth as the seasons change. It can be related to how children discover more about their world as they grow older.

Borten, H. *Do you move as I do?* New York: Abelard, 1963. The book tells how children experience their world by movement. It is best for older kindergarteners because of the complexity of the language.

Brenner, B. *Faces.* New York: E. P. Dutton, 1970. The book focuses on the similarities and differences between children. It has expressive photographs and a simple text.

Brenner, B. *Bodies.* New York: E. P. Dutton, 1973. An excellent book; in words and photographs it explores our bodies and discusses each person's uniqueness.

Brothers, A. & Holeslaw, C. *Just one me.* Chicago: Follett, 1967. The book aims to develop self acceptance and striving for success. The child's father tells him he can be anything he wants to be. He wonders what he might be and ends with the words "If there's just one me, that's what I really want to be."

Brown, M. B. *Sandy signs his name.* New York: Franklin Watts, 1967. The book portrays the satisfaction of a kindergartener who learns to write his name and his pleasure in his accomplishment.

Craig, M. J. *Where do I belong?* New York: Four Winds, 1971. This warm story about a bear who finds where he belongs is more appropriate for older kindergarteners.

Ets, M. H. *Just me.* New York: Viking, 1965. A child learns what he can do.

Fassler, J. *Howie helps himself.* Chicago: Albert Whitman, 1975. This is a story about a child who is physically handicapped. It honestly and sensitively shows his unique problems and needs that are similar to those of normal children.

Green, M. M. *Is it hard? Is it easy?* New York: Young Scott, 1960. The well-illustrated book focuses on sharing and a discussion of individual skills.

Goodsell, J. *Katie's magic glasses.* Boston: Houghton Mifflin, 1965. Katie is a five-year-old girl who needs glasses. It is more appropriate for an older kindergartener.

Horn, A. *You can be taller.* Boston: Little, Brown, 1974. What can be seen from different bodily positions is depicted by black-and-white photographs and a simple text.

Horvath, B. *Hooray for Jasper.* New York: Franklin Watts, 1966. The simple story effectively touches on how it feels to be little and the desire and joy of accomplishment which make one feel big.

Johnson, C. *Harold and the purple crayon.* New York: Harper & Row, 1958. This old favorite shows how a child gains self-confidence using a purple crayon.

Krasilovsky, P. *The shy little girl.* Boston: Houghton Mifflin, 1970. A child dislikes her physical appearance, but with time she makes a friend and gains positive feelings about herself.

Krasilovsky, P. *The very little boy.* New York: Doubleday, 1962. A boy grows from a little boy to a big boy who can push his little sister in the carriage.

Krasilovsky, P. *The very little girl.* New York: Doubleday, 1953. A girl grows from a little to a bigger person.

Krauss, R. *Growing story.* New York: Harper & Row, 1947. This classic book shows the joy a child feels about growing from season to season.

Krauss, R. *I write it.* New York: Harper & Row, 1970. The book reveals the joy a child has when he learns to write his name and he writes it all over.

Lasker, J. *He's my brother.* Chicago: Albert Whitman, 1974. This is a sensitively written book about a learning disabled child as described by his older brother.

Lenski, L. *Big little Davy.* New York: Henry Z. Walck, 1956. The joy of growing up is simply expressed for the young child.

Lionni, L. *Pezzettino.* New York: Pantheon, 1975. Pezzettino, a small creature, is convinced he is a piece of another creature. He is sent to look for these pieces on a barren island, but becomes shattered. He puts himself together and realizes he is complex and whole. The story and illustrations are well-done.

Raebeck, L. *Who am I? Activity songs for young children.* Chicago: Follett, 1967. These songs can help children discriminate and strengthen their self-images.

Raskin, E. *Spectacles.* New York: Atheneum, 1968. The humorous story and illustrations depict a girl who couldn't see and didn't want spectacles but ended up getting them.

Rice, E. *Ebbie.* New York: Greenwillow, 1975. The need for a child to be called by his rightful name is humorously told.

Rockwell, H. *My dentist.* New York: Greenwillow, 1975. By the use of clear, vivid illustrations and text, this book prepares children for their first visit to the dentist.

Schlein, M. *Billy, the littlest one.* Chicago: Albert Whitman, 1966. A simply told story with appropriate illustrations describes the feelings of a child who is the littlest one but who soon grows and finds someone littler than he.

Showers, P. *Follow your nose.* New York: Thomas Y. Crowell, 1963. The simple, well-written and illustrated book accurately describes what our noses do.

Showers, P. *Look at your eyes.* New York: Thomas Y. Crowell, 1962. A Negro child is shown becoming aware of the wonder of his eyes and eyesight. The text and illustrations are good. It is meant for an older child to read to himself, but it can be read selectively to younger children.

Showers, P. *Your skin and mine.* New York: Thomas Y. Crowell, 1965. For older children, but it can be used selectively with younger ones to develop knowledge and positive feelings about skin and skin color.

Stanley, J. *It's nice to be little.* Chicago: Rand McNally, 1965. In text and illustration, the book simply discusses the fun of growing up, but also some of the pleasures of being little.

Supraner, R. *Would you rather be a tiger?* Boston: Houghton Mifflin, 1973. The book stresses that even though expectations for animals may be less, being a child has its compensations.

Vasilu, M. *The world is many things.* New York: John Day, 1967. This book puts into words children's experiences with their senses. The words and illustrations are simple and explicit.

Yashimo, T. *Umbrella.* New York: Viking, 1967. This beautifully illustrated story is about a Japanese girl who finds delight in doing something grown up: using an umbrella.

Zolotow, C. *Over and over.* New York: Harper & Row, 1957. This beautifully illustrated and sensitive book about holidays ends with the child's special day—her birthday.

SEXUAL AND RACIAL BODY IMAGE

Pride and acceptance of our sex and race means that there has to be an acceptance of our biological endowment. Questions occur before the age of three. Therefore, it is mandatory that negative feelings be discussed openly with the preschool and kindergarten child. Nonwhite children particularly need to have their physical characteristics discussed and compared realistically with those of the majority group child in an atmosphere where value judgements are not attached to these discussions. It is common for adults to evade the issue and refuse to discuss racial and sexual problems openly. This gives the children a feeling that there is something wrong with the difference and adds to the anxiety of a child who has been denigrated by another and further decreases self-esteem.

It is hard to separate the physical aspects from the social and academic aspects. In Chapter 8, there is further discussion of ways to enhance the sexual and the racial self in the social dimension.

BODY FEELINGS

Not visible like a part of the body, but a significant aspect that makes for "wholeness" of self are one's feelings. A key goal of every classroom teacher should be to make children aware of their feelings. Teachers have to be in touch with their own feelings and to share them with the children. One should say things like "I am sad because the dog died," or "I am so happy your daddy is back home," or "Your screaming makes me angry." When children experience tragic loss or triumph experiences, encourage them to express their feelings and sympathize or celebrate with them.

Creativity in art, music, language, and play gives the child another channel for expression of feelings. A psychoanalytic principle regarding creativity is that children should be allowed to regress by using their creative processes, so that they can better cope with reality. Kris (1952) termed it "regression in the service of the ego." Kubie (1952) believed that too much emphasis on convergent thinking (getting the right answer) in early life leads to a neurotic distortion of the creative process. When children do not have an outlet for their fantasy life and adults focus only on the logical processes, children become frightened by their illogical fantasies that they cannot control but that continue to control them. Expression of these fantasies should be encouraged by parents and teachers.

Feelings About a New Baby

Feelings of security are threatened when a new baby enters the life of a child. Teachers and parents have to accept the emergence of the normal feelings of jealousy that are present during this time. In addition, the child has to be prepared for every aspect of the mother's condition, hospitalization, and the baby's arrival. There has to be explicit sympathy for the child's verbalizations and actions and encouragement of feelings if she doesn't express them. The child should have props to act out her feelings about the new sibling, and to express her own need to be babied. This is critical because every child believes that wishes to harm this rival (by whom she feels replaced) can become a reality. It scares her that this harm will occur, so she feels dangerous and bad for having the wishes. She needs to feel that they aren't so bad and that she won't be allowed to actually physically hurt the baby, but she can hit a doll and say that she hates the baby.

Separation Feelings

An experience that can leave long-lasting scars is separation. Separation, with support and without trauma for short periods of time in the later part of early childhood, should not cause difficulty if the child has had a stable early life. However, separations can lead to serious problems later in life if a child is very young, if he has had inconsistent love experiences with significant others, or if the separation is excessively traumatic, for example, where there is bodily threat—as in hospitalization—or loss of a loved one—as in death (Kliman, 1971). Divorce, which has become a common experience in the lives of more and more young children lately, is another kind of separation that can be traumatic. This is especially true if the events preceding the divorce were stormy, if the parent who left the home is inconsistent in visitation or has abandoned the child or the parents deprecate one another in front of the child. The feelings related to hospitalization, divorce, and death should be openly discussed (as should all feelings) to allow angry, scary, or sad emotions to emerge. Accurate information in answer to questions has to be given. As much preparation as possible is recommended in advance of a child's hospitalization.

Young children until the age of seven or eight see death, which is the ultimate separation, as being reversible. They want and expect the dead person to come back and are angry at them for not doing so. Additionally, anger, which is normal in the relationship between loved ones, is thought by the child to have caused the death and disappearance in the first place. That is, a young child believes that his wishes can become reality, and when something happens to a parent, the power of his wishes becomes frightening to him and creates tremendous guilt. This, of course, happens when there is a divorce as well as when there is a death of a loved one.

For children who have had a death in their families, the teacher may be the only person who is available enough for them at such a tragic time, as others close to them may be too emotionally involved with the death to pay enough attention to the children. Any teacher who has difficulty doing so should get professional help in dealing with a child who experiences the death of a close relative. For more information on how to handle the emotions and questions of children who have experienced death, a recent series (Open Family Book Series, Stein, 1974) copes with this issue as well as that of hospitalization, a new baby in the family, reproduction, and physical handicaps. These books combine excellent photographs and a text for children with notes for parents and teachers that explain the concepts given.

The first real separation of average young children on a daily extended basis occurs when they begin school. It is a mammoth step away from the first "significant other" in their lives—the mother or mother substitute. Self-concept development is significantly affected by how that separation is made. Teachers and parents working together can decrease the negative impact of the first school experience, if they understand and cope appropriately with feelings in this extremely vital area. Many people do not understand the significance. It is for this reason that an extended discussion on this topic will be presented, focusing on the child's feelings, the mother's feelings, and the teacher's feelings, followed by a general discussion.

CHILD'S FEELINGS. It is the first day of school, Johnny's mother has been telling him for weeks that he is going to school; she has said that big boys go to school. He remembers visiting there the previous spring. He liked the boys to play with there, but he was scared his mother would leave him. That lady who was at the school was nice, but would she help him when he is hurt or understand when he wants to go to the bathroom? He wants to grow up and read and write like his brothers, who go to public school, but he also likes staying home with Mommy and being taken care of by her. When he feels like climbing into her lap, she usually lets him and he wonders whether the lady at school will have a lap for him to climb into. When he visited the school all the children were playing and seemed to enjoy being there, but he is scared about going into that strange place without Mommy. He feels that Mommy will be upset with him if he doesn't go into school like a "big boy" and he doesn't want to lose her love, so he will try not to cry if he is unhappy. On the other hand, from the sound of Mommy's voice, it sounds like she is not so sure she wants him to grow up. Does she want him to cry and to miss her, or does she want him to be a big boy and go to school with a stiff upper lip?

MOTHER'S FEELINGS.   Mother has enrolled Johnny in a pre-kindergarten program because she wants to make sure he has the advantages of new friends and learning before going to public school, both of which she cannot offer him at home. When she visited the school the previous spring, the children seemed so independent. The teacher gave them attention when they needed it, but generally the children were on their own. She wonders whether Johnny will be taken care of as well as she takes care of him. There is the disquieting feeling that maybe she doesn't easily accept the idea that he is growing up, but she is ready for some time for herself. Is he ready to be independent? Suppose he doesn't like it? Does that mean that she hasn't done a good job? She realizes that he is a reflection of her. Will he behave right and act as though she has done a good job of bringing him up?

TEACHER'S FEELINGS.   At college, she was taught that young children should have a slow separation from their mothers. She is uncomfortable about having mothers in the room. They are evaluating her actions with the children. There are those children who hover around their mothers, others who just sit and refuse to participate in anything, and the most difficult to handle are those who cry and whine as soon as their mothers say they have to leave. Fortunately, these kind of children are not in the majority. Most of the children eagerly participate in the activities and she is relieved to have children like this, as an indication to her that she is doing a good job. What sometimes puzzles her is that many of these apparently adjusted children later don't want to go to school. The sooner she can get rid of the mothers, the better she will feel. Most of the crying children will stop after their mothers leave; that is easier to handle than having mothers around. The worst problem is the mother who insists on staying when it appears her child doesn't need her. How does a teacher help her to realize that it is not good for her child for her to continue to stay? There are some children who continue to cry; perhaps they are emotionally disturbed or too young to start school.

DISCUSSION.   Separation feelings have their roots in children's fantasies that their aggressive feelings will overwhelm them when they are away from their mother, and that without her controlling presence, the feelings will come to the surface (Furman, 1966). Mothers may also worry about their children's aggressive feelings coming to the surface. These feelings and the ambivalence that mothers may feel about their children's growing up is felt by their children. The need to be loved puts pressure on the children to do what their mothers want, which may be not crying and showing only good behavior. This, of course, adds to the problem since it means hiding their true feelings and it puts greater pressure on them to repress their aggressive feelings. If the mother is from a minority group, her anxiety may be greater because she may remember the denigration she might have received when she went to school. Her white teachers tried to be nice, but sometimes hostility lurked behind that niceness. Her mother kept impressing on her the need to be "good" and to "behave." She would like her child to behave because people sometimes say that nonwhite children are badly brought up.

Most of us have some tense feelings when we enter a strange group without someone we know. Normal adults can cope with these feelings, having been strengthened by past positive experiences that allow them to open themselves up to new strange situations and to continue to grow. We know that if separation is forced on children before they are emotionally ready for it, they will not continue to be open to new experiences and separation anxiety can reach the point of debilitation.

Mahler (1963, 1975) has studied extensively the stages that eventually lead to healthy separation of a child from the mother. According to Mahler, children learn to cope with separation as a result of their emotional relationships with the mother that should be in tune with their internal growth and development. As they grow, the mother must be emotionally and physically available, but she also has to be able to encourage their emerging autonomy. Mahler calls this the "separation-individuation process," which has four subphases: the differentiation phase, the practicing period, the reapproachment stage, and the object constancy phase. The differentiation phase, which takes place from birth to about ten months, is when babies become more and more able to separate themselves from the mother. Not only can they differentiate themselves from her by the end of the period, but a bond is developed between them. In the second phase, the practicing period, which lasts until about eighteen months, children become able to move away physically from the mother, yet they still come back to her for comforting. During the reapproachment phase, which occurs from about eighteen to twenty-four months, toddlers are increasingly concerned with where mother is, as awareness of separation grows. They show more ambivalence about separation, and as their cognitive abilities increase, they want mother to share their increased skills and experiences. The object-constancy phase lasts until about thirty months. At this time, children, whose mothers were available and acceptant of their needs at each previous level, have reached emotional object constancy; that is, they have internalized an inner image of the mother that enables them to function separately, despite moderate degrees of tension and discomfort.

In sum, during these stages, the normal child moves from symbiotic union (no separation, as the "I" is not as yet

separated from the "non-I"), through awareness of separation, to a sense of self and separation of self from mother.
When object constancy is achieved, the child has the mother's picture in her mind, she feels and knows that even if
she is not there, mother will be back for her; she has a
separate identity and she doesn't need mother's presence
to control her. Additionally, the child should have attained
and continue to maintain self-esteem in the context of object constancy. This means that by the end of the separation-individuation phase, the child should have positive
object constancy as well as a unified self-image and both
should be based on true ego identifications.

This relates to self-concept, in that children who can
separate themselves from their mothers and have object
constancy, can devote their energies to exploring and dis-
covering new things in their environment, instead of having to keep their fears and aggressive impulses in check.
Therefore, early childhood separation experiences starting
from birth affect the openness with which a child faces life
and its contingencies. Acceptance of feelings also leads to
positive self-concept. A child who is obsessed because of a
real fear that his mother will not be back, but is told that
he should not cry, is made to feel ashamed for his feelings
that he can't help having. One important dimension of
body self is one's feelings. "Significant others" help the
child to form evaluations about this body self; denigration
or denial of one part of it is destructive to self-esteem.

The role of teachers and parents as it relates to separation should be, first of all, to recognize that there is nothing
wrong if a child needs a parent in school to help make the
home–school transition an easier one. Instead of the attitude being "what is the matter with you that you need your
mother here," which instills negative self-feelings, the attitude should convey the idea that it is all right to have
mother stay. This is especially important for a child who
defends against separation feelings by denying them. After
the denial is removed, sadness, fear, and anger may

become evident (Furman, 1966). Furman (1966) feels that the job of separation resolution has not been accomplished until all three of these emotions have come to the surface. This may occur at home or at school. In addition, the teacher should convey the feeling to the child that as soon as the child feels comfortable, the teacher knows he will let his mother leave. This shows faith in the child that he will let his mother go when he is ready. Children want to grow up and will do so when given time and a choice. Maslow (1971) feels that if the choice is a free one and if the child is not crippled, he will choose forward progression. However, if he is forced to move ahead, pseudo-growth takes place. He wrote: (p. 119)

> A kind of pseudo-growth takes place very commonly when the person tries (by repression, denial, reaction formation, etc.) to convince himself that an ungratified basic need has really been gratified, or doesn't exist. He then permits himself to grow on to higher—need—levels, which of course, forever after, rest on a very shaky foundation. I call this "pseudo-growth" by bypassing the ungratified need.

This means that the teacher has to allow parents to be around for varying periods of time. The teacher's security about his role as a teacher is related to his comfort in doing so. He has to be able to reassure parents before school starts that it is normal for some children to need their mothers, or mother substitutes, that they should remain, and that the time needed to stay varies from child to child. The key message conveyed to parents is the need to think of each child as an individual and that norm expectations are detrimental to individual children. The parent and the teacher should cooperatively discuss the needs of that parent and her child regarding separation when problems arise, but before school starts it is a good idea for teachers to discuss the normal process of separation and to ask each parent to expect to stay until the parent and the teacher feel it is time for the parent to leave.

There is recognition that the very child who needs the mother the most will more likely than not be the one whose mother explicitly or implicitly expects the child to stay in school without her. This mother cannot emotionally accept the teacher's intellectual argument that it is all right for the child to need her. The problem goes deeper than this situation. This child would undoubtedly have difficulty already, and it is incumbent on the teacher to recognize that there are a few alternatives he can use to help the child. They are: (1) to work with the child in school and allow the mother to leave the child, (2) insist that the mother stay and meet with him to offer reassurance and guidance, (3) terminate the school experience, and (4) recommend outside psychological help for the child. Whichever one of these procedures is followed, alone or in combination, depends on many factors. Let us take each one separately and evaluate them.

1. Work with the child in school allowing the mother to leave the child.

This may be necessary if the mother works and a substitute is not available. However, if the child is terrified as shown by his screaming in terror and he cannot be consoled, or he withdraws from any contact, there may have to be pressure put on the mother or a mother substitute to stay. For a child who is not unduly distraught, the teacher has the opportunity to work openly with the separation problem. She can verbalize the feeling that children have when they miss their mothers, since children who seem to be adjusted to the separation have these feelings also. Verbalizing these feelings to children who are in great stress reassures the other children at the same time and allows the teacher to show them that she understands their feelings. Fassler (1974) has compiled a bibliography of children's story books that might aid children in coping with separation fears suitable for the three- to five-year-old range. These books could help the child to gain information, reassurance and an opportunity to share some inner concerns regarding separation experiences.

2. Insist that the mother stay and meet with the teacher to offer reassurance and guidance.

This would be the ideal alternative if the mother has the time to stay and can emotionally cope with the problem and if the child cannot tolerate being without her at all. A teacher has to be available during the mother's stay to help her to cope with her feelings about the child and the school. If a social worker or administrator are available to do this, the teacher's role could be supported by them. Reassurance rather than criticism are essential. Statements such as "I know how you feel and how hard it is for you to—(stay, leave, etc.) are appropriate. The teacher has to verbalize the child's feelings also and know the time to praise the child for an action that indicates growth, without forcing that growth.

One of the most difficult problems to deal with is the ambivalence some mothers have about leaving their children. While they say that they want their children to adjust to this new situation, they convey a message such as "but I don't think he can make it without me." Children sense this unspoken message; they see themselves as not being able to make it and feel they have to live up to their mothers' expectations. After all, children learn about their adequacies or inadequacies by their perceptions of significant others' evaluations of them.

These evaluations do not have to be verbalized to be felt. It is for this reason that it is incumbent on professional school personnel to work with the ambivalence that parents have. It is fine to say, "I understand that you are not sure you want your son (daughter) to grow up," or "It's hard to turn the care of your child over to someone else." The teacher should also verbalize to parents that children are not sure the parent has faith in their being able to make it in school and that eventually parents have to convey the message that they believe children can make it without them. Obviously, she has to feel that way herself first. Then the teacher has to help the parent leave the child. The school has to build up the parents' feelings of adequacy and continue guiding them to help children develop positive feelings and skills. As the teacher sees signs of strength in the child, the mother will be reassured on two scores. First, she will feel that she obviously did something right in the past and second that the child is making discernible progress.

School personnel can be successful with most parents, but occasionally we encounter very troubled parents who cannot be helped by the teacher. Their children are most frequently the more disturbed children. A decision has to be made as to whether terminating the school experience is the best alternative for these children.

3. Terminating the school experience.

Children who scream and are aggressive are obviously more difficult for teachers than those who withdraw and quietly refuse to participate in any activities. Passive resistance resulting from fear of separation is certainly easier to cope with than disruption, but not necessarily less pathological. A school would more likely terminate a disruptive child than a withdrawn one, although the underlying reason for the behavior may be the same. It would be preferable if the school and the parents worked cooperatively to keep the child in school. Unless the child is helped to cope with and overcome the problem, another failure situation is added to the already-existing problem. To keep the child in school without a family member present may require additional classroom assistance. A high school student or volunteer could serve this purpose. With supervision, someone who is warm, consistent, and engenders trust can develop the skill to help children express their feelings.

This may enable children to stay in school while other simultaneous measures such as parent guidance or psychiatric help are being implemented. There will still be children so lacking in trust and positive self-feelings that they cannot function in school at all without outside psychotherapy. For these infrequent cases, the fourth alternative may be the only possible one.

4. Recommend outside psychological help for the child.

It would be preferable if the child could remain in school while this help is being initiated. If the child is to be recommended to a special school, it is important that the school that made the referral does not exclude the child before he starts in the new situation. If a school is not available, there should be a referral to a psychologist, psychiatrist, or social worker. The transfer and separation from the old school to the new situation must be done gradually and carefully because the self-concepts of children in trouble are not helped by removing them before adequate help is available to repair some of this damage. As previously discussed, children with special needs are generally much better off in classes with normal children and if at all possible this should be encouraged. However, this can only be done if the school is able to meet their psychological needs in regular classrooms. This usually requires having additional personnel and psychiatric services. The resources for psychological help outside the school for disturbed families and children are far from adequate at this time. The psychological needs of the poor, among whom we find many more multiproblem families, are barely being met. This makes it essential that prekindergartens and kindergartens develop adequately trained staffs who can support parents psychologically and help them to handle the separation problems of their children. Except for seriously disturbed parents, there is much success that can be effected by sensitive, secure teachers who are in touch with their feelings and can accept and constructively reflect children's and parents feelings.

Curricular Suggestions to Focus on Feelings

1. After reading stories, discuss the feelings of the characters; relate them to the children's experiences.

2. Play "feeling games" where the children are asked to act out what makes them sad, happy, angry, and so on.

3. Role play feelings when they are encountered in real school situations. For example, if one child hurts another child, let the first child reverse roles with the other child and see if the aggressor can imagine being hurt and the aggressed imagine she is the perpetrator. This may be difficult for very young children to do, but it is a valuable social learning experience for older children.

4. Sing songs like "If You're Happy and You Know It—(clap your hands, smile or whatever)," or "If You're Sad and You Know It—(cry or whatever)."

5. Have children look at themselves in the mirror when they express feelings to focus on how the body shows our emotions.

6. Have general discussions on what makes them happy, angry, sad, and the like.

7. Show the scholastic filmstrips "Joy of Being You" and "All Kinds of Feelings." They are in the "Who Are You" series (1972).[1]

8. Have a doctor kit in every classroom.

9. Encourage children to draw pictures of any emotionally charged experience they have had, such as hospitalization, death, or a happy trip they want to remember.

10. Bibliotherapy is a way a child can identify with a story book character to gain insights into his feelings (Gilpatrick, 1969; Newton, 1969; Schulters, 1970; Fassler, 1974). A picture book that is well done touches on children's experiences so that they can identify and grow with

the characters in the book as they solve their problem. Gilpatrick (1969) suggested that a book's power lies in its subliminal influence and that its often unguessed hidden symbols and literary devices act below the surface of overt knowing; the child benefits through tacit knowing. In recent years more and more children's books have focused on feelings (check book list below).

11. Bernstein (1976) has an annotated list of children's and adult's books, cassettes, films and recent ERIC materials which deal with death and separation.[2]

Children's Books on Universal Emotions

Anglund, J. W. *Love is a special way of feeling.* New York: Harcourt, Brace, Jovanovich, 1960. Words and pictures superbly capture the nice feeling of love.

Babbitt, N. *Something.* New York: Farrar, Straus & Giroux, 1970. The book discusses in humorous verse and black-and-white illustrations how a child feels and comes to grips with his nighttime fears.

Behrens, J. *How I feel.* Chicago: Children's Press, 1973. The book verbalizes children of every race experiencing positive and negative emotions such as anger and joy. The photographs depicting the emotions are excellent.

Berger, T. *I have feelings.* New York: Human Sciences, 1971. The book covers the feelings that children in the early grades have; most of the situations are geared to the older child.

Brown, M. B. *Benjy's blanket.* New York: Franklin Watts, 1962. The sensitively told story is about a little boy who had to have his blanket for security and when he was ready to give it up. The illustrations and text are excellent.

Ciardi, J. *You know who.* Philadelphia: Lippincott, 1964. This book of poems is about children who realistically express their inner fantasies and express their feelings.

Ets, M. H. *Talking without words.* New York: Viking, 1968. This book stresses how non-verbal communication conveys feelings.

Hazen, B. S. *The gorilla did it.* New York: Atheneum, 1974. This excellent book is about a little girl who blames an imaginary gorilla for the mess she makes in her room.

Hickman, M. *I'm moving.* New York: Abington, 1974. This book explains accurately the problems of moving to a new home.

Hitte, K. *Boy, was I mad.* New York: Parents', 1969. The little boy in the story was mad and ran away from home. His humorous adventures are depicted in picture and story, but he is glad to be home at the end.

Holland, R. *Bad day.* New York: David McKay, 1964. The book touches on a common experience and the feelings attached to it: having a bad day.

Klein, N. *If I had my way.* New York: Pantheon, 1974. A child fantasizes that she reprimands her parents like they reprimand her. A humorous well-illustrated story.

Lund, D. *Did you ever?* New York: Parents', 1965. The book captures the joy of being.

Mayer, M. *You're the scaredy-cat.* New York: Parents', 1974. The story humorously tells about two brothers who camp outdoors. After the older one tells a spooky story about monsters, he scares himself and his brother, so they both go back into the house.

Miles, B. *Around and around – Love.* New York: Alfred A. Knopf, 1975. By the use of excellent photographs and descriptive words, this book describes the universal emotion of love.

Simon, N. *I know what I like.* Chicago: Albert Whitman, 1971. In this book a child reflects on his likes and dislikes in a realistic way. The good illustrations and text are excellent for discussion of varying likes and dislikes of children.

Stein, S. B. *About handicaps: An open family book for parents and children together.* New York: Walker, 1974. By the use of vivid photographs and text, this book provides accurate simple information that focuses on the feelings children have about handicaps. The child's text is supplemented by written material for adults that allows them to handle questions raised by the material in the book.

Tobias, T. *Moving day.* New York: Alfred A Knopf, 1976. Here is another book which should help young children prepare for a move to a new home.

Viorst, J. *Alexander and the terrible, horrible, no good, very bad day.* New York: Atheneum, 1972. The book vividly expresses how a child feels on a day when everything seems to go wrong for him.

Watson, J. W., Switzer, R. E., & Hirschberg, J. C. *Look at me now!* Racine, Wis.: Golden, 1971. The book reviews what a two-year-old child has accomplished up to that time. The note to parents at the beginning of the book, on the development of the self, is particularly good.

Watson, J. W., Switzer, R. E., & Hirschberg, J. C. *Sometimes I get angry.* Racine, Wis.: Golden, 1971. The book simply expresses the things that make children angry and why. There is an excellent introduction for parents.

Watson, J. W., Switzer, R. E., & Hirschberg, J. C. *Sometimes I'm afraid.* Racine, Wis.: Golden, 1971. An excellent book on how children feel about scary things. There is a good introduction for parents to explain the text.

Zolotow, C. *Hating book.* New York: Harper & Row, 1969. The book touches on an emotion that is frequently ignored with young children. In picture and verse, it shows that we can hate someone at one time, discuss the feeling, and then become friends again. It is best for older kindergarteners.

Zolotow, C. *May I visit?* New York: Harper & Row, 1976. When her older sister returns home for a visit, a little girl asks her mother if she will be allowed to come back to visit if she is as well-behaved as her sister. Her mother assures her that she would be welcomed just as she is.

Children's Books on Death

Bartoli, J. *Nonna.* New York: Harvey House, 1975. In illustration and text, this book describes realistically a child's feelings and experiences after the death of a grandmother.

Brown, M. W. *The dead bird.* New York: Young Scott Books, 1965. This is a story about a dead bird that is found and buried. There is excellent sensitivity to children's feelings about death in illustration and text.

dePaola, T. *Nana upstairs and Nana downstairs.* New York: G. P. Putnam's Sons, 1973. The book tells of a four-year-old child's special relationship with a grandmother and a great-grandmother and their ultimate deaths.

Gackenbach, D. *Do you love me?* New York: Seabury, 1975. The book, which is more appropriate for older children deals with the accidental death of a bird and a child's recognition of the need to treat animals as individual creatures.

Kantrowitz, M. *When Violet died.* New York: Parents', 1973. A bird dies and its friends have a funeral and mourn its loss and remember it. The text and illustrations are well done and capture the mood effectively.

Stein, S. B. *About dying: An open family book for parents and children together.* New York: Walker, 1974. The book sensitively and accurately portrays the feelings of a child relating to death. The vivid photographs and simple text for children is accompanied by more written material for adults to extend their understanding in order to help them to answer other questions raised by children regarding the material.

Viorst, J. *The tenth good thing about Barney.* New York: Atheneum, 1975. The book expresses the sadness a child feels when her cat dies. It sensitively answers some questions about what happens to the body after death.

Zolotow, C. *My grandson Lew.* New York: Harper & Row, 1974. A child and his mother share their memories of grandpa and their love for him. The story is beautifully and sensitively told.

Children's Books about Temporary Separation

Adams. E. *Mushy eggs.* New York: G. P. Putnam's Sons, 1973. Two children in a home where the mother is divorced are taken care of by a baby sitter. She leaves them and their sadness at her departure is touchingly expressed.

Breinberg, P. *Shawn goes to school.* New York: Thomas Y. Crowell, 1974. This book is about a black child who panics on the first day at nursery school, showing the separation concerns of normal young children.

Hurd, E. T. *Come with me to nursery school.* New York: Coward, McCann & Geoghegan, 1970. This simple story with realistic photographs describes what a child does in nursery school. The book can be used to prepare a child for this new experience away from the mother.

Rockwell, H. *My nursery school.* New York: Greenwillow, 1976. This is a simple, well-illustrated book which realistically introduces young children to the routine of nursery school.

Rogers, H. S. *Morris and his brave lion.* New York: McGraw Hill, 1975. The book has excellent illustrations but a rather long text which deals with a child's feelings about divorce. Although it is somewhat didactic, it can be used selectively.

Sharmat, M. W. *I want Mama.* New York: Harper & Row, 1974. The feelings of a child whose mother goes to the hospital, realistically told and illustrated.

Sonneborn, R. *Lollipop party.* New York: Viking, 1967. The book sensitively touches on the fearful feelings of a little boy who waits alone for his mother to come home.

Waber, B. *Ira sleeps over.* Boston: Houghton Mifflin, 1972. This is a humorous story about a boy who sleeps over at a friend's house. He has a conflict about needing a teddy bear. It is a relief when he finds his friend needs one too.

Children's Books on Hospitalization

Collier, J. L. *Danny goes to the hospital.* New York: Norton, 1970. Danny goes to the hospital to have an eye operation. The book prepares a child for such an event in a simple and informative way.

Shay, A. *What happens when you go to the hospital.* Chicago: Reilly & Lee, 1969. The book uses real photographs taken in a hospital and accurately explains what happens when a child enters a hospital to have a tonsillectomy.

Sobol, H. L. *Jeff's hospital book.* New York: Henry Z. Walck, 1975. Realistic photographs and accurate story portray all the hospital procedures a child will have to have done when he goes into the hospital to have an eye operation.

Stein, S. B. *A hospital story: An open family book for parents and children together.* New York: Walker, 1974. By text and photograph, this book sensitively and accurately describes the feelings and experiences of a child who has to have her tonsils out. An accompanying text for adults enables them to answer children's further questions about hospitalization.

Tamburine, J. *I think I will go to the hospital.* New York: Abington, 1965. The book tells what happens when a child goes to the hospital to have her tonsils out.

Children's Books about a New Sibling

Alexander, M. *Nobody asked me if I wanted a baby sister.* New York: Dial, 1971. The book is about a little boy who can't stand the fuss over his new baby sister. He packs her into a wagon and tries to find her a new home, but at the end he decides to keep her. It is done with humor and the pictures are good and descriptive.

Andry, A. C., & Kratka, S. C. *Hi, new baby.* New York: Simon & Schuster, 1970. The book speaks simply and directly to children about the feelings they have when a sibling is added to their family.

Brown, M. B. *Amy and the new baby.* New York: Franklin Watts, 1965. The book discusses the reality of having a new baby brother join the family.

Hoban, R. *Baby sister for Frances.* New York: Harper & Row, 1964. This book is about Frances, a young badger whose mother has a new baby. Frances runs away because everyone seems to attend only to the baby's needs and have little time for her needs. At the end, she does recognize that she has special importance to her parents.

Hobson, L. Z. *I'm going to have a baby.* New York: John Day, 1967. The book has good illustrations and accurate information to prepare a young child for a new sibling.

Holland, V. *We are having a baby.* New York: Scribner's, 1972. Real photographs explain what happens while a mother is in the hospital having a baby and a child's feelings after the baby comes home, all excellently depicted.

Iwasaki, C. *A new baby is coming to my house.* New York: McGraw-Hill, 1972. The book honestly conveys a little girl's mixed feelings about a new sibling.

Keats, E. J. *Peter's chair.* New York: Harper & Row, 1967. A black child discovers that there are advantages to being grown up. At first, he's not sure he likes being replaced by a new baby.

Schick, E. *Peggy's new brother.* New York: Macmillan, 1970. The book expresses a child's feelings about having a new sibling. It ends up being happy (maybe too much so) in that she likes the idea after all.

Stein, S. B. *That new baby: An open family book for parents and children together.* New York: Walker, 1974. Realistic photographs and honest text sensitively portray a child's feelings when a sibling is born. There is an accompanying adult text to help in handling questions brought up by the child.

Vigna, J. *Couldn't we have a turtle instead?* Chicago: Albert Whitman, 1975. A humorous story in illustration and text tells about a child's feelings regarding having a new baby in the family.

Wolde, G. *Betsy's baby brother.* New York: Random House, 1975. The book illustrates the realities of having a new baby brother by the use of vivid pictures and simple text for a young child.

Children's Books on Sex and Reproduction

Andry, A. C., and Schepp, S. *How babies are made.* New York: Time-Life Books, 1968. The book tells accurately and in detail how animals and children are conceived and born. It has an easy to read text and explicit illustrations for use by the older child.

Bewley, S., & Sheffield, M. *Where do babies come from?* New York: Knopf, 1973. Beautiful, softly colored illustrations and direct text sensitively and accurately describe reproduction, birth, and sexuality.

Cole, J. *My puppy is born.* New York: Morrow, 1973. Superb photographs and text show the birth of a puppy and how it changes from a helpless creature to a more independent animal who can leave its mother.

Dragonwagon, C. *Wind rose.* New York: Harper & Row, 1976. The miracle of childbirth is beautifully told in black and white wash drawings and flowing language.

Gordon, S. and Gordon, J. *Did the sun shine before you were born?* New York: Third, 1974. This is a simple, clear book on sex and reproduction to be read to children by their parents. It shows different kinds of families (extended, one-parent, etc.) and different races.

Gruenberg, S. *Wonderful story of how you were born.* Garden City, N. Y.: Doubleday, 1952. This is a classic book about sex and birth to be read on a one-to-one basis to children. The facts are well stated. The book is more appropriate for the older child.

Selsam, M. E. *How puppies grow.* New York: Four Winds, 1972. A simple text and photographs trace the growth of six puppies from birth until they are six weeks of age.

Showers, P., & Showers, K. S. *Before you were a baby.* New York: Thomas Y. Crowell, 1968. The book simply and accurately tells about how a sperm and egg join and the fetus develops.

Stein, S. B. *Making babies: An open family book for parents and children together.* New York: Walker, 1974. This accurate photographic book with simple verbal explanations discusses the development and birth of a baby. There is an accompanying text for adults to continue discussion with the child.

SUMMARY

The body image dimension of self-concept includes the value an individual puts on his physical, sexual, and racial characteristics. Encouragement of the expression of feelings as they relate to self-experiences help to make children feel whole and in touch with themselves and comfortable with both positive and negative feelings. Of particular importance is the need to help children and parents cope with separation feelings, so that children can separate from their mothers without emotional stress and scarring. Negative societal values placed on sexual and racial differences have to be recognized as problems for some children. The curriculum has to be utilized to elevate these children's self-concepts. Techniques and materials that foster positive attitudes about the individuality of each child's body and separateness as a worthwhile human being have to be utilized with all the children.

NOTES

1. Available from Scholastic Early Childhood Center, 904 Sylvan Ave., Englewood Cliffs, N.J. 07632.
2. Available from the Publications Office, College of Education/ University of Illinois, 805 West Pennsylvania Ave., Urbana, Illinois 61801. The cost is $1.85.

Chapter 8

SOCIAL SELF-CONCEPT

Research quoted in Chapter 3 indicated that children who feel positively about themselves are more likely to be accepted by their peers. They are more assertive and independent and seek out children more than adults. One of the goals in socialization is to help children feel adequate as members of society; in early childhood, their first group is the family and later it expands to include the peer group in school and in the neighborhood. As children's social life moves beyond that of the family, they act in accordance with how they think others expect them to act, based on their early socialization experiences in the family group. In other words, some continuity in self-concept is to be expected, since it is organized before a person enters a new situation. However, if significant people in the new social situation no longer reward previously expressed behavior, it is difficult to maintain the old self-image and behavior will most likely change. This is particularly true with young children, for their defenses are not yet stabilized. This places great responsibility on the early childhood teacher and success is more possible if there is early intervention. In interacting with children, the teacher makes the children's group experiences successful by overt and directed interventions focused on children's area of difficulty.

SOCIAL SELF AS MALE OR FEMALE

Each individual regardless of sex should be treated as an individual and have an equal opportunity to develop his or her full potential. When children are channeled into sex-role stereotypes, both boys and girls are deprived of freedom of choice. They and society suffer for it. The media and the educational, sociological, and psychological literature continue to perpetuate many stereotypic standards for each sex. If we believe that these standards are not productive for societal growth, there have to be conscious changes in school and, simultaneously, we have to work with parents to try to begin to eradicate stereotyped expectations of males and females. Our society would become psychologically healthier if we defined what "human" qualities we want to develop in *all* of our children and if we respected and utilized individual differences to enhance those qualities. Parents have to be involved in discussions focusing on this question. It is essential that fathers be involved, since they are usually firmer in maintaining sex differences than are mothers. Separate fathers' groups have worked with this writer.

Models of males and females in a variety of roles and occupations should be provided by real experiences or books, so that the children can have the opportunity to expand their knowledge of possibilities for both sexes. The models at school must encompass the characteristics we define as *human*. If we continue to search for males as teachers, without considering their attitude toward each sex, our schools can be counterproductive to sex-role change. Teachers and administrators are being urged to eliminate sex bias in their school practices and materials. In their haste to add males to school faculties, care should be taken not to hire males (or females for that matter) who reinforce the very stereotypes the new materials are meant to eliminate.

Peer influences strengthen existent patterns. Children who are brought up in homes not based on traditional patterns may become anxious when teased about manifesting nonstereotypic behaviors by children not so brought up. If teachers hear stereotypic statements by children such as, "boys don't take care of babies," "boys don't cry, you're a baby," or "girls can't drive trains," they must surely take some time during the day to counter that stereotype in some way. To decrease such conflict, there is a need for the teacher to explicitly support children who manifest nonconformist behavior in this sphere as in all other spheres of behavior. This, plus the teacher's total teaching program, should convey the attitude that it is all right for a boy to cry or to play with dolls and for a girl to drive a train.

Children need adult role models in literature as well as in life to develop a stronger sense of self. In *Dick and Jane as Victims* (1972),[1] 134 elementary school readers, poems, and fairy tales published before 1972 and used in a New Jersey town were evaluated, and a content analysis was made of the number and kinds of quotations made by each sex. They found that girls and women were generally characterized as being passive, they were more involved with emotions than with things, they were more involved in activities related to taking care of children than were boys and men, and very few worked outside of the home; if they did they were teachers, librarians, or nurses. Although there has been some recent change in textbooks, many of the picture books and beginning reading books still show girls watching boys climb while girls continue to enact maternal roles. There are too few examples in the literature of women as doctors, engineers, or other nontraditional female roles. This is a distortion of what really exists in society. Even in their follow-up of textbooks published after 1972, the group that did the original evaluation for the 1972 edition of Alroy et al. (1975) still found that women for the most part were depicted as mothers, and that the creative aspects of motherhood were not generally shown. However, more females were found to be clever, competent, and initiating and a few males were found to be expressing their real emotions. Teachers' guides have included directions for dealing with sexism. Additionally, women as well as men were shown in a wider variety of occupations than in the earlier study.

Curricular Ideas That Are Nonsexist

1. Cut figures such as carpenters, doctors, dentists, and so on, on sturdy composition board that is light in weight and that is child sized and headless; they can be cut out so that hand holds are made to help children secure the boards against themselves; to attract girls there would be duplicates portrayed in pigtails; a full-length mirror placed near the area where these are kept would be a good idea (Lasky, 1974).

2. Find pictures that illustrate nonsexist roles; glue them to heavy cardboard and protect them by clear adhesive plastic.

3. Make a ring-toss game by filling with sand or plaster two quart-sized milk cartons and seal them and then paint them; draw and cut out and then paste to each carton one male and one female dressed to do the same job; rings can be made from pipe cleaners or coat hangers to toss onto the figures (Lasky, 1974).

4. Have children dictate and tape record their fantasies related to nonsexist roles they would like to assume; the teacher would precede this by a discussion of roles.

5. Use labels and words that eliminate sex stereotypes, such as "Garbage Person", "People At Work" (Lasky, 1974).

6. Make flannel board figures showing men and women in counterpart roles.

7. Take trips observing people doing jobs that are not sex stereotypic; make a class book with pictures taken of these people and have the children dictate the text.

8. Place pictures on the bulletin board that show both sexes in all occupations.

9. Locate and bring in parents who engage in nonsexist activities in their jobs or hobbies.

10. Have the record "Free to be You and Me" available for children to listen to.[2]

11. Assign chores equally to boys and girls.

12. Eliminate separation by sex in any activity; sort children by things such as color of clothes or other classification that is nonsexist.

13. Consciously accommodate and provide motivation for both boys and girls in every activity area in the classroom.

14. Encourage boys as well as girls to express emotions such as fear, anger, tenderness, and so on.

15. Have a representative sampling of books about boys and about girls; discuss unreal ways men and women are portrayed in books, TV, and other media.

16. Draw pictures (or write) on "Some things mommies and daddies can both do to help at home."

17. Discuss tape sounds of various vocations (e.g., typewriter, pneumatic drill); ask the children who they think will be doing it; discuss what is available in society for boys and girls focusing on these activities (Bernstein, 1974).

18. Discuss feelings that are commonly used to describe boys and those to describe girls; try to eliminate the stereotypic notion that these activities are only related to one sex or the other (Bernstein, 1974).

19. Discuss cause and effect of sex typing in classroom situations.

20. Woman's Action Alliance, 370 Lexington Avenue, New York, N.Y. 10017, has block accessories, puzzles, records, a curriculum guide, and books that can be purchased for early childhood classrooms. The curriculum guide (Sprung, 1974) evaluates the available materials.

21. Feminist Resources for Equal Education, P.O. Box 3185, Framingham, Mass. 01701, has sixteen pictures of women in a variety of nonstereotypic roles.

Children's Nonsexist Books

Burton, V. L. *Katy and the big snow*. Boston: Houghton Mifflin, 1943. This classic is about a strong tractor named Katy who plows out a snowed-in city.

Eickler, M. *Martin's father*. North Carolina: Lollipop Power, 1971. The story tells about a father who plays with and takes care of his son.

Gaeddert, L. A. *Noisy Nancy Norris*. New York: Doubleday, 1971. The book describes a little girl who can be noisy.

Gaeddert, L. A. *Noisy Nancy Norris and Nick*. New York: Doubleday, 1970. The book is about Noisy Nancy and her friend, Nick who explore the city together. The illustrations are humorous, but it is a little long for a very young child.

Gauch, P. *Christina Katrina and the box*. New York: Coward, McCann & Geoghegan, 1971. The book shows how boys and girls can use their imaginations and create different things from a large box.

Hopkins, L. B. *Girls can too: A book of poems*. New York: Franklin Watts, 1972. This book of poems is about things that girls can do that parallel boys activities. The illustrations are not as good as the text since they tend to be somewhat cluttered.

Katz, B. *Nothing but a dog*. New York: Feminist, 1972. The book has illustrations that show a girl doing things that boys are usually shown to do; some of these things are climbing trees and working at a workbench. The soft illustrations and simple story about a girl who wants a dog are well done.

Kaufman, J. *Busy people and how they do their work*. Racine, Wis.: Golden, 1973. Beautiful pictures and text depict male and female jobs simply, accurately, and in a nonstereotypic manner. Females are shown as telephone installers, postal workers, and physicians.

Klagsbrun, F. (Ed.) *Free to be you and me.* New York: McGraw-Hill, 1974. The book has all the music for the songs on the record. Some of the poems are appropriate for young children and can be read to them.

Klein, N. *Girls can be anything.* New York: E. P. Dutton, 1973. The story tells about a kindergarten girl who discovered that a girl can be a doctor, a pilot, and even a president.

Krasilovsky, P. *The Man who didn't wash his dishes.* New York: Doubleday, 1950. This amusing book is about a man who kept house for himself and didn't like doing the dishes.

Leaf, M. *The story of Ferdinand.* New York: Viking, 1936. This classic story is about a nonstereotypic bull who is gentle, quiet, and peace loving and does not like to fight. The book is best for older children because some of the language is advanced for very young children.

Levy, E. *Nice little girls.* New York: Delacorte, 1974. This book focuses on the problems of a girl who is not the stereotype of a girl in the classic sense. The story and text reveal the feelings of adults and children and the conflicts created by such a situation.

Mangi, J. *ABC workbook.* New York: Feminist, 1975. Black-and-white line drawings and ABC rhymes depict that girls can do anything boys can do. The line drawings are a little cluttered.

Merriam, E. *Mommies at work.* New York: Scholastic Book Services, 1973. The book shows realistically the varying jobs that are held by women.

Preston, E. M. *Temper tantrum book.* New York: Viking, 1969. Using animals, the book humorously shows that expressing feelings should be all right for boys and girls.

Rockwell, H. *My doctor.* New York: Macmillan, 1973. A story about visiting a female doctor is simple, accurate, and well illustrated.

Simon, N. *I was so mad!* Chicago: Albert Whitman, 1974. This well-illustrated and simply written book is about universal feelings experienced by girls, such as sibling rivalry and school differences.

Skorpen, L. M. *Mandy's grandmother.* New York: Dial, 1975. The girl in this story finally gets accepted by her grandmother, even though she isn't a typical little girl.

Udry, J. M. *What Mary Jo wanted.* Chicago: Albert Whitman, 1968. Mary Jo is a black child who gets a dog. The book focuses on her relationship with him.

Wolde, G. *Tommy and Sarah dress up.* Boston: Houghton Mifflin, 1972. The text describes how two children (a boy and a girl), dress up and enjoy both feminine and masculine clothes.

Wolde, G. *Tommy goes to the doctor.* Boston: Houghton Mifflin, 1972. The book is about a boy who goes to a female doctor. It handles receiv-

ing an injection and his coming to grips with it by explaining the
procedure to his teddy bear.

Zolotow, C. *The summer night.* New York: Harper & Row, 1974. A warm
story of a father tells how he takes care of his little girl on a summer
night when she can't fall asleep.

Zolotow, C. *William's doll.* New York: Harper & Row, 1972. The excellent
message and language describe the feelings towards a boy who
wants a doll to nurture. His grandmother understands how much he
wants it and he wins out.

MINORITY GROUP SOCIAL SELF-CONCEPT

Any preconceived notions teachers have about children
who differ from them socioeconomically, racially, or ethni-
cally will consciously or unconsciously affect their reactions
to the children. These reactions could result in hostility,
denial, or patronizing behaviors that affect both the minority group children's attitudes toward themselves and other
children's reactions to them. Bernstein and DiVesta (1971)
taught white and black boys favorable and unfavorable
phrases, depicting white and black situations. They found
that favorable attitudes were learned more easily than unfavorable ones and that positive attitudes were more resistant
to change than were negative attitudes. This result provides optimistic evidence that children can be easily helped
to overcome whatever negative attitudes they might have
developed from previous experiences. Teacher's attitudes
and techniques contribute to the level of social success
among peers whose ethnic backgrounds differ from one
another. First and foremost, teachers must learn as much
as possible about the culture and values of every child
within the group that they are teaching. The Navajo Indians' culture is quite different from the Puerto Rican culture, which is quite different from the black urban child's
culture. This information can be gained from reading or
courses taken at local colleges. General problems relating
to poverty and language differences should also be studied.

Second, teachers should be involved in group discussions with their peers to air their attitudes about working with children whose values may be different from their own. These discussions are valuable when working with any children, but essential when there are children from minority groups in the class. In a newly desegregated school, there should be such discussions before the children begin school.

Recently, a few investigators have reported on programs that have enhanced children's self-concepts (Lloyd, 1967; Trowbridge, 1970; Zirkel, 1972; Brown & Cleary, 1973; Felker et al., 1973; Landry and Pardew, 1973; Howard, 1974). Felker et al. (1973) had a twelve-week training program for teachers of grades one to six from eight inner-city schools with predominantly black populations in order to increase the self-rewarding behavior of the children. The classes of teachers in the program made more gains in self-concept and in reduction of anxiety than did the classes of the teachers in the control group. Brown and Cleary (1973) investigated the impact of an in-service program that for six consecutive weeks focused on teacher interaction with third- to sixth-grade children. They found that as a result of this opportunity for teachers to discuss and analyze their behavior via videotape, there were significant and positive changes in the children's self-perceptions. The children saw themselves as being more worthwhile and adequate. The gains were more pronounced for grades three and four than for grades five and six, suggesting that younger pupils may be more easily influenced than older ones. In a three-year project in Florida, Howard (1974) found that children's self-concepts were enhanced by positive changes in the teacher's classroom management techniques by improved methods of relating to the children, and by the use of motivating learning techniques. Landry and Pardew (1973) had an experimental program that used techniques to enhance self-concept in thirty-four, four-year-old, middle-class children. Significant change in the self-concepts of these children occurred, but not in a control group not in the program. He focused on all areas of development (physical, intellectual, emotional, and social self-concept areas). Teachers' ratings and children's self-reports indicated very significant increases on the factor scales of happiness, sociability, sharing, lessened fear of things and people, independence, self-confidence, and sensitivity to others. Trowbridge (1970) and Zirkel (1972) reported a significant positive effect on disadvantaged children's self-concepts as a result of teacher education programs.

There seems no question that in-service courses for teachers are valuable for work with any child, but it is particularly important for teachers who are unprepared to work with children with whom they have not previously had experience. This would be true for teachers in schools that are newly desegregated and for teachers who have just begun working in programs that have minority group children. Familiarity with curricular materials for minority group children comes from reading professional journals as well as from attending workshops. Increased classroom emphasis on a child's culture had a positive effect on his self-concept, as reported in a few studies (Van Koughnett & Smith, 1969; Golin, 1970.) In their programs for black upper elementary school children, the goal was to develop racial awareness and pride. They reported that the goal was achieved. If enhancement of self-esteem is possible with children eleven or twelve years of age, the possibilities for change in early childhood are greater.

Curricular Ideas For Cultural Diversity

1. Demonstrate acceptance of their home language in all of the contacts with children.
2. Utilize knowledge of the child's values and socialization practices; make sure that expectations in school do

not conflict with such practices. For example, in the Navajo culture, competition runs counter to the accepted behavior; a teacher who fosters competition for Navajo children is not accepting the child and his values.

3. Introduce cultural history and events, including holidays about every child in the class throughout the year.

4. Teach songs to the whole class about each child's culture.

5. Cook and eat foods representative of each child's culture.

6. Teach key words of the languages of every child represented in the classroom.

7. Make available dolls, representing every racial and ethnic group in the classroom.

8. Make sure there are enough books bearing on the realistic experiences of minority group children; this means that positive and negative feelings have to be covered in books and in class discussion.

9. Encourage the children to dictate creative stories into a tape recorder to be transcribed later by the teacher; topics such as, "Black Is . . .," "Foods My Family Likes," and so on, are suggested.

10. Display photographs of men and women from every ethnic group.

11. Invite older children from the ethnic groups represented in the classroom to come in and work with the younger ones.

12. If possible, take trips into each child's neighborhood, take pictures, and discuss sights and sounds experienced during the trip.

13. The parents should be totally involved in the program; they should be encouraged to come in dressed in their native costumes, to cook native foods, to tell a story about their ethnic group, and to teach native songs.

14. Make the school available to the total community for cultural events, speakers, and the like.

BOOKS ON RACE AND ETHNICITY

Children's Books About Black Children

Adoff, A. *Black is brown is tan.* New York: Harper & Row, 1973. A beautifully illustrated poem that warmly expresses the variations of skin color in a family. Skin colors range from light to dark.

Adoff, A. *Big sister tells me that I'm black.* New York: Holt, Rinehart and Winston, 1976. This is an image enhancing book for black children written in poetry.

Baker, B. F. *What is black?* New York: Franklin Watts, 1969. An excellent book with black-and-white photographs to help us recognize that black has positive connotations by showing us black objects all around us.

Beim, J. *Swimming hole.* New York: William Morrow, 1951. An older book about a child who refuses to play with a Negro boy and how he discovers after he gets a sunburn and is mocked that color doesn't matter.

Blue, R. *Black, black, beautiful black.* New York: Franklin Watts, 1969. The book talks about beautiful black objects encountered by a black girl. At the end she looks in the mirror and sees she's beautiful. The illustrations are a little cluttered.

Bond, J. C. *Brown is a beautiful color.* New York: Franklin Watts, 1969. A story in poetry that stresses the beauty of the color brown and aims to develop self pride for a Negro child.

Caines, J. *Abby.* New York: Harper & Row, 1973. About an adopted black child who looks at her baby book and the feeling that exists in a family who wants an adopted child. A nice story but it really doesn't tell about adoption.

Clifton, L. *My brother fine with me.* New York: Holt, Rinehart & Winston, 1975. This is a tender story told in black dialect depicting a child's feelings about taking care of a younger sibling while the parents are at work. It is more appropriate for the older child.

Clifton, L. *Everett Anderson's friend.* New York: Holt, Rinehart & Winston, 1976. This book depicts a black child's feelings and encounters with a new Spanish girl who moves next door to him.

Gerson, M. J. *Omoteji's baby brother.* New York: Henry Z. Walck, 1974. A beautifully illustrated book about a boy living in Nigeria can be used with older children when discussing the cultural background of the black child.

Greenberg, P. *O Lord, I wish I was a buzzard.* New York: Macmillan, 1968. A black dialect story about a little girl and her brother who work in a cotton field with their father.

Grifalconi, A. *City rhythms*. Indianapolis: Bobbs–Merrill, 1965. This is a beautifully illustrated book that poetically depicts a black child's experiences in the city in which he lives.

Keats, E. J. *Goggles*. New York: Macmillan, 1969. The book accurately portrays, in word and picture, the life of the small black child in the city.

Keats, E. J. *Hi, cat*. New York: Macmillan, 1970. This is a beautifully illustrated and told story of Peter and a new cat on the block.

Keats, E. J. *Louie*. New York: Greenwillow, 1975. Colorful pictures and a simple story depict a black city child's love for a puppet he saw in a puppet show.

Keats, E. J. *Snowy Day*. New York: Viking, 1962. A black child's vivid experiences with snow are beautifully illustrated.

Keats, E. J. *Whistle for Willie*. New York: Viking, 1964. A story about a black boy, who learns to whistle, with excellent illustrations.

Kempner, C. *Nicholas*. New York: Simon & Schuster, 1968. The experiences and feelings of a black boy, who gets lost when taking a subway train, are accurately depicted.

Lexau, J. M. *Benji*. New York: Dial, 1964. Older children would enjoy this story of a bashful black child living with his grandmother and his search for an earring she lost.

Lexau, J. M. *Benji on his own*. New York: Dial, 1970. Benji's grandmother, with whom he lives alone, gets sick and his experiences are realistically told in this book for older kindergartners.

McGovern, A. *Black is beautiful*. New York: Four Winds, 1969. In words and black-and-white illustrations, the book reveals the beauty of the color black.

Pomeranz, C. *The moon pony*. New York: Young Scott Books, 1967. A beautifully illustrated story that depicts a child's wishes in a dream and the realities of life living in the city. The book is best for older children.

Prather, R. *New neighbors*. New York: McGraw Hill, 1974. This book discusses the mixed feelings of a black child who moves to a new neighborhood.

Randall, B. E. *Fun for Chris*. Chicago: Albert Whitman, 1956. A white child befriends a black one and becomes aware of their racial differences and asks questions regarding them. A good book to use for classroom discussion regarding race.

Rosenbaum, E. *Ronnie*. New York: Parents', 1969. This is a realistically told story about a day in the life of a black boy who lives in the city.

Scott, A. *Big cowboy western*. New York: Lothrop, Lee & Shepherd, 1965. A five-year-old black boy in the city receives two toy guns and a cowboy hat and imagines himself a cowboy. The book is warmly written and well illustrated.

Steptoe, J. *Stevie.* New York: Harper & Row, 1969. The story is about a black boy and the feelings he has when a younger boy is taken care of by his mother.

Stone, E. H. *I'm glad I'm me.* New York: G. P. Putnam's Sons, 1971. The simple words and clear illustrations describe the joy a black boy feels at being himself.

Van Leeuwen, J. *Timothy's flower.* New York: Random House, 1967. The story warmly tells about a black boy who lives in the city.

Children's Books About Puerto Rican Children

Belpré, P. *Santiago.* New York: Frederick Warne, 1969. This is a beautifully illustrated book about a lonely kindergarten Puerto Rican boy in New York who wins new friends.

Binzen, B. *Carmen.* New York: Coward, McCann & Geoghegan, 1970. Excellent photographs and story show a Puerto Rican girl who moves to New York City and finds a friend.

Blue, R. *I am here: Yo estoy aqui.* New York: Franklin Watts, 1971. The feelings of a Puerto Rican child in a new school and with a new language are described.

Brenner, B. *Barto takes the subway.* New York: Alfred A. Knopf, 1961. This story is about a Puerto Rican boy and his experiences on the subway. It has excellent black-and-white illustrations. It is appropriate for the older kindergartner.

Felt, S. *Rosa-too-little.* New York: Doubleday, 1950. This story about a little Puerto Rican girl, who has a sense of competence after learning to write her own name, is most appropriate for an older child.

Fern, E. *Pepito's story.* New York: Ariel Books, 1960. This book is about a lonely boy who helped a lonely girl and how he became glad to be himself. It is best for older children.

Keats, E. J., & Cherr, P. *My dog is lost.* New York: Thomas Y. Crowell, 1960. It is about a boy who just arrived in New York from Puerto Rico and could speak only Spanish. He lost his dog and the story recounts his experiences looking for his dog in the city.

Kesselman, W., & Holt, N. *Angelita.* New York: Hill & Wang, 1970. A beautiful book of real photographs shows Puerto Rico and New York and depicts the feelings and experiences of a child who comes to New York from Puerto Rico. It is rather long but well written.

Sonneborn, R. *Seven in a bed.* New York: Viking, 1968. This book is about a Spanish-speaking family with seven children who have to sleep in one bed. It touches on the experiences of some urban children who have to live in crowded conditions.

Sonneborn, R. *Friday night is papa night.* New York: Viking, 1970. This warm, realistic story depicts a Puerto Rican family whose father comes home only once a week because of job responsibilities.

Children's Books About Other Ethnic Groups

Clark, A. N. *Along sandy trails.* New York: Viking, 1969. This story depicts a Papago Indian grandmother showing her granddaughter the beauty of the desert home of this Southwestern Indian tribe. It has beautiful pictures and a lyrical story with somewhat difficult language, showing and naming the cactus, flowers, trees, and birds of the Arizona Desert.

Clark, A. N. *In my mother's house.* New York: Viking, 1941. This long but excellent book discusses simply the life of the Pueblo Indians. It is best for the older child.

Ets, M. H. *Bad boy, good boy.* New York: Thomas Y. Crowell, 1967. The book movingly portrays a Mexican boy's experiences. He can't speak English and his curiosity gets him into trouble. He gradually has an easier time after he enters school. It is appropriate for the older kindergartner because of its length.

Ets, M. H. *Gilberto and the wind.* New York: Viking, 1969. The experiences of a Mexican child with the wind are related.

Hitte, K. & Hayes, W. D. *Mexicalli soup.* New York: Parents', 1970. A Mexican-American family moves to the city and the children want to become like their new friends. The book humorously depicts the result.

Miles, M. *Annie and the old one.* Boston: Little, Brown, 1971. A beautifully illustrated story tells about a Navajo child's experiences with her grandmother. She learns about the inevitability of death and the continuity of life. It is for the older and more mature child.

Morrow, S. *Inatuk's friend.* Boston: Little Brown, 1968. There are few realistic, well-illustrated stories about Eskimo life. This is one for older children.

Parish, P. *Snapping turtle's all wrong day.* New York: Simon & Schuster, 1970. This humorous story tells about the misadventures of an Indian boy that ends happily when he gives his mother a birthday surprise.

Perrine, M. *Salt boy.* New York: Houghton Mifflin, 1968. This is a beautifully told and well-illustrated story for the older child about a Navajo boy and his father.

Politi, L. *Rosa*. New York: Scribner's, 1963. This story is about a Mexican girl who wanted a doll and ended up by having a real baby sister. There is an unrealistic assumption that the child can play with her baby sister. However, books about Mexican children are rare and the pictures are excellent.

Politi, L. *Moy Moy*. New York: Scribner's, 1960. This is one of the few books that touches on the experiences of a Chinese child (Chinese New York). It is best for an older child.

Reich, H. *Children of many lands*. New York: Hill & Wang, 1964. The book has exquisite photographs of children from all over the world.

Taylor, M. *Time for flowers*. San Carlos, California: Golden Gate Jr. Books, 1967. Colorful pictures and a well-written text tell the story of two Japanese children who sell flowers against their father's wishes to buy new eye glasses for their grandfather.

Yashimo, T. & Yashimo, M. *Mono's kitten*. New York: Viking, 1961. Here is a beautiful story about Mono, a Japanese child who finds a cat that has kittens.

Zemach, H. *Mommy buy me a china doll*. Chicago: Follett, 1966. This beautifully illustrated book is based on an Ozark song. It is about a child who wants a china doll.

FAMILY RELATIONSHIPS

The caring responses that a teacher makes to each child's contributions to the group, regardless of the child's race, sex, or familial situation, can do much to enhance his social self-esteem. The sexual and racial aspects of this have already been discussed. Family structure, the child's place in that structure and the roles of family members need to be discussed in the classroom. This means that children without fathers (or mothers) and foster children have to be encouraged to talk openly about their experiences and feelings. On Father's (or Mother's) Day the teacher should spend time with children lacking fathers and/or mothers. When children with differing family experiences are ignored, they feel that there is something wrong with their families. They, no doubt, have felt this in their experiences with others, but teachers have an opportunity to build up children's self-feelings by consciously planning activities that include *all* the familial patterns in their classrooms. Sharing experiences and feelings in discussion and play with a significant group, including teachers and peers who care, aids children toward growing into more adequate members of society.

Curricular Ideas to Enhance Feelings About Family

1. Have the children bring in pictures of family members and discuss them.

2. Make drawings of family members doing varying activities and compare similarities and differences among children.

3. Arrange a bulletin board display of family photographs.

4. Talk about the roles of family members.

5. Role play experiences children have in their families.

6. Discuss the ways family members can help each other.

7. Have the children make books about their family lives.

8. Discuss problems and happy experiences with siblings.

9. Discuss experiences with other family members, such as grandparents, uncles, aunts, and cousins.

10. Invite family members to share skills with the class.

11. Discuss and compare what younger and older members of the family can or cannot do and compare them.

12. Make sure that there is discussion and activities related to all kinds of families (e.g., one-parent families, foster families, adoptive families, etc.).

13. The Scholastic Early Childhood Center[3] has available some excellent filmstrips about children and families;

Five Children and *Five Families* are two that discuss children and families from varying parts of the United States.

14. Have block accessories and puppets of family members readily available.

Children's Books on Family Relationships

Abbott, S. *Where I begin.* New York: Coward, McCann and Geoghegan, 1970. The book is like a photo album with sepia pictures about a child's ancestors.

Adoff, A. *Make a circle, keep us in: Poems for a good day.* New York: Delacorte, 1975. By the use of poetry and pleasant pen and ink drawings, the book depicts a child's experiences in a warm family.

Alexander, M. *I'll be the horse if you'll play with me.* New York: Dial, 1975. A vivid story shows the problems in playing with an older brother.

Alexander, M. *And my mean old mother will be sorry.* New York: Dial, 1972. The book captures a universal feeling of children who get angry at their mothers and their fantasies of how to cope with these feelings.

Amoss, B. *Tom in the middle.* New York: Harper & Row, 1968. In words and pictures, the book depicts well the experiences of the middle child.

Anglund, J. W. *Look out the window.* New York: Harcourt, Brace, Jovanovich, 1959. The book expresses a child's feelings about his own special place in the world with his pets, his house, and his parents.

Borack, B. *Grandpa.* New York: Harper & Row, 1967. The special relationship of a child with her grandfather is well expressed in text and illustration.

Brown, M. W. *The runaway bunny.* New York: Harper & Row, 1972. This classic captures the warm feelings of belonging between a mother and her child.

Brownstone, C. *All kinds of mothers.* New York: David McKay, 1969. This simple story portrays the variations of maternal personality and behaviors.

Buckley, H. E. *Grandfather and I.* New York: Lothrop, Lee & Shepard, 1959. The book stresses the warm relationship between a grandfather and his grandson.

Buckley, H. E. *Grandmother and I.* New York: Lothrop, Lee & Shepard, 1969. The special relationship between a young child and her grandmother is well related and illustrated in this book.

Buckley, H. E. *Wonderful little boy.* New York: Lothrop, Lee & Shepard, 1970. The book shows how it feels to be the smallest child in the family. Everyone in his family criticizes what he does but his grandmother, who makes him feel important.

Carton, L. C. *Daddies.* New York. Random House, 1963. The book depicts the experiences and warm feelings that can exist between fathers and their children.

Charlip, R., & Moore, L. *Hooray for me.* New York: Parents', 1975. The book does a good job in exploring a child's relationship to his family, friends and pets.

Clifton, L. *Don't you remember?* New York: E. P. Dutton, 1973. The story is about a black four-year-old who was upset that her family didn't remember what they said they'd do, but at the end they do remember. The vivid illustrations and text touch on common experiences.

Ehrlich, A. *Zeke Silver Moon.* New York: Dial, 1972. The book focuses on the everyday happenings in the life of a child with his parents. The photographs are exquisite and the story affectionate. It is best for older children.

Fassler, J. *All alone with daddy.* New York: Behavioral Publications, 1969. The book describes the normal feelings a four-year-old girl has when her mother goes away for a short while and she tries to take her place.

Fassler, J. *The man of the house.* New York: Behavioral Publications, 1969. The book is about a four-year-old boy who is left to take care of his mother when his father goes on a trip, but is relieved when his father comes home again.

Fisher, A. *My mother and I.* New York: Thomas Y. Crowell, 1967. This beautifully illustrated story poem tells about the joy of having a mother.

Flack, M. *Ask Mr. Bear.* New York: Macmillan, 1958. This old favorite tells about the warm gift a child gives his mother on her birthday.

Goff, B. *Where is daddy? The story of a divorce.* Boston: Beacon, 1969. The book simply and accurately describes a young child's feelings and experiences when her parents separate.

Gray, G. *Send Wendell.* New York: McGraw-Hill, 1974. The story tells about a six-year-old black boy and his warm family feelings.

Hanson, J. *I don't like Timmy.* Minneapolis, Minn.: Carolrhoda Books, 1972. An accurate and humorously illustrated book describes the negative feelings that a child has toward a younger sibling.

Hazen, B. S. *Why couldn't I be an only kid like you, Wiggen?* New York: Atheneum, 1975. Why it would be nice to be an only child is simply told. The illustrations are a little cluttered.

Hogan, C. G. *Eighteen cousins.* New York: Parents', 1968. The story is about a child who goes to a farm and meets eighteen cousins for the first time. It is an excellent book for the younger preschoolers.

Hutchins, P. *Titch.* New York: Macmillan, 1971. The book is about the problems of the youngest child in the family.

Jarrell, M. *The knee baby*. New York: Farrar, Straus & Giroux, 1973. Striking illustrations sensitively portray a young child's feelings about having to share his mother's lap with a younger sibling.

Krauss, R. *Bundle book*. New York: Harper & Row, 1951. The book expresses the warm feelings that a young child experiences when he knows his mother cares for him and his need for her.

Lapsley, S. *I am adopted*. New York: Bradbury, 1975. This simple warm story is about an adopted child who belongs. It is meant for a very young child.

Lenski, L. *Debbie and her grandma*. New York: Henry Z. Walck, 1967. The book touches on the special loving relationship between a grandmother and her grandchild.

Lexau, J. M. *Emily and the klunky baby and the next door dog*. New York: Dial, 1972. This story, with vivid illustrations and warm understanding, focuses on the frustrations of a child in a one–parent home. Her mother is busy and she has to keep her baby brother quiet. She gets lost trying to run away to live with her father.

Meeks, E. *Families live together*. Follett Family Life Education Program. Chicago: Follett, 1969. This beautifully illustrated book is about some common experiences and feelings that exist within families.

Mizumura, K. *If I were a mother*. New York: Thomas Y. Crowell, 1968. The book tells about what mothers do for their children and ends with the thought that the child would be just like his mother. It has enchanting illustrations and simple text.

Ness, E. *Exactly alike*. New York: Scribner's, 1964. The story is about a girl who had four brothers who looked exactly alike and how she learned to identify each and to get along with them. There are colorful photographs. The story is more appropriate for older children.

Parsons, E. *Rainy day together*. New York: Harper & Row, 1971. A warmly illustrated and narrated story tells about a rainy day spent together by a little girl and her mother.

Radlauer, R., & Radlauer, E. *Father is big*. Glendale, Cal.: Bowmar, 1967. Beautiful full-page color photographs and simple text show a black child's pride in his father.

Raynor, D. *This is my father and me*. Chicago: Albert Whitman, 1973. The beautifully illustrated book is about fathers and sons all over the world.

Schick, E. *City in the winter*. New York: Macmillan, 1973. This realistic story is about a boy who lives with his mother and his grandmother. His grandmother takes care of him and they spend a snowy day together when his mother goes to work.

Scott, A. *On mother's lap*. New York: McGraw-Hill, 1972. A universal experience depicts an Eskimo mother and her child. He likes being on his mother's lap and is concerned that his mother won't find a place for him when the baby cries but she does.

Scott, A. H. *Sam.* New York: McGraw-Hill, 1967. Sam, a black child, seems to get in the way of his family as the youngest child and his universal feelings are sensitively depicted by the sepia illustrations and the text.

Segal, L. *Tell me a Mitzi.* New York: Farrar, Straus & Giroux, 1970. Three stories about family life that mix reality and fantasy in a humorous way. The illustrations are strong and add to the enjoyment of the stories. Recommended primarily for older children.

Simon, N. *All kinds of families.* Chicago: Albert Whitman, 1975. This book, with good illustrations, describes many varieties of family life. It is best for the older child.

Simon, N. *How do I feel?* Chicago: Albert Whitman, 1970. The book discusses differences in the feelings of two children who are twins.

Steptoe, J. *My special best words.* New York: Viking, 1974. This book is narrated by a young black child and deals realistically with her life. She is brought up by her father. The language and situations are concerned with the realities in the lives of three year olds (toileting, runny noses, curse words, etc.)

Thayer, J. *Where's Andy?* New York: William Morrow, 1954. This older book is about a little boy who hid from his mother and discovers at the end that she missed him and loves him. It is humorously and realistically done.

Williams, B. *If he's my brother.* New York: Harvey House, 1976. This book deals with a child's needs to do what he wants with his possessions. The text is humorous and the illustrations pleasantly soft-hued.

Wood, J. *Grandmother Lucy in her garden.* Cleveland, Ohio: Collins World, 1975. The book for older children discusses a day a child has with her grandmother.

Udry, J. M. *What Mary Jo shared.* Chicago: Albert Whitman, 1966. This excellent, sensitive book is about a black child who brings her father to share with her class.

Viorst, J. *I'll fix Anthony.* New York: Harper & Row, 1969. A child's negative feelings about his older brother, who says he stinks, are presented.

Watson, N. D. *Tommy's mommy's fish.* New York: Viking, 1971. The book is about a little boy's desire to get his mother a special birthday present and his success in doing so because he liked his mother quite a lot.

Wesson, V. *The chosen baby.* New York. Lippincott, 1950. This classic on adoption should be read on a one-to-one level.

Zalben, J. B. *Cecilia's older brother.* New York: Macmillan, 1973. A mouse family is used to discuss the problems of sibling rivalry in a humorous way.

Zindel, P. *I love my mother.* New York: Harper & Row, 1975. Vivid illustrations and text sensitively capture a child's feelings for his mother in a one-parent family.

Zolotow, C. *Big sister and little sister.* New York: Harper & Row, 1966. This is a sensitive story about the relationship between sisters.

Zolotow, C. *A father like that.* New York: Harper & Row, 1971. This is a story of a little boy who idealizes the father he wishes he had.

Zolotow, C. *If it weren't for you.* New York: Harper & Row, 1966. The honest feelings of an older brother who has to share with a younger sibling are dealt with in a simple way.

PARENT INTERACTION TO ENHANCE CHILDREN'S SELF-CONCEPTS

The first "significant others" in the lives of children are their parents. In the review of theory and empirical research, it was found that a child's self-concept is related to how she is treated (the looking-glass theory) and how the mother sees herself. It was further hypothesized in Chapter 3 that the child imitates her mother's feelings towards her (the "modeling theory"). Both the "looking glass" and "modeling" theories must operate at the same time, since theory and research has supported the premise that "significant others'" behavior and attitude toward a child are affected by his or her self-acceptance and self-feelings and the child identifies with these feelings very early in life. Those children who feel negatively about themselves are more likely to have parents who also feel negatively about themselves. Teachers cannot be therapists and treat the parents, but they can serve a very important role by helping parents explore ways of becoming more effective. The specific behavior of parents is less important than their attitude conveying warmth, firmness, support, consistency, and encouragement of appropriate autonomy. The teacher's role is not so much to give parents specific advice as to build a parent's confidence in his role. Those who are succeeding need to know this; those who are having difficulty need to feel that teachers will listen to them and help them without blaming them. A mother who responds primarily to her own needs, rather than to those of her child probably has low self-esteem. One of the goals of professionals should be to build up the mother's esteem. The teacher can explore ways to help a parent feel more effective in her interactions with her child. A teacher may not have the expertise to help a parent in trouble, but just listening is important and after sufficient trust is developed, the teacher may successfully refer the parent to other trained professionals.

Lower-income parents who have few other supports to help with child-rearing concerns have more difficulty in getting involved in their children's education. A few studies of lower-income parents have found that there is a relationship between positive maternal self-concept, their children's self-concept and maternal confidence, and involvement in school and community affairs (Lopate et al., 1969; Holmes et al., 1973; Samuels 1973). Holmes et al. (1973) found in a study of parents at seven parent-child centers, that those parents who were outgoing and involved, were likely to feel that they determined in large part what happened in their lives. They were confident of their abilities and they tended to be assertive and decisive. Samuels (1973) found that lower-income children with higher self-concepts were more likely to have mothers who were actively involved in community affairs. Lopate et al., (1969), in a review paper on the issue of decentralization, observed that participation in the decision-making process resulted in positive changes in the effective behavior of participants. It is hard to know which is cause and which is effect since the mother's self-concept was not measured prior to her involvement. Theory suggests that those who were socially competent and assertive would feel positive about themselves and would be more likely to be actively involved in such a program in the first place. However, even if the parents had positive self-feelings before their involvement in school or other community affairs, the sense of powerlessness felt by minority group parents in society would be lessened if they did actively involve themselves in the decisions affecting their children.

Parents are the most significant people in young children's lives and the ones with whom the children spend the majority of their time.[4] Without communication and cooperation with the child's family, teachers are limited in being able to help children grow fully in positive self-esteem. One frequently hears the statement "Johnny's mother isn't interested in how her son is doing in school, so what can you expect? She was invited to come in for a conference, but she didn't show up." All too often the teacher uses an experience like this one to explain a child's problems and does no more to contact the home. This unfortuante situation is more likely to occur with nonwhite and lower-class children. The self-fulfilling prophecy operates with parents as well as with children; the little cooperation teachers expect from parents is just what happens. Thus the myth is perpetuated that parents in poor economic circumstances are not interested in their children. Actually, such parents want their children to do better educationally than they did. It is precisely in the area of cognitive self-concept that most lower-income parents feel inadequate and they painfully recognize the need for their children to do better academically. These parents resent the failure of the school to educate their children. Often there is a wide gap between their needs and the school's knowledge of their needs. Actually, the goal of the school and the parent are the same and that is to educate the children. The communication gap results in the children becoming victims because they more likely than not identify with their parents' anger. Their openness and confidence about the value of school is undermined if this anger occurs. As a result, many lower-income children don't internalize school failure as their own (Trowbridge & Trowbridge, 1972). Therefore, lack of communication between home and school tends to increase this externalization and distance the child and the family from the school. Guttentag (1972) found that children with parents who had frequent contacts with teachers in a community-controlled school had higher academic achievement than children in a neighboring district whose parents were not so involved in the school. The children also saw the school, teachers, and parents as being more powerful in helping them to succeed or to fail.

The school bears the major responsibility for initiating good relationships with parents, and for involving them in a meaningful way in their children's education. This means that the teacher must evaluate underlying problems and take steps to remedy them. As in the case of a child, he must first examine his feelings about the parents and try to understand their problems, value, and cultural backgrounds. Parents readily perceive a teacher's negative attitudes about their family life and treatment of a child. These attitudes can be communicated in subtle ways. The parent may not even have to meet the teacher, for this disdain can be communicated by a child who reports what a teacher has said about her manner of dress or her speech. A note to a mother telling her to put her child to bed earlier, to dress the child differently, or to send money to school to take a trip may show lack of understanding of divergent family patterns and financial problems. If the parents' way of life differs, or if they can't provide the money for a requested item, they may feel that they are inadequate or they may become angry. Both of these reactions are counterproductive to helping the child.

Previous parental difficulties with authorities also may make it difficult for parents to come to school or to communicate with the school. People who have been controlled, harrassed, and intimidated by those in power find it difficult to trust any person or institution representing authority. Many of these parents remember their own experiences of failure in school and how humiliating it was when their parents were called in. In essence, they identify with their children. Unfortunately, their feelings of alienation and powerlessness are reinforced by society, which also blames the home and parents for the difficulties children experience.

Many parents, particularly those from lower economic groups, view conferences between parents and teachers as times of conflict. Protecting oneself from disagreeable situations by evading them is a normal human reaction. Who wants to come into a setting that reinforces negative feelings one has had all one's life? It is easy to understand why some parents would rather stay at home than risk being uncomfortable with a critical teacher.

When parents come in for conferences or meetings, their attitudes create problems in communication for the teacher. Parents may remain silent or launch a verbal attack. The hostility revealed by either of these reactions may make it difficult for teachers not to become angry. Yet if the teacher reacts defensively or implies that the parent is responsible for the child's inadequacies, any chance for a successful conference and for helping the child are shattered. A constructive approach is for a teacher to listen without showing disapproval. The teacher must believe that parents have as much information to share as she does. Sometimes, the teacher may find it difficult to listen and be accepting, especially when she hears something with which she completely disagrees. This writer remembers a conference with a mother who said she routinely beat her son with a strap. It was all one could do to suppress the urge to cry out in defense of the child. However, as attention was paid to the parent's anger and frustration with her son and as she realized there was understanding, she said, "but it doesn't help, he's sorry for a few minutes, but he does the same thing again later on." This led to a discussion of how one feels after physical punishment. The mother said that she was beaten as a child and that it didn't change her behavior either. From there, it was possible to discuss alternative ways of discipline that the mother decided to try. Had the mother been reprimanded for beating her son, communication would have come to an abrupt end. The self-concepts of both the mother and the child were dealt with in this situation.

Conferences should be frequent and have as their purpose the mutual exploration of problems and the cooperative quest for solutions. Every conference should end on a constructive and encouraging note and include a plan for cooperative action. To continue showing her interest, the teacher should follow up with a note or phone call to encourage further discussion.

One good way to reach parents and to have them become a part of school life is to provide an open room to which they may come anytime. There should be a coffee pot, magazines, child development materials, displays of children's work, and notices for parents in the room. With the help of trained (preferably indigenous) leaders, sewing classes, discussion groups, and other planned activities can be scheduled for parents. These situations provide natural opportunities for parents to share their concerns with each other. While making a dress, it is common for a parent to talk about her child and a skilled group leader can help to make the discussion constructive.

Somehow, we must discover parental skills and talents and utilize them in school. Contributions in the classroom, such as helping children to cook an ethnic food, or teaching a song, or in being involved on a school board and having decision-making powers, create feelings of pride in parents and their children. Visits to the classroom to observe, especially before parent-teacher conferences, should be encouraged. The observation could stimulate discussions that could lead to solutions of problems that neither the teacher nor the parent could solve alone.

A school can have a newsletter that tells what the children are doing and welcomes feedback from parents. Additionally, teachers can send notes home or make phone calls telling parents about the positive things their children are doing.

Development of trust and acceptance by parents takes time. Confidence is built after much contact and good experience. This is particularly true with parents who do not feel positively about themselves. Nevertheless, the school should initiate and continue to look for ways of reaching the parents of every child.

SOCIAL RELATIONSHIPS

Some children with negative self-feelings may be withdrawn or aggressive. These are the most challenging students for the teacher to cope with, because frequently the teacher's feeling interferes with his objective evaluation and constructive reaction. It is essential that teachers try to recognize their negative reactions to children with social problems. If one can open oneself up to observation by videotape or can share with colleagues some of the "objective" records taken of children, others may spot subjective reactions. This would allow blind spots to be uncovered. Self-evaluation is difficult but can serve the same purpose. A teacher who can ask himself why he overreacted when a child hit another child or didn't do anything when another student sat in one spot all day will be better able to intervene in the future to help these children more effectively. A child who feels left out needs adults who seek out ways to redirect such behavior actively, so that she will be more acceptable to herself and others. Knowledge of "normal" social development of young children is needed, since teachers' expectations of children have to be within the framework of such information. Ames (1952) observed a maximum of seventy-five "normal" children aged eighteen months to four years for a period of two years to get clues to their developing sense of self. She observed child behavior, child-teacher, and child-child interactions that were self-initiated, responsive, and nonverbalized. The results indicated that at eighteen months children are primarily egocentric; "no" is the favorite word, and they treat other children as things. At twenty-one months, they still treat other children impersonally. At two years children are most occupied with their own individual activities and they are still consolidating their sense of self by obtaining and hoarding possessions. At two-and-a-half they obtain objects aggressively, are less impersonal and begin to break away from adults. At three, they no longer seem to affirm and embellish themselves with many possessions and they begin to say "we." At three-and-a-half they establish themselves with other children, treat them as individuals, and seem to be able to adapt to the needs of others and prefer cooperative play. At the earlier ages, their selves are more related to adults, but after three they relate more to their peers.

The classroom teacher, who has realistic expectations, helps children move from solitary play to parallel play to cooperative play and from more to less egocentricity. Children up until the age of six or seven are basically egocentric (Piaget & Inhelder, 1969); that is, they are focused on themselves and their perceptions. It is cognitively impossible for them to put themselves in others people's positions. The teacher has to verbalize things such as "I know you want the ball and it is hard to give it up," indicating acceptance of the child's normal inability to understand why another child's turn has come up, but she also helps the child to move to a higher level by adding "but it is another child's turn to have the ball." In accordance with her knowledge of child development, she should have told him in advance that in a little while it will be the other child's turn, giving him enough time to complete the activity. The child should also be reassured that he can have another turn later. This example indicates that when children have difficulty in their social relationships, the teacher should verbalize the feeling and difficulties and use active means to help children overcome them.

Young children who are fearful and anxious tend to have lower self-concepts. They also tend to be more dependent on adults than on peers (see Chapter 3). A teacher's normal reaction might be to reassure such children that there is nothing to be afraid of, and to subtly or directly force peer interaction. Unfortunately, dealing with the symptom in this way frequently doesn't work. A fearful child must first feel comfortable in the environment as a result of feeling trust for the adults there. Although it is difficult for some teachers to have a child hover around them, this may be necessary until that trust is developed. A hovering child is more related than a child who completely withdraws. Gradually, the teacher should help to move the child into the group. At first, the teacher may need to be present when she helps the child work with one other child. It would be best if the teacher chose a child who is likely to accept him and one to whom he can easily relate. With time, as the child gains more confidence, he will move out into the group. Actions that would exacerbate the problem would be the rejection of his behavior or his being pushed into the group too fast. At the same time that she slowly builds up his self-confidence in school, the teacher has to work with his parents to try to effect some change in their interactions with him. Children who completely withdraw from adults as well as from children should be evaluated by a psychologist or a psychiatrist.

The child who is aggressive with other children is harder to deal with than the withdrawn child, since direct action by the teacher has to be taken to prevent other children from getting hurt. A differentiation has to be made between children who occasionally hit out because their development and experience has not enabled them to learn more appropriate techniques for coping with stress or the desire to play with other children and children who consistently and excessively hit out in anger. If there is excessive, consistent anger, we can be relatively sure that the child has negative self-feelings. Coopersmith (1967) found that the low-self-esteem children in his study of fifth- and sixth-grade elementary school children, were more destructive than the high-self-esteem children. The negative self-concept, which is apt to be at the root of the aggression, is harder to deal with because the threat to other children is more likely to engender counteranger in the teacher. This tends to increase the child's anger and does little for the basic problem. The issue is not whether the teacher has to stop the child or not. Obviously, she has to protect him and his peers. Young children believe their thoughts will actually become reality. When they lose control and get punished or feel their thoughts of hurting others will become reality, they become overwhelmed. The child needs to know that adults will protect him from this aggression that is so frightening. The teacher must also accept the child's feelings by saying "I know you are angry, but I have to help you stop hurting John." If the child has to be removed from a situation, an adult should make it a removal not for punishment, but to help her gain control. The adult should give the child the power to return and help her to return when she has gained that control. The child has to be helped to recognize that self-control is possible and that the adult will help her to develop that control. In all other interactions with such children, there has to be a concerted effort to make sure that there are successful experiences and a gradual socialization process that redirects the aggression to verbal expressions of anger. Supportive nonjudgmental teachers are needed to go beyond the child's behavior to get a glimpse of the distress and to implement programs to alleviate it.

There are children who are too disturbed to be helped in a normal classroom. It is folly to keep a child with little control in a classroom where there is not enough teacher help to keep the child from hurting others, or where the adults react with counteranger. Unfortunately, the parent is often forced to remove the child without a referral. As discussed earlier, it is preferable if a referral for psychological help is made before the child leaves the school, because the withdrawal will increase the child's distress and his fears of his distructive powers. The child's self-concept is further diminished when he fails in his first school experience. Moreover, his family's reaction to a "flunkout" can augment these feelings.

Children's Books on Relationships with Peers

Anglund, J.W. *A friend is someone who likes you.* New York: Harcourt, Brace, Jovanovich, 1958. This book captures well the good feelings in having friends.

Beim, L., & Beim, J. *Two is a team.* New York: Harcourt, Brace, Jovanovich, 1945. This is a well-illustrated story about a realistic problem that occurs between friends and how they solve the problem.

Cohen, M. *Best friends.* New York: Macmillan, 1971. The book describes a typical experience of children who reject one another and then become friends again.

Cohen, M. *Will I have a friend?* New York: Collier Books, 1967. The story is about a little boy who feels insecure about whether he will have friends at the beginning of his first day at school. He becomes more secure as he makes many friends during the day.

Iwaski, C. *Will you be my friend?* New York: McGraw-Hill, 1974. Illustrations that appear crayoned depict a warm story of a girl who wants to befriend a new neighbor and how she does it.

Krasilovsky, P. *Shy little girl.* Boston: Houghton-Mifflin, 1970. This sensitive story is about a girl who doesn't feel good about herself, but who gradually gains confidence after she makes a friend.

Krasilovsky, P. *Susan sometimes.* New York: Macmillan, 1962. A little girl wished for a real playmate and one day she found one next door.

Lionni, L. *Little blue and little yellow.* New York: Astor–Honor. 1959. The joy of friendship is creatively depicted by the use of the colors blue and yellow.

Lystad, M. *That new boy.* New York: Crown, 1973. Even though the new boy is different, having him for a friend and sharing his interests is fun.

Mayer, M., & Mayer, M. *Mine.* New York: Simon & Schuster, 1970. A funny story with simple black-and-white pictures tells how a young boy learns what he can and can't call his own.

McGovern, A. *Scram, kid!* New York: Viking, 1974. The book depicts how it feels to be prevented from taking part in a game. The child then finds another friend.

Mallett, A. *Here comes tagalong.* New York: Parents', 1971. A little five-year-old finds himself a tagalong when he plays with older boys, but able to be part of the group when he finds peers of his own age.

Mannheim, G. *Two friends.* New York: Alfred A. Knopf, 1968. Excellent photographs depict the experiences of a black and a white child who become friends in kindergarten; there is a subtheme about the black child's family.

Schick, E. *5A and 7B.* New York: Macmillan, 1967. This simple story is about the difficulties in making friends if you live in the city, and the joys that result when you do so.

Schick, E. *Making friends.* New York: Macmillan, 1969. Superb line-drawn illustrations without words for young children depict the joys of friendship.

Sherman, I. *I do not like it when my friend comes to visit.* New York: Harcourt, Brace, Jovanovich, 1973. A perceptive view is given of how children feel when friends come to visit and the pain that this sometimes causes.

Udry, J. M. *Let's be enemies.* New York: Harper & Row, 1961. The simple story tells about the realities involved in having friends.

Vogel, I.-M. *Hello Henry.* New York: Parents', 1965. This delightful story is about two children with the same name who get lost in a supermarket and become friends.

Ziner, F., & Galdone, P. *Counting carnival.* New York: Coward, McCann & Geoghegan, 1962. A simple rhyming story teaches the concept of numbers as they relate to the joys of having friends.

Zolotow, C. *Hold my hand.* New York: Harper & Row, 1972. This beautifully illustrated and simply written book for young children is about
the joys of sharing experiences with a friend.

Zolotow, C. *Janey.* New York: Harper & Row, 1973. This beautiful sepia-
colored illustrations and simple text describe the feeling of loss a
child experiences when a friend moves away.

Zolotow, C. *My friend John.* New York: Harper & Row, 1968. The book
perceptively talks about the affection and secrets good friends share
with one another.

Zolotow, C. *New friend.* New York: Abelard–Schuman, 1968. The book
sensitively discusses the hurt and disappointment a child feels when
losing a friend.

SUMMARY

A key goal of the school must be to help children to function as contributing members of society. Children's experiences at home lay the groundwork for their feelings of
adequacy as a member of a group. They are fortunate if
they have a sense of belonging and feel they are contributing members of their family. They will then enter school
with confidence and find it easier to become part of a peer
group. For the underconfident child who has not developed a stable foundation of social worth at home, the
teacher's job is more difficult. The teacher has to intervene
with the child's peers and act as a trusting model as a new
"significant other" to help the child develop positive social
self-esteem. Children from a different social class or race
need added support and acceptance, for society's negative
evaluation of them has to be explicitly countered by the
educational system. The stereotypic expectations of boys
and girls deprive both of a full range of possibilities in life.
The school has to prepare all children regardless of sex or
race to be comfortable in any role in the society they are
intellectually capable of reaching. The parents of the children we teach are the most "significant others" in the lives
of these children. The teacher can have a significant role in

helping parents explore ways to become more effective, thus building their self-esteem as parents and their children's total self esteem. Providing conditions to enable parents to become actively involved in their children's education should be a key goal of the school. This would be most important for lower-income parents who feel powerless in our society. Greater closeness of home to school, developed as a result of home-school cooperation, would make education a more central area for children whose parents feel alienated from the mainstream of American education.

NOTES

1. Alroy et al. (1972) has been updated with new data in 1975.
2. Available from *Ms.* magazine, 370 Lexington Avenue, New York, N.Y. 10017.
3. Scholastic Early Childhood Center, 904 Sylvan Ave., Englewood Cliffs, N.J.
4. Portions of this section are taken from this author's article "Johnny's Mother Isn't Interested", *Today's Education*, February 1973, 36–38.

REFERENCES

Abraham, K. Manifestations of the female castration complex (1920). In *Selected papers of Karl Abraham.* New York: Basic Books, 1954.

Adams, E. B., & Sarason, I. G. Relation between anxiety in children and their parents. *Child Development*, 1963, **134**, 237–246.

Adkins, D. C. et al. *Physical activities for preschool.* (ERIC, ED060949) Washington, D.C.: Office of Economic Opportunity, 1971.

Adler, A. *The practice and theory of individual psychiatry.* New York: Harcourt, Brace and Co., 1927.

Adler, A. *The neurotic constitution.* New York: Dodd, Mead and Co., 1930.

Ainsworth, L. & Alford, G. *Responsive environment program. Program for Spanish-American children evaluation report, 1971–72.* (ERIC, ED068219) Lubbock, Texas: Adobe Educational Services, June 1972.

Akert, R. U. Interrelationships among various dimensions of the self-concept. *Journal of Counseling Psychology*, 1959, **6**, 199–201.

Allport, G. W. *Personality: A psychological interpretation* New York: Holt, Rinehart and Winston, 1937.

Allport, G. W. The ego in contemporary psychology. *Psychological Review,* 1943, **50**, 451–68.

Allport, G. W. *Becoming.* New Haven, Conn.: Yale University Press, 1955.

Allport, G. W. *The nature of prejudice.* Garden City, N.Y.: Doubleday Anchor Books, 1958.

Allport, G. W. *Pattern and growth in personality.* New York: Holt, Rinehart and Winston, 1961.

Almy, M. *Ways of studying children.* New York: Bureau of Publications, Teachers College, Columbia University, 1959.

Alroy, P. et al. *Dick and Jane as victims.* Princeton, N.J.: Women on Words and Images, 1975.

Ames, L. B. The sense of self of nursery school children as manifested by their verbal behavior. *Journal of Genetic Psychology,* 1952, **81**, 193–232.

Ames, R. E. Methodology of inquiry for self-concept, *Educational Theory,* 1975, **25**, 314–22.

Anderson, J. G. & Safar, D. The influence of differential community perceptions on the provisions of equal educational opportunities. *Sociology of Education,* 1967, **40**, 219–23.

Armstrong, J. G. Intellectual competence and coping behavior in preschool children. *Dissertation Abstracts,* 1969, **29** (12–B), 4837–4838.

Asher, S. R., & Allen, V. L. Racial preference and social comparison processes. *Journal of Social Issues,* 1969, **25**, 157–166.

Aspy, D. N. The effect of teacher inferred self-concept upon student achievement. Paper presented at the annual meeting of the American Educational Research Association, Los Angeles, 1969.

Atkinson, J. W. *An introduction to motivation.* Princeton, New Jersey: D. Van Nostrand Company, 1964.

Atkinson, J. W., & Feather, N. T., (Eds.) *A theory of achievement motivation.* New York: John Wiley and Sons, 1966.

Ausuble, D. P. *Ego development and the personality disorders.* New York: Grune and Stratton, 1952.

Ausuble, D. P., & Ausuble, P. Ego development among segregated Negro children. In A. H. Passow, (Ed.), *Education in depressed areas.* New York: Teacher's College Press, 1963.

Bandura, A. Social learning theory of identificatory processes. In D. A. Goslin, (Ed.), *Handbook of socialization theory and research.* Chicago: Rand McNally, 1969.

Bandura, A., & Kupers, C. J. Transmission of patterns of self-reinforcement through modeling. *Journal of Abnormal and Social Psychology,* 1964, **69**, 1–9.

Bandura, A., Ross, D., & Ross, S. Transmission of aggression through imitation of aggressive models. *Journal of Abnormal and Social Psychology,* 1961, **63**, 575–582.

Bandura, A., Ross, D., & Ross, S. Imitation of self-mediated aggressive models. *Journal of Abnormal and Social Psychology*, 1963, **66**, 3–11.

Bandura, A., & Walters, R. H. *Social learning and personality development.* New York: Holt, Rinehart and Winston, 1963.

Barry, H., III, Bacon, M. K., & Child, I. L. A. A cross-cultural survey of some sex differences in socialization. *Journal of Abnormal and Social Psychology*, 1957, **55**, 327–332.

Baughman, E. E., & Dahlstrom, W. G. *Negro and white children: A psychological study in the rural south.* New York: Academic Press, 1968.

Baumrind, D. Child care practices anteceding three patterns of preschool behavior. *Genetic Psychological Monographs*, 1967, **75**, 43–88.

Baumrind, D. From each according to her ability. *School Review*, 1972, **80**, 161–197.

Baumrind, D., & Black, A. E. Socialization practices associated with dimensions of competence in preschool boys and girls. *Child Development*, 1967, **38**, 291–327.

Bayer, L. A., & Bayley, N. Growth pattern shifts in healthy children: Spontaneous and induced. *Journal of Pediatrics*, 1963, **62**, 631–45.

Behrens, M. L. Child rearing and the character structure of the mother. *Child Development*, 1954, **25**, 225–38.

Benedek, T. Parenthood as a development phase. *Journal of the American Psychoanalytic Association*, 1959, **7**, 389–417.

Berg, R. C. et al. *Exploring music: Music for young Americans series* (2nd ed., Book 3) Cincinnati, Ohio: American Book Co., 1966.

Berger, E. M. The relation between expressed acceptance of self and expressed acceptance of others. *Journal of Abnormal Psychology*, 1952, **47**, 778–782.

Bernstein, J. *Helping children cope with death and separation: Resources for teachers.* Urbana, Illinois: ERIC/Early Childhood Education. 1976.

Bernstein, J. E., & Newman, S. Non-sexist ideas for the language arts curriculum. In S. R. Rausher & T. Young (Eds.), *Sexism: teachers and young children.* New York: Early Childhood Education Council of New York, 1974.

Bernstein, M. E., & Vesta, F. J. D. The formation and reversal of an attitude as function of assumed concept, race and socioeconomic class. *Child Development*, 1971, **42**, 1417–31.

Biber, H., Miller, L. B., & Dyer, J. L. Feminization in preschool. *Developmental Psychology*, 1972, **7**, 86.

Bibring, E. The mechanism of depression. In P. Greenacre (Ed.) *Affective disorders.* New York: International Universities Press, 1953.

Bilby, R. W. et al. Parental variables as predictors of student self-conceptions of ability. (ERIC ED081479) Paper presented at the annual meeting of the American Educational Research Association, New Orleans, February 26–March 1, 1973.

Biller, H. B., & Borstelman, L. J. Masculine development: An integrative review. *Merrill-Palmer Quarterly*, 1967, **13**, 253–294.

Binswanger, L. *Being-in-the-world: Selected papers of Ludwig Binswanger.* New York: Basic Books, 1963.

Bledsoe, J. C. Self-concepts of children and their intelligence, achievement, interests and anxiety. *Journal of Individual Psychology*, 1964, **20**, 55–58.

Bloom, B. *Stability and change in human characteristics.* New York: John Wiley and Sons, 1964.

Bogo, N., Winget, C., & Gleser, G. C. Ego defenses and perceptual styles. *Perceptual and Motor Skills*, 1970, **30**, 599–604.

Borowitz, G. H., Hirsch, J. G., & Costello, J. Play behavior and competence in ghetto four-year olds. *The Journal of Special Education*, 1970, **4**, 215–221.

Boss, M. *Psychoanalysis and daseinsanalysis.* New York: Basic Books, 1963.

Brennan, M. Urban lower class Negro girls. In M. Grossack (Ed.) *Mental health and segregation.* New York: Springer Publishing Company, 1963.

Bridgeman, B., & Shipman, V. C. *Disadvantaged children and their first school experiences ETS—head start longitudinal study: Predictive value of measures of self-esteem and achievement motivation in four to nine year old low-income children.* Princeton, New Jersey: Educational Testing Service, 1975.

Brim, O. G. Personality development as role-learning. In I. Iscoe & H. Stevenson (Eds.), *Personality development in children.*, Austin: University of Texas Press, 1960.

Brody, E. B. Color and identity conflict in young boys. *Psychiatry*, 1963, **26**, 188–201.

Brody, G. F. Relationship between maternal attitudes and behavior. *Journal of Personality and Social Psychology*, 1965, **2**, 317–323.

Brody, S., & Axelrad, S. *Anxiety and ego formation in infancy.* New York: International Universities Press, 1970.

Brookover, W. B., Shailer, T., & Paterson, A. Self-concept of ability and school achievement. *Sociology of Education*, 1964, **37**, 271–279.

Brophy, J. E., & Good, T. L. Teachers' communication of differential expectations for children's classroom performance: Some behavioral data. *Journal of Educational Psychology*, 1970, **61**, 365–374.

Brophy, J. E., & Good, T. L. Teacher expectations: Beyond the pygmalion controversy. *Phi Delta Kappan*, 1972, **54**, 276–278.

Brophy, J. E. & Good, T. L. Of course the schools are feminine, but let's stop blaming women for it. *Phi Delta Kappan,* 1973a, **54,** 73–75.

Brophy, J. E., & Good, T. L. Feminization of American elementary schools. *Phi Delta Kappan,* 1973b, **54,** 564–566.

Broverman, I. K., Broverman, D. M., & Clarkson, F. E. Sex-role stereotypes and clinical judgments of mental health. *Journal of Consulting and Clinical Psychology,* 1970, **34,** 1–7.

Brown, B. R. The assessment of self-concept among four year-old Negro and white children: A comparative study using the Brown-IDS self-concept referents test. Unpublished paper, Institute for Developmental Studies, School of Education, New York University, New York, 1966.

Brown, D. G. Sex role preference in young children. *Psychological Monographs,* 1956, **70** (No. 421), 1–19.

Brown, D. G. Masculinity femininity development in children. *Journal of Consulting Psychology,* 1957, **21,** 197–202.

Brown, J. A., & Cleary, M. A. The impact of teacher consultation on the self-perceptions of elementary school children. *Education,* 1973, **93,** 339–345.

Bruch, H. Perceptual and conceptual disturbances in anorexia nervosa. *Psychosomatic Medicine,* 1962, **24,** 187–194.

Bruck, M., & Bodwin, R. The relationship between self-concept and the presence and absence of scholastic underachievement. *Journal of Clinical Psychology,* 1962, **18,** 181–182.

Brunswick, E. Mechanism of self-deception. *Journal of Social Psychology,* 1939, **10,** 409–420.

Bunton, P. L., & Weissbach, T. A. Attitudes toward blackness of black preschool children attending community controlled or public schools. *Journal of Social Psychology,* 1974, **92,** 53–59.

Burchinal, L. G. Parents attitudes and adjustment of children. *Journal of Genetic Psychology,* 1958, **92,** 69–79.

Burchinal, L., Gardner, B. & Hawkes, G. R. Children's personality adjustment and social-economic status in their families. *Journal of Genetic Psychology,* 1958, **92,** 149–159.

Butts, H. F. Skin color perception and self-esteem. *Journal of Negro Education,* 1963, **32,** 122–128.

Caliguri, J. The self-concept of the poverty child. *Journal of Negro Education,* 1966, **35,** 280–282.

Caplan, P. J. The role of classroom conduct in the promotion and retention of elementary school children. *Journal of Experimental Education,* 1973, **41,** 8–11.

Caplin, M. D. Self-concept level of aspiration and academic achievement. *Journal of Negro Education,* 1968, **37,** 435–439.

Carlson, R. Identification and personality structure in preadolescents. *Journal of Abnormal and Social Psychology*, 1963, **67**, 566–573.

Carlton, L., & Moore, R. H. The effects of self-directive dramatization on reading achievement and self-concept of culturally disadvantaged children. *Reading Teacher*, 1966, **20**, 125–130.

Carpenter, T. R., & Busse, T. V. Development of self-concept in Negro and white welfare children. *Child Development*, 1969, **40**, 935–939.

Carter, T. P. The negative self-concept of Mexican-American students. *School and Society*, 1968, **96**, 217–219.

Chang, T. S. The self-concept of children in ethnic groups: Black-American and Korean-American, *Elementary School Journal*, 1975, **76**, 52–58.

Chodorkoff, B. Self-perception, perceptual defense and adjustment. *Journal of Abnormal and Social Psychology*, 1954, **49**, 508–512.

Clark, E. T. The Clark U-scale. Unpublished test, St. John's University, New York, copyright 1967.

Clark, K. B., & Clark, M. P. The development of consciousness of self and the emergence of racial identification in Negro preschool children. *Journal of Social Psychology*, 1939, **10**, 591–599.

Clark, K. B., & Clark, M. P. Skin color as a factor in racial identification of Negro preschool children. *Journal of Social Psychology*, 1940, **11**, 159–169.

Clark, K. B., & Clark, M. P. Emotional factors in racial identification and preference in Negro children. *Journal of Negro Education*, 1950, **19**, 341–350.

Clark, K. B., & Clark, M. P. Racial identification and preference in Negro children. In G. E. Swanson, T. M. Newcomb, & E. L. Hartley (Eds.), *Readings in social psychology*. New York: Henry Holt and Co., 1952.

Cohen, D. H., & Stern, V. *Observing and recording the behavior of young children*. New York: Bureau of Publications, Teachers College, Columbia University, 1958.

Coleman, J. S. *Abnormal psychology and modern life*. Glenview, Ill: Scott Foresman and Co., 1972.

Coleman, J. S. et al. *Equality of educational opportunity*. Washington, D.C.: U.S. Government Printing Office, 1966.

Coles, R. *Children of crisis: A study of courage and fear*. Boston: Little, Brown, 1967.

Combs, Arthur W. (Ed.) *Perceiving, behaving, becoming: A new focus for education*. Washington, D.C.: Association for Supervision and Curriculum Development, 1962.

Combs, A. W. *The professional education of teachers: A perceptual view of teacher preparation*. Boston: Allyn & Bacon, 1965.

Combs, A. W. et al. *Florida studies in the helping professions*. University of Florida Press. 1969.

Combs, A. W., Avila, D. L. & Purkey, W. W. *Helping relationships: Basic concepts for the helping professions*. Boston: Allyn & Bacon, 1971.

Combs, A. W., & Snygg, D. *Individual behavior: A perceptual approach to behavior*. New York: Harper and Bros., 1959.

Combs, A. W., & Soper, D. W. The self, its derivate terms and research. *Journal of Individual Psychology*, 1957, **13**, 135–145.

Combs, A. W., Soper, D. W. & Courson, C. C. The measurement of self-concept and self-report. *Educational and Psychological Measurement*, 1963, **23**, 493–500.

Cooley, C. *Human nature and the social order*. New York: Charles Scribner, 1902.

Coopersmith, S. A method for determining types of self-esteem. *Journal of Abnormal and Social Psychology*, 1959, **59**, 87–94.

Coopersmith, S. *The antecedents of self-esteem*. San Francisco: W. H. Freeman and Co., 1967.

Cox, S. H. Family background effects on personality development and social acceptance. (ERIC, ED020020) Fort Worth: Texas Christian University Institute of Behavioral Research, 1966.

Cox, S. H. The association of peer acceptance-rejection with children's perception of parental behaviors. *Psychology in the Schools*, 1974, **2**, 222–225.

Crandall, V. J. Achievement. In H. W. Stevenson (Ed.), *Child psychology*, 63rd Yearbook of the National Society for the Study of Education. Chicago: The National Society for the Study of Education, 1963.

Crandall, V. J., Katkovsky, W., & Preston, A. A conceptual formulation for some research on children's achievement development. *Child Development*, 1960a, **31**, 787–797.

Crandall, V. J., Katkovsky, W., & Preston, A. Motivational and ability determinants of young children's intellectual achievement behaviors. *Child Development*, 1962, **33**, 643–661.

Crandall, V. J., Preston, A., & Robson, A. Maternal reactions and the development of independence and achievement behavior in young children. *Child Development*, 1960b, **31**, 243–251.

Crandall, V. C., Crandall, V. J., & Katkovsky, W. A children's social desirability questionnaire," *Journal of Consulting Psychology*, 1965a, **29**, 27–36.

Crandall, V. C., Katkovsky, W., & Crandall, V. J. Children's beliefs in their own control of reinforcements in intellectual-academic achievement situations. *Child Development*, 1965b, **36**, 92–109.

Crowne, D. P., & Stephens, M. W. Self-acceptance and self-evaluative behavior: A critique of methodology. *Psychological Bulletin*, 1961, **58**, 104–121.

Cummings, S. An appraisal of some recent evidence dealing with the mental health of black children and adolescents, and its implications for school psychologists and guidance counselors. *Psychology of the Schools*, 1975, **12**, 234–8.

David, A. Self-concept and mother-concept in black and white preschool children. *Child Psychiatry and Human Development*, 1973, **4**, 30–43.

David, A., & White, A. A. Effects of success, failure, and social facilitation on level of aspiration in emotionally disturbed and normal children. *Journal of Personality*, 1958, **26**, 77–93.

Davidson, H. H., & Greenberg, J. W. *School achievers from a deprived background.* New York: Associated Educational Services Corp., 1967.

Davidson, H. H., & Lang, G. Children's perceptions of their teacher's feelings toward them related to self-perception, school achievement, and behavior. *Journal of Experimental Education*, 1960, **29**, 107–118.

Davidson, K. S. Interviews of parents of high anxious and low anxious children. *Child Development*, 1959, **30**, 341–351.

Davis, O. L., Jr., & Slobodian, J. Teacher behavior toward boys and girls during first-grade reading instruction. *American Educational Research Journal*, 1967, **4**, 261–269.

De Saussure, J. Some complications in self-esteem regulation caused by using an archaic image of the self as an ideal. *International Journal of Psychoanalysis*, 1971, **52**, 87–97.

Deutsch, H. *The psychology of women.* Vol. I. New York: Grune and Stratton, 1944.

Deutsch, M. Minority group and class status as related to social and personality factors in scholastic achievement. In Grossack, M. (Ed.), Mental health and segregation. New York: Springer Publishing Co., 1963.

Deutsch, M. *Theories in social psychology.* New York: Basic Books, 1965.

Diggory, J. C. *Self-evaluation: Concepts and studies.* New York: John Wiley and Sons, 1966.

Dion, K. L., & Miller, N. Determinants of task-related self-evaluations in black children. *Journal of Experimental Social Psychology*, 1973, **9**, 466–479.

Dixon, J. C. Development of self recognition. *Journal of Genetic Psychology*, 1957, **91**, 251–256.

Doyle, W., Hancock, G., & Kifer, E. Teachers' perceptions: Do they make a difference?'' Paper presented at the annual meeting of the American Educational Research Association, 1971.

Dreyer, A. S., & Haupt, D. Self evaluation in young children. *Journal of Genetic Psychology,* 1966, **108,** 185–197.

Durrett, M. E., & Davy, A. J. Racial-awareness in young Mexican-American, Negro and Anglo children. *Young Children,* 1970, **26,** 16–24.

Edwards, A. L. *The social desirability variable in personality assessment.* New York: Dryden Press, 1957.

Engel, M. The stability of the self-concept in adolescence. *Journal of Abnormal and Social Psychology,* 1959, **58,** 211–215.

Epps, E. G. Interpersonal relations and motivation: Implications for teachers of disadvantaged children. *Journal of Negro Education,* 1970, **39,** 14–25.

Epstein, S. The self-concept revisited: On a theory of a theory. *American Psychologist,* 1973, **28,** 404–416.

Erikson, E. H. *Childhood and society.* New York: Norton, 1950.

Erikson, E. H. Growth and crisis of the healthy personality. In C. Kluckholm & H. Murray (Eds.), *Personality in nature, society and culture.* New York: Alfred A. Knopf, 1955.

Erikson, E. H. *Identity: Youth and crisis.* New York: Norton, 1968.

Everhart, R. W. Literature survey of growth and developmental factors in articulatory maturation. *Journal of Speech and Hearing Disorders,* 1960, **25,** 59–69.

Fagot, B. I., & Patterson, G. R. An in vivo analysis of reinforcing contingencies for sex-role behaviors in the preschool child. *Developmental Psychology,* 1969, **1,** 563–568.

Fassler, J. Children's literature and early childhood separation experiences. *Young Children,* 1974, **29,** 311–323.

Felker, D. W. Predictions of specific self-evaluations from performance and personality measures. *Psychological Reports,* 1972, **31,** 823–826.

Felker, D. W. *Building positive self-concepts.* Minneapolis, Minn.: Burgess Publishing Company, 1974.

Felker, D. W., & Bahlke, S. *Learning deficit in the ability to self-reinforce as related to negative self-concept.* Washington, D.C.: American Educational Research Association, 1970.

Felker, D. W., Stanwyck, D. J., & Kay, R. S. The effects of a teacher program in self-concept enhancement on pupil's self-concept, anxiety and intellectual achievement responsibility. *Journal of Educational Research,* 1973, **66,** 443–445.

Felker, D. W., & Thomas, S. B. Self-Initiated verbal reinforcement and positive self-concept. *Child Development,* 1971, **42,** 1285–1287.

Fenichel, O. *The psychoanalytic theory of neurosis.* New York: Norton, 1945.

Fenichel, O. Identification. In H. Fenichel & D. Rapaport (Eds.), *The collected papers of Otto Fenichel.* New York: Norton, 1953.

Feshbach, N. D. Student teacher preferences for elementary school pupils varying in personality characteristics. *Journal of Educational Psychology*, 1969, **60**, 126–132.

Feshbach, N. D. How not to succeed in the professions without really trying or the seven stages of women. *Educational Horizons*, Winter 1973–1974, **52**, 67–71.

Festinger, L. *A theory of cognitive dissonance.* Stanford, Cal.: Stanford University Press, 1957.

Fish, J. E. & Larr, C. J. A decade of change in drawings by black children. *American Journal of Psychiatry*, 1972, **129**, 421–426.

Fisher, S., & Cleveland, S. E. *Body image and personality.* New York: Dover Publications, 1968.

Fleming, E. S., & Auttomen. R. G. Teacher expectancy as related to the academic and personal growth of primary-age children. *Monographs of the Society for Research in Child Development*, 1971, **36**, 1–31.

Flynn, T. M. The personality characteristics of school readiness in disadvantaged preschool children. *Journal of Instructional Psychology*, 1974, **1**, 45–52.

Fox, D. J., & Jordan, V. B. Racial preference and identification of black American, Chinese, and white children. *Genetic Psychology Monographs*, 1973, **88**, 229–286.

Frazier, E. *Black bourgeoisie.* Glencoe: The Free Press, 1957.

Frerichs, A. H. Relationship of self-esteem of the disadvantaged to school success. (ERIC ED040223). Paper presented at the annual meeting of the American Educational Research Association, March 1970.

Freud, A. *The ego and the mechanisms of defense.* New York: International Universities Press, 1946.

Freud, S. Group psychology and the analysis of the superego (1921). In *The standard edition*, Vol. 18. London: Hogarth Press, 1957.

Freud, S. The dissolution of the Oedipus-complex (1924). In *The standard edition*, Vol. 19. London: Hogarth Press, 1961.

Freud, S. On narcissism: An introduction (1925a). In *Collected papers*, Vol. 4. London: Hogarth Press, 1956.

Freud, S. Some psychological consequences of the anatomical distinction between the sexes (1925b). In *Collected papers*, Vol. 5. New York: Basic Books. 1959.

Freud, S. Female sexuality (1931). In *Collected papers*, Vol. 5. New York: Basic Books, 1959.

Freud, S. The psychology of women. In *New introductory lectures on psychoanalysis.* New York: Norton, 1933.

Freud, S. *General introduction to psychoanalysis.* New York: Doubleday, 1953.

Freud, S. *The ego and the id.* London: Hogarth Press, 1962.

Friend, R. M., & Neale, J. M. Children's perceptions of success and failure: An attributional analysis of the effects of race and social class. *Developmental Psychology,* 1972, **7,** 124–128.

Fromm, E. Selfishness and self-love. *Psychiatry,* 1939, **2,** 507–523.

Furman, R. A. Experiences in nursery school consultations. *Young Children.* 1966, **22,** 84–95.

Garai, J. E., & Scheinfeld, A. Sex differences in mental and behavioral traits. *Genetic Psychology Monographs,* 1968, **77,** 169–299.

Gardner, D. B. *Development in early childhood.* New York: Harper & Row, 1973.

Gecas, V., Calonico, J. M., & Thomas, D. L. The development of self-concept vs. the child: Mirror theory versus model theory. *Journal of Social Psychology,* 1974, **92,** 67–76.

Gergen, K. J. The effects of interaction goals and personalistic feedback on the presentation of self. *Journal of Personality and Social Psychology.* 1965, **1,** 413–424.

Gergen, K. J. Personal consistency and the presentation of self. In C. Gordon & K. J. Gergen (Eds.), *The self in social interaction.* New York: John Wiley and Sons, 1968.

Gergen, K. J. Self-theory and the process of self-observation. *The Journal of Nervous and Mental Disease,* 1969, **148,** 437–448.

Gergen, K. J. *The concept of self.* New York: Holt, Rinehart and Winston, 1971.

Getsinger, S. H. et al. Self-esteem measures and cultural disadvantagement. *Journal of Consulting and Clinical Psychology,* 1972, **38,** 149.

Gibby, R. G. S., & Gabler, R. The self-concept of Negro and white children. *Journal of Clinical Psychology,* 1967, **23,** 144–148.

Gill, M. P. *Pattern of achievement as related to the perceived self.* (ERIC ED029336) Washington, D.C.: American Educational Research Association, 1969.

Gilpatrick, N. Power of picture books to change child's self-image. *Elementary English,* 1969, **46,** 570–574.

Ginsburg, H. *The myth of the deprived child.* Englewood Cliffs, N.J.: Prentice-Hall, 1972.

Gitter, A. C., & Satow, Y. Color and physiognomy as variables in racial misidentification among children. (ERIC ED034584) Paper presented at the 77th annual convention of the American Psychological Association, Washington, D.C., 1969.

Goff, R. M. Culture and the personality development of minority peoples. In V. A. Clift, A. W. Anderson, & H. G. Hullfish (Eds.), *Negro education in America.* New York: Harper & Bros., 1962.

Goldberg, S., & Lewis, M. Play behavior in the year-old infant: Early sex differences. *Child Development,* 1969, **40,** 21–31.

Goldfarb, W. Self-awareness in schizophrenic children. *Archives of General Psychiatry,* 1963, **8,** 47–60.

Golin, S. et al. Psychology in the community: Project self-esteem. *Psychological Reports,* 1970, **26,** 735–740.

Good, T., & Brophy, J. Questioned equality for grade one boys and girls. *The Reading Teacher,* 1971, **25,** 247–252.

Goodman, M. E. *Race awareness in young children.* New York: Collier Books, 1964.

Gordon, I. *Studying the child in the school.* New York: John Wiley and Sons, 1966.

Gordon, I. J. *On early learning: The modifiability of human potential.* Washington, D.C.: Association for Supervision and Curriculum Development, 1971.

Gorelick, M. C. The effectiveness of visual form training in a prereading program. *Journal of Educational Research,* 1965, **58,** 315–318.

Greenberg, J. Comments on self-perceptions of disadvantaged children. *American Educational Research Journal,* 1970, **7,** 627–630.

Greenberg, J. W. et al. Attitudes of children from a deprived environment toward achievement related concepts. *Journal of Educational Research,* 1965, **59,** 57–62.

Greene, J. F., & Zirkel, P. A. Academic factors relating to the self-concept of Puerto Rican pupils. (ERIC ED054284) Paper presented at the annual convention of the American Psychological Association, Washington, D.C., 1971.

Greenwald, H. J., & Oppenheim, D. B. Reported magnitude of self-misidentification among Negro children—artifact. *Journal of Personality and Social Psychology,* 1968, **8,** 49–52.

Gregor, A. J., & McPherson, D. A. Racial attitudes among white and Negro children in a deep-south standard metropolitan area. *Journal of Social Psychology,* 1966, **68,** 95–106.

Grier, W., & Cobbs, P. *Black Rage.* New York: Basic Books, 1968.

Grossman, B. D. Enhancing the self. *Exceptional Children,* 1971, **38,** 248–254.

Guggenheim, F. Self-esteem and achievement expectations for white and Negro children. *Journal of Projective Techniques and Personality Assessment,* 1969, **33,** 63–71.

Guttentag, M. Children in Harlem's community-controlled schools. *Journal of Social Issues,* 1972, **28,** 1–20.

Hall, C. S., & Lindzey, G. *Theories of personality.* New York: John Wiley & Sons, 1970.

Halpern, F. Self-perceptions of black children and the civil rights movement. *American Journal of Orthopsychiatry,* 1970, **40**, 520–526.

Hamburg, D. A., & Lunde, D. T. Sex hormones in the development of sex differences in human behavior. In E. Maccoby (Ed.), *The development of sex differences.* Stanford, Cal.: Stanford University Press, 1966.

Hampson, J. L. Determinants of psychosexual orientation. In F. A. Beach (Ed.), *Sex and behavior.* New York: John Wiley and Sons, 1965.

Harris, S., & Braun, J. R. Self esteem and racial preference in black children. Proceedings of the annual convention of the American Psychological Association, Washington, D.C., 1971.

Hartley, R. E. Children's concepts of male and female roles. *Merrill-Palmer Quarterly,* 1960, **6**, 83–91.

Hartley, R. E. A developmental view of female sex-role definition and identification. *Merrill-Palmer Quarterly,* 1964, **10**, 3–16.

Hartley, R. E. Sex role pressures and the socialization of the male child. In J. Stacey, S. Bereaud, & J. Daniels (Eds.), *And Jill came tumbling down: sexism in American education.* New York: Dell Publishing Co., 1974.

Hartmann, H. Comments on the psychoanalytic theory of the ego. *The Psychoanalytic Study of the Child,* 1950. **5**, 74–96.

Hartmann, H. *Ego psychology and the problem of adaptation.* New York: International Universities Press, 1958.

Haynes, L. E., & Kaufer, F. H. Academic rank, task feedback and self-reinforcement in children. *Psychological Reports,* 1971, **28**, 967–974.

Heath, D. H. *Explorations of maturity: Studies of mature and immature college men.* New York: Appleton-Century-Crofts, 1965.

Heathers, G. Emotional dependence and independence in nursery school play. *The Journal of Genetic Psychology,* 1955, **87**, 37–57.

Hebert, D. J. Reading comprehension as a function of self-concept. *Perceptual and Motor Skills,* 1968, **27**, 78.

Heidegger, M. *Being and time.* New York: Harper & Row, 1962.

Heiss, J. & Owens, S. Self-evaluation of blacks and whites, *American Journal of Sociology,* 1972, **78**, 360–70.

Helper, M. M. Parental evaluation of Children and Children's self-evaluations. *Journal of Abnormal and Social Psychology,* 1958, **56**, 190–194.

Henderson, E. H., & Long, B. H. Personal-social correlates of academic success among disadvantaged school beginners. *Journal of School Psychology,* 1971, **9**, 101–113.

Henderson, E. H., Long, B. H. & Ziller, R. C. Self-social constructs of achieving and nonachieving readers. *Reading Teacher,* 1965, **19**, 114–118.

Hilgard, E. Human motives and the concept of self. *American Psychologist,* 1949, **4,** 374–82.

Hoffer, W. Mouth, hand and ego-integration. In *The Psychoanalytic Study of the Child.* 1949, **3/4,** 49–56.

Hoffer, W. Development of the body ego. *The Psychoanalytic Study of the Child,* 1950, **5,** 18–23.

Holmes, M. et al. *The impact of the parent-child centers on parents: A preliminary report.* Vol. II (ERIC ED084038). New York: Center for Community Research, February 1973.

Horner, M. Toward an understanding of achievement-related conflicts in women. *Journal of Social Issues,* 1972, **28,** 157–175.

Horney, K. *The neurotic personality of our time.* New York: Norton, 1937.

Horney, K. *New ways in psychoanalysis.* New York: Norton, 1939.

Horowitz, R. E. Racial aspects of self-identification in nursery school children. *Journal of Psychology,* 1939, **7,** 91–99.

Horrocks, J. E., & Jackson, D. W. *Self and role: A theory of self-process and role behavior.* Boston: Houghton Mifflin, 1972.

Hovland, C. I., Janis, I. L., & Kelley, H. H. *Communication and persuasion: Psychological studies of opinion change.* New Haven: Yale University Press, 1953.

Howard, D. P. The needs and problems of socially disadvantaged children as perceived by students and teachers. *Exceptional Children,* 1968, **34,** 327–335.

Howard, N. K. *Self-concept: An abstract bibliography.* University of Illinois, Urbana: ERIC Clearinghouse on Early Childhood Education, May 1974.

Hraba, J., & Grant, G. Black is beautiful: A reexamination of racial preference and identification. *Journal of Personality and Social Psychology,* 1970, **16,** 398–402.

Hunt, J. McV. *Revisiting Montessori: Introduction to the Montessori method.* New York: Schocken Books, 1964.

Hyman, H. H. *The psychology of status.* No. 269. New York: Archives of Psychology, 1942.

Iglitzin, L. B. A child's eye view of sex roles. *Today's Education,* 1972, **67,** 23–25.

Jacklin, C. N., Maccoby, E. E., & Dick, A. E. Barrier behavior and toy preference: Sex differences (and their absence) in the year-old child, *Child Development,* 1973, **44,** 196–200.

Jacobson, E. *The self and the object world.* New York: International Universities Press, 1964.

James, M. Premature ego development: Some observations on disturbances in the first three months of life. *International Journal of Psychoanalysis,* 1960, **41,** 288–294.

James, W. *Psychology.* New York: Henry Holt and Co., 1893.

Jersild, A. T. *Child psychology.* Englewood Cliffs, N.J.: Prentice-Hall, 1968.

Joffe, C. As the twig is bent. In J. Stacey, S. Bereaud, & J. Daniels (Eds.), *And Jill came tumbling down: Sexism in American education.* New York: Dell Publishing Co., 1974.

Johnson, D. Racial attitudes of Negro freedom school participants and Negro and white civil rights participants. *Social Forces,* 1966, **45**, 266–272.

Jones, S. C. Self and interpersonal evaluations: Esteem theories. *Psychological Bulletin,* 1973, **79**, 185–199.

Kagan, J. Acquisition and significance of sex typing and sex role identity. In M. L. Hoffman & L. W. Hoffman (Eds.), *Review of child development research.* Vol. I. New York: Russell Sage Foundation, 1964a.

Kagan, J. The child's sex-role classification of school objects. *Child Development,* 1964b, **35**, 1051–1056.

Kagan, J. *Understanding children.* New York: Harcourt, Brace, 1971.

Kagan, J. The emergence of sex differences. *School Review,* 1972, **80**, 217–227.

Kagan, J., & Moss, H. A. *Birth to maturity: A study in Psychological development.* New York: John Wiley and Sons, 1962.

Kamii, C. A sketch of the Piaget-derived preschool curriculum developed by the Ypsilanti early education program. In J. L. Frost (Ed.), *Revisiting early childhood education: Readings.* New York: Holt, Rinehart and Winston, 1973.

Kaplan, H. B., & Pokorny, A. D. Sex related correlates of adult self-derogation: Reports of childhood experiences. *Developmental Psychology,* 1972, **6**, 536.

Kardiner, A., & Ovesey, L. *The mark of oppression: Explorations in the personality of the American Negro.* New York: The World Publishing Co., 1951.

Katahn, M. Interaction of anxiety and ability in complex learning situations. *Journal of Personality and Social Psychology.* 1966, **3**, 475–479.

Katz, I. Review of evidence relating to effects of desegregation on the intellectual performance of Negroes. *American Psychologist,* 1964, **19**, 381–399.

Katz, I. Some motivational determinants of racial differences in intellectual achievement. *International Journal of Psychology,* 1967a, **2**, 1–12.

Katz, I. The socialization of academic motivation in minority group children. In D. Levine (Ed.), *Nebraska symposium on motivation.* Lincoln, Neb.: University of Nebraska Press, 1967b.

Katz, I. Factors influencing Negro performance in the desegregated school. In M. Deutsch, I. Katz, & A. Jensen (Eds.), *Social class, race and psychological development.* New York: Holt, Rinehart and Winston, 1968.

Katz, I., Cole, O. J. & Baron, R. M. Self evaluation, social reinforcement, and academic achievement of black and white schoolchildren, *Child Development,* 1976, **47**, 368–374.

Keller, S. The social world of the urban slum child: Some early findings. *American Journal of Orthopsychiatry.* 1963, **33**, 823–831.

Kellogg, R. L. A direct approach to sex-role identification of school-related objects. *Psychological Reports,* 1969, **24**, 839–841.

Kelly, E. L. Consistency of the adult personality. *American Psychologist,* 1955, **10**, 659–681.

Kelly, H. H. Two functions of reference groups. In G. E. Swanson, T. M. Newcomb., & E. L. Hartley (Eds.), *Readings in social psychology.* New York: Henry Holt and Co., 1952.

Kernberg, O. F. Factors in the psychoanalytic treatment of narcissistic personalities. *Journal of the American Psychoanalytic Association,* 1970, **18,** 51–85.

Kernberg, O. F. Contrasting viewpoints regarding the nature and psychoanalytic treatment of narcissistic personalities: A preliminary communication. *Journal of the American Psychoanalytic Association,* 1974, **22**, 255–267.

Kernberg, O. F. *Borderline conditions and pathological narcissism.* New York: Jason Aronson, Inc., 1975.

Kifer, E. Relationships between academic achievement and personality characteristics: A quasi–longitudinal study, *American Educational Research Journal,* 1975, **12**, 191–210.

Kinch, J. W. A formalized theory of self-concept. *American Journal of Sociology,* 1963, **68**, 481–486

Kirshner, E. P., & Vondracek, S. I. What do you want to be when you grow up? Vocational choice in children aged three to six. (ERIC, ED076244) Paper presented at the Society for Research in Child Development, Phildelphia, Penn., March 29–April 1, 1973.

Kleiner, R., & Parker, S. Status position, mobility, and ethnic identification of the Negro. *Journal of Social Issues,* 1964, **20**, 85–102.

Kliman, G. *Psychological emergencies of childhood.* New York: Grune and Stratton, 1971.

Kohlberg, L. A cognitive developmental analysis of children's sex-role concepts and attitudes. In E. E. Maccoby (Ed.), *The development of sex differences.* Stanford, Cal.: Stanford University Press, 1966.

Kohn, M. & Rosman, B. L. Social-emotional, cognitive and demographic determinants of poor school achievement: Implications for a strategy of intervention, *Journal of Educational Psychology,* 1974, **66,** 267–276.

Kohut, H. *The analysis of the self.* New York: International Universities Press, 1971.

Kohut, H. Thoughts on narcissism and narcissistic rage. *Psychoanalytic Study of the Child,* 1972, **27,** 360–400.

Kolb, L. C. The body image in schizophrenic reaction. In A. Auerback (Ed.), *Schizophrenia: An integrated approach.* New York: Ronald Press, 1959a.

Kolb, L. C. Disturbances of the body-image. In S. Arieti (Ed.), *American handbook of psychiatry.* New York: Basic Books, 1959b.

Kravitz, H. Sex distribution of hospitalized children with acute respiratory diseases, gastroenteritis and meningitis. *Clinical Pediatrics,* 1965, **4,** 484–491.

Kris, E. *Psychoanalytic exploration in art.* New York: International Universities Press, 1952.

Kubie, L. S. *Neurotic distortions of the creative process.* New York: Noonday Press, 1952.

Kurtz, R. M. Body attitude and self-esteem. Proceedings of the annual convention of the American Psychological Association, Washington, D.C., 1971, **6,** 467–468.

L'Abate, L. Personality correlates of manifest anxiety in children. *Journal of Consulting Psychology.* 1960, **24,** 342–348.

LaBenne, W. A theoretical framework for behavioral analysis and interpretation. *Psychology,* 1968, **5,** 14–19.

Labov, W. *Language in the inner city: Studies in the black English vernacular.* Philadelphia, Penn.: University of Pennsylvania Press, 1973.

Laing, R. D. *The politics of experience.* New York: Ballantine, 1967.

Laing, R. D. *The divided self.* New York: Pantheon, 1969.

Landreck, B. *Songs to grow on.* New York: Edward B. Marks Music Corp., 1950.

Landreth, C., & Johnson, B. C. Young children's responses to a picture and inset test designed to reveal reactions to persons of different skin color. *Child Development,* 1953, **24,** 63–80.

Landry, R. G., & Pardew, M. E. Self-concept of preschool children. (ERIC, ED081490) Paper presented at meeting of the American Educational Research Association, New Orleans, La., February 26–March 1, 1973.

Lasky, L. Ways and means: Some tips for teachers. In S. R. Rausher., & T. Young (Eds.), *Sexism: Teachers and young children.* New York: Early Childhood Education Council of New York City, 1974.

Lavatelli, C. S. *Piaget's theory as applied to an early childhood curriculum.* Boston: American Science and Engineering, Inc. 1970.

Lecky, P. *Self-consistency: A theory of personality.* New York: Island Press, 1945.

Lee, P. C., & Gropper, N. B. Sex–role, culture and educational practice, *Harvard Educational Review,* 1974, **44**, 369–410.

Leeds, D. S. The role of self-concept in the psychological and educational development of the individual. *Reading World,* 1971, **11**, 161–176.

Leonetti, R., & Miller, D. G. The Spanish-surnamed child: Self-concept and school, *Elementary School Journal,* 1976, **76**, 246–255.

Levitin, T., & Chananie, J. D. Responses of female primary school teachers to sex-typed behaviors in male and female children, *Child Development,* 1972, **43**, 1309–1316.

Levy, B. The school's role in the sex-role stereotyping of girls: A feminist review of the literature. *Feminist Studies.* 1972, **1**, 5–23.

Lewin, K. *A dynamic theory of personality.* New York: McGraw-Hill, 1935.

Lewis, M., & Brooks-Gunn, J. *Self, other and fear: The reaction of infants to people.* Princeton, N.J.: Educational Testing Service, 1972.

Lichtenberg, J. D. The development of the sense of self. *Journal of the American Psychoanalytic Association,* 1975, **23**, 453–484.

Liebow, E. *Tally's corner: A study of Negro streetcorner men.* Boston: Little, Brown, 1967.

Linton, R. *The study of man.* New York: Appleton-Century-Crofts, 1936.

Linton, T. H. A study of the relationship of global self-concept, academic self-concept, and academic achievement among Anglo and Mexican-American sixth grade students. (ERIC, ED063053) Paper presented at the annual meeting of the American Educational Research Association, Chicago, Ill., April 3–7, 1972.

Lipsitt, L. P. A self-concept scale, for children and its relationship to the children's form of the manifest anxiety scale. *Child Development,* 1958, **29**, 463–472.

Little, J., & Ramirez, A. Ethnicity of subject and test administrator: Their effect on self-esteem, *Journal of Social Psychology,* 1976, **99**, 149–150.

Lloyd, J. The self-image of the small black child. *Elementary School Journal,* 1967, **67**, 406–411.

Long, B. H. Critique of Soares and Soares "Self-perceptions of culturally disadvantaged children." *American Educational Research Journal,* 1969, **6**, 710–711.

Long, B. H., & Henderson, E. H. Self-social concepts of disadvantaged school beginners. *Journal of Genetic Psychology,* 1968, **113**, 41–51.

Looft, W. R. Sex differences in the expression of vocational aspirations by elementary school children. *Developmental Psychology,* 1971, **5**, 366.

Lopate, C. et al. Some effects of parent and community participation on public education, (ERIC, ED027359) Washington, D.C.: Office of Education, 1969.

Ludwig, D. J., & Maehr, M. L. Changes in self-concept and stated behavioral preferences. *Child Development,* 1967, **38**, 453–467.

Lynd, H. M. *On shame and the search for identity.* New York: Harcourt, Brace, and Co., 1958.

McAdoo, H. P. Self concepts and racial attitudes of Northern and Southern black preschool children. (ERIC, ED062496) Washington, D.C.: U.S. Government Printing Office, 1970.

McCandless, B. R., Bilous, C. B., & Bennett, H. L. Peer popularity and dependence on adults in preschool age socialization. *Child Development,* 1961, **32**, 511–518.

McCarthy, J. D., & Yancey, W. L. Uncle Tom and Mr. Charlie: Metaphysical pathos in the study of racism and personal disorganization. *American Journal of Sociology,* 1971, **76**, 648–672.

McClelland, D. C. et al. *The achievement motive.* New York: Appleton-Century-Crofts, 1953.

Maccoby, E. E., & Jacklin, C. N. *The Psychology of sex differences.* Stanford, Cal.: Stanford University Press, 1974.

McDaniel, E. L. Relationships between self-concept and specific variables in a low-income culturally different population. (ERIC, ED019124). Final report of Head Start evaluation and research to the Institute for Educational Development, Section VII, August 31, 1967.

McDevitt, J. B. Preoedipal determinants of an infantile neurosis. In J. B. Settlage, & C. F. Settlage (Eds.), *Separation-individuation essays in honor of Margaret S. Mahler.* New York: International Universities Press, 1971.

McDill, E. L., Meyer, E. D., Jr., & Rigsby, L. *Sources of Educational Climates in High Schools.* Baltimore, Md: Department of Social Relations, Johns Hopkins University, 1966.

McDonald, M. *Not by the color of their skin: The impact of racial differences on the child's development.* New York: International Universities Press, 1970.

McNeil, J. D. Programmed instruction versus usual classroom procedures in teaching boys to read. *American Educational Research Journal,* 1964, **1**, 113–120.

McNelly, F. W., Jr. Development of the self-concept in childhood, (ERIC, ED086318) Washington, D.C.: U.S. Government Printing Office, 1972.

Mahler, M. S. Thoughts about development and individuation. *The Psychoanalytic Study of the Child,* 1963, **18**, 307–324.

Mahler, M. S., Pine, F., & Bergman, A. *The psychological birth of the human infant: Symbiosis and individuation.* New York: Basic Books, 1975.

Malone, C. E. The psychosocial characteristics of the children from a developmental viewpoint. In E. Pavenstedt (Ed.), *The drifters: Children of disorganized lower class families.* Boston: Little, Brown, 1967.

Martin, R. Student sex and behavior as determinants of the type and frequency of teacher–student contacts, *Journal of School Psychology,* 1972, **10**, 339–347.

Maslow, A. H. *Motivation and personality.* New York: Harper & Row, 1954.

Maslow, A. H. Some basic propositions of a growth and self-actualization psychology. In A. W. Combs (Ed.), *Perceiving, behaving, becoming: A new focus for education.* Washington, D.C.: Association for Supervision and Curriculum Development, 1962.

Maslow, A. H. *Toward a psychology of being.* (2nd ed.) Princeton, N.J.: D. Van Nostrand, 1968.

Maslow, A. H. Defense and growth. In R. H. Anderson & H. G. Shane (Eds.), *As the twig is bent.* Boston: Houghton Mifflin, 1971.

Maw, W. H., & Maw, E. W. Self-concepts of high- and low-curiosity boys. *Child Development,* 1970, **41**, 123–129.

May, R. *Existential psychology.* New York: Random House, Inc., 1969a.

May, R. Love and will. *Psychology Today.* 1969b, **3**, 17–64.

Mead, G. H. *Mind, self and society from the standpoint of a social behaviorist.* Chicago: The University of Chicago Press, 1934.

Mead, G. H. Self: The self and the organism. In A. Strauss (Ed.), *The social psychology of George Bernard Mead.* Chicago: University of Chicago Press, 1956.

Mead, M. *Sex and temperament in three primitive societies.* New York: Morrow, 1935.

Medinnus, G. R., & Curtis, E. J. The relation between maternal self-acceptance and child acceptance. *Journal of Consulting Psychology,* 1963, **27**, 542–544.

Merton, R. K. *Social theory and social structure.* New York: The Free Press, 1968.

Minuchin, P. Correlates of curiosity and exploratory behavior in preschool disadvantaged children. *Child Development,* 1971, **42**, 939–950.

Mischel, W. Sex typing and socialization. In P. H. Mussen (Ed.), *Carmichael's manual of child psychology.* New York: John Wiley and Sons, 1970.

Monahan, L., Kuhn, D., & Shower, P. Intrapsychic versus cultural explanations of the fear of success motive. *Journal of Personality and Social Psychology,* 1974. **29**, 60–64.

Money, J. *Sex research: New developments.* New York: Holt, Rinehart and Winston, 1965.

Money, J., & Ehrhardt, A. *Man and woman: Boy and girl.* Baltimore, Md: Johns Hopkins University Press, 1973.

Moore, S., & Updegraff, R. Sociometric status of preschool children related to age, sex, nurturance-giving and dependency. *Child Development,* 1964, **35**, 519–524.

Morland, J. K. Racial recognition by nursery school children in Lynchburg, Virginia. *Social Forces,* 1958, **37**, 132–137.

Morland, J. K. Racial self-identification: A study of nursery school children. *American Catholic Sociological Review,* 1963, **24**, 231–242.

Moses, E. G., Zirkel, P., & Greene, J. F. Measuring self-concept of minority group pupils. *Journal of Negro Education,* 1973, **42**, 93–98.

Moss, H. A. Sex, age and state as determinants of mother-infant interaction. *Merrill-Palmer Quarterly,* 1967, **13**, 19–36.

Murphy, G. *Personality: A biosocial approach to origins and structure.* New York: Harper and Bros., 1947.

Mussen, P. H. Differences between TAT responses of Negro and white boys. *Journal of Consulting Psychology,* 1953, **17**, 373–376.

Mussen, P. H. Early sex role development. In D. Goslin (Ed.), *Handbook of socialization theory and research.* Chicago: Rand McNally, 1969.

Mussen, P. H., & Distler, L. Masculinity, identification and father–son relationship. *Journal of Abnormal and Social psychology,* 1959, **59**, 350–356.

Mussen, P. H., & Distler, L. Child rearing antecedents of masculine identification in kindergarten boys. *Child Development,* 1960, **31**, 89–100.

Mussen, P. H., & Rutherford, E. Parent-child relations and parental personality in relation to young children's sex-role preferences. *Child Development,* 1963, **34**, 589–607.

Newcomb, T. M. *Social psychology.* New York: The Dryden Press, 1950.

Newton, E. S. Bibliotherapy in the development of minority group self-concept. *Journal of Negro Education,* 1969, **38**, 257–265.

Nobles, W. W. Psychological research and the black self-concept: A critical review. *Journal of Social Issues,* 1973, **29**, 11–31.

Omwake, K. T. The relation between acceptance of self and acceptance of others shown by three personality inventories. *Journal of Consulting Psychology,* 1954, **18**, 443–446.

Ozehosky, R. J., & Clark, E. T. Children's self-concept and kindergarten achievement. *Journal of Psychology,* 1970, **75**, 185–192.

Ozehosky, R. J., & Clark, E. T. Verbal and non-verbal measures of self-concept among kindergarten boys and girls. *Psychological Reports,* 1971, **28**, 195–199.

Palardy, J. M. For Johnny's reading sake. *Reading Teacher,* 1969, **22**, 720–724.

Palermo, D. S. Racial comparisons and additional normative data on the children's manifest anxiety scale. *Child Development,* 1959, **30**, 53–57.

Parker, J. The relationship of self report to inferred self concept. *Educational and Psychological Measurement,* 1966, **26**, 691–700.

Payne, D. E., & Mussen, P. H. Parent-child relations and father identification among adolescent boys. *Journal of Abnormal and Social Psychology,* 1956, **52**, 358–362.

Peller, L. E. Language and development. In P. Neubauer (Ed.), *Concepts of development in early childhood.* Springfield, Ill.: Charles C. Thomas, 1965.

Perkins, C. W., & Shannon, D. T. Three techniques for obtaining self-perceptions in preadolescent boys. *Journal of Personality and Social Psychology,* 1965, **2**, 443–447.

Piaget, J. *The language and thought of the child.* New York: Harcourt, Brace, and World, 1926.

Piaget, J. *The origins of intelligence in children.* New York: International Universities Press, 1952.

Piaget, J. *The construction of reality in the child.* New York: Basic Books, 1954.

Piaget, J. *Six psychological studies.* New York: Vintage Books, 1967.

Piaget, J., & Inhelder, B. *The psychology of the child.* New York: Basic Books, 1969.

Piers, E. V., & Harris, D. B. Age and other correlates of self-concepts in children. *Journal of Educational Psychology,* 1969, **55**, 91–95.

Porter, J. D. *Black child, white child. The development of racial attitudes.* Cambridge, Mass: Harvard University Press, 1971.

Poussaint, A. F. The Negro American: His self-image and integration. *Journal of the National Medical Association,* 1966, **58**, 419–423.

Powell, G. J. Self-concept in white and black children. In C. V. Willie, B. M. Kramer & B. S. Brown (Eds.), *Racism and mental health.* Pittsburgh: University of Pittsburgh Press, 1973.

Proshansky, H., & Newton, P. The nature and meaning of Negro self-identity. In M. Deutsch, I. Katz., & A. R. Jensen (Eds.), *Social class, race and psychological development.* New York: Holt, Rinehart and Winston, 1968.

Purkey, W. W. *Self-concept and school achievement.* Englewood Cliffs, N.J.: Prentice-Hall, 1970.

Purkey, W. W. Building self-concepts in students and teachers. University of Florida Unpublished Paper, 1974.

Purkey, W. W., & Cage, B. N. The Florida key: A scale to infer learner self-concept. *Educational and Psychological Measurement*, 1973, **33**, 979–984.

Purkey, W. W., & Graves, W. Self-perceptions of students enrolled in an experimental elementary school. (ERIC, ED037794) Paper presented at the American Educational Research Association Convention, Minneapolis, Minn., March 2–6, 1970.

Radke, M. J., & Trager, H. G. Children's perceptions of the social roles of Negroes and whites. *Journal of Psychology*, 1950, **29** 3–33.

Radke, M. J., Trager, H. G., & Davis, H. Social perceptions and the attitudes of children. *Genetic Psychological Monographs*, 1949, **40**, 327–447.

Rainwater, L. Crucible of identity: The Negro lower class family. *Daedalus*, 1966, **95**, 172–216.

Raymer, E. *Race and sex identification in preschool children*. (ERIC, ED041634) Washington, D.C.: Office of Economic Opportunity Report No. OEO-4117, 1969.

Reich, A. Pathologic forms of self-esteem regulation. *Psychoanalytic Study of the Child*, 1960, **15**, 215–232.

Retish, P. M. Changing the status of poorly esteemed students through teacher reinforcement. *Journal of Applied Behavioral Science*, 1973, **9**, 44–50.

Richmond, B. O., & White, W. F. Sociometric predictors of the self-concept among fifth and sixth grade children. *Journal of Educational Research*, 1971, **64**, 425–429.

Rist, R. C. Student social class and teacher expectations: The self-fulfilling prophecy in ghetto education. *Harvard Educational Review*, 1970, **40**, 411–451.

Robbins, L., & Robbins, E. Comment on: Toward an understanding of achievement related conflicts in women. *Journal of Social Issues*, 1973, **29**, 133–137.

Rogers, C. R. *Client-centered therapy*. Boston: Houghton Mifflin, 1951.

Rogers, C. R. A theory of therapy, personality and interpersonal relationships as developed in the client-centered framework. In S. Koch (Ed.), *Psychology: A study of a science*. Vol. III. New York: McGraw-Hill, 1959.

Rosenberg, M. *Society and the adolescent self-image*. Princeton, N.J.: Princeton University Press, 1965.

Rosenberg, M. Psychological selectivity in self-esteem formation. In C. Gordon & K. J. Gergen, (Eds.), *The self in social interaction*. New York: John Wiley and Sons, 1968.

Rosenberg, M. Race, ethnicity, and self-esteem. In S. S. Guterman (Ed.), *Black psyche: The modal personality patterns of black Americans*. Berkeley, Cal.: The Glendessary Press, 1972.

Rosenkantz, P. S. et al. Sex role stereotypes and self-concepts in college students. *Journal of Consulting and Clinical Psychology,* 1968, **32,** 287–295.

Rosenthal, B. G. Developments of self-identification in relation to attitudes towards the self in the Chippewa Indians, *Genetic Psychology Monographs,* 1974, **90,** 43–141.

Rosenthal, R., & Jacobson, L. *Pygmalion in the classroom.* New York: Holt, Rinehart and Winston, 1968.

Roth, R. W. How Negro fifth grade students view "black pride" concepts. *Integrated Education,* 1970, **8,** 24–27.

Rotter, J. B. Generalized expectancies for internal versus external control of reinforcement. *Psychological monographs.* 1966, **80** (Whole No. 609).

Rowe, M. B. Science, silence, and sanctions, *Science and Children,* 1969, **7,** 11–13.

Rowen, B. Emerging identity through movement. (ERIC, ED073854) Coral Gables, Fla.: School of Education, Miami University, November 1972.

Rutter, M. Normal psychosexual development. *Journal of Child Psychology and Psychiatry and Allied Disciplines,* 1971, **11,** 259–283.

St. John, N. H. *School desegregation: Outcomes for children.* New York: John Wiley and Sons, 1975.

Samuels, S. C. An investigation into the self-concepts of lower and middle class black and white kindergarten children. *Journal of Negro Education,* 1973, **42,** 467–472.

Samuels, S. C. Johnny's mother isn't interested. *Today's Education,* 1973, **62,** 36–38.

Sandler, J., Holder, A. & Meers, D. The ego ideal and the ideal self. *Psychoanalytic Study of the Child,* 1963, **18,** 139–158.

Santrock, J. W. & Ross, M. Effects of social comparison on facilitative self-control in young children, *Journal of Educational Psychology,* 1975, **67,** 193–7.

Sarason S. et al. *Anxiety in elementary school children.* New York: John Wiley & Sons, 1960.

Sarbin, T. R. A preface to a psychological analysis of the self. *Psychological Review,* 1952, **59,** 11–22.

Schilder, P. *Image and appearance of the human body: Studies in constructive energies of the psyche.* New York: John Wiley and Sons, 1950.

Schonfeld, W. A. Body image in adolescents: A psychiatric concept for the pediatrician. *Pediatrics,* 1963, **31,** 845–854.

Schulthers, M. Building a better self-concept through story book guidance. (ERIC, ED044251) Paper presented at the Language Arts and

Reading Conference, Ball State University, Muncie, Ind., June 22–23, 1970.

Schwartz, S. Parent-child interaction as it relates to the ego functioning and self-concept of the preschool child. Unpublished Ed. D. dissertation, Columbia University, Teachers College, New York, 1966.

Sciara, F. A study of the acceptance of blackness among Negro boys. *Journal of Negro Education,* 1972, **41**, 151–155.

Sears, P. S. Levels of aspiration in academically successful and unsuccessful children. *Journal of Abnormal and Social Psychology,* 1940, **35**, 498–536.

Sears, P. S. Child-rearing factors related to playing of sex-typed roles. *American Psychologist,* 1953, **8**, 431.

Sears, P. S. Effective reinforcement for achievement behaviors in disadvantaged children: The first year. (ERIC, ED067442) Washington, D.C.: Office of Education, August 1972.

Sears, P. S. & Feldman, D. Teacher interaction with boys and girls. *The National Elementary Principal,* 1966, **46**, 30–37.

Sears, P. S., & Hilgard, E. R. The teacher's role in the motivation of the learner. In E. Hilgard (Ed.), *Theories of learning and instruction.* 63rd Yearbook of the National Society for the Study of Education. Chicago, Ill.: University of Chicago Press, 1964.

Sears, R. R. Relations of early socialization experience to self-concepts and gender role in middle childhood. *Child Development,* 1970, **41**, 267–289.

Sears, R. R., Maccoby, E. E., & Levin, H. *Patterns of child rearing.* New York: Row, Peterson 1957.

Sears, R. R., Rau, L. & Alpert, R. *Identification and Child Rearing.* Stanford, California: Stanford University Press, 1965.

Secord, P. F., & Backman, C. W. Personality theory and the problem of stability and change in individual behavior: An interpersonal approach. *Psychological Review,* 1961, **68**, 21–32.

Secord, P. F., & Jourand, S. M. The appraisal of body-cathexis: Body cathexis and the self. *Journal of Consulting Psychology,* 1953, **17**, 343–347.

Serbin, L., O'Leary, D., Kent, R. N., & Tonick, I. J. A comparison of teacher response to the preacademic and problem behavior of boys and girls. *Child Development,* 1973, **44**, 796–804.

Sewell, W. H. Social class and childhood personality. *Sociometry,* 1961, **24**, 340–356.

Sewell, W. H., & Haller, A. O. Social status and personality adjustment of the child. *Sociometry,* 1965, **19**, 114–125.

Sexton, P. C. *The feminized male.* New York: Random House, 1969.

Shaw, M. C., & Alves, G. J. The self-concept of bright academic under-achievers: Continued. *Personnel and Guidance,* 1963, **42,** 401–403.

Sheerer, E. T. An analysis of the relationship between acceptance of and respect for self and acceptance of and respect for others in 10 counseling cases. *Journal of Counseling Psychology,* 1949, **13,** 69–75.

Sherif, M., & Sherif, C. W. *Groups in harmony and tension.* New York: Octagon Books, 1966.

Sigel, I. E. et al. Social and emotional development of young children. In J. L. Frost (Ed.), *Revisiting early childhood education: Readings.* New York: Holt, Rinehart and Winston, 1973.

Simon, W. E., & Bernstein, E. The relationship between self-esteem and perceived reciprocal liking: A sociometric test of the theory of cognitive balance. *Journal of Psychology,* 1971, **79,** 197–201.

Singer, J. L. *The child's world of make-believe: Experimental studies of imaginative play.* New York: Academic Press, 1973.

Sisk, D. Relationship between self-concept and creativity: Theory into practice. *Gifted Child Quarterly,* 1972, **16,** 229–234.

Smart, M. S., & Smart, R. C. *Children: Development and Relationships.* (2nd ed.) New York: Macmillan, 1972.

Smirnoff, V. *The scope of child analysis.* New York: International Universities Press, 1971.

Smith, D. F. Yes American schools are feminized. *Phi Delta Kappan,* 1973, **54,** 703–704.

Smith, M. B., The phenomenological approach in personality theory: Some critical remarks. *Journal of Abnormal and Social Psychology,* 1950, **45,** 516–522.

Smith, P. A factor analytic study of the self concept. *Journal of Consulting Psychology,* 1960, **24,** 191.

Soares, A., & Soares, L. M. Self perceptions of culturally disadvantaged children, *American Educational Research Journal,* 1969, **6,** 31–45.

Soares, A., & Soares, L. M. Critique of Soares and Soares self-perceptions of culturally disadvantaged children—a reply. *American Educational Research Journal,* 1970, **7,** 631–635.

Spaulding, R. L. Achievement, creativity and self-concept correlates of teacher-pupil transactions in elementary schools. In C. B. Stendler (Ed.), *Readings in child behavior and development.* New York: Harcourt, Brace, and World, 1954.

Spitz, R. A. *No and yes: On the genesis of human communication.* New York: International Universities Press, 1957.

Sprung, B. *Guide to non-sexist early childhood education.* New York: Women's Action Alliance, 1974.

Spurlock, J. D. Problems of identification in young black children—static or changing? *Journal of the National Medical Association,* 1969, **61,** 504–507.

Stabler, J. R. & Johnson, E. E. Children's perception of black and white boxes and bobo dolls as a reflection of how they regard their own and other's racial membership. (ERIC, ED069406) Paper presented at the American Psychological Association, Washington, D.C., September 2–8, 1972.

Stabler, J. R., Johnson, E. E. & Jordon, S. E. The measurement of children's self-concepts as related to racial membership. *Child Development,* 1971, **42,** 2094–2097.

Stagner, R. Homeostasis as a unifying concept in personality theory. *Psychological Review,* 1951, **58,** 5–17.

Stanchfield, J. M. *Sex differences in learning to read.* Bloomington, Ind.: Phi Delta Kappa Educational Foundation, 1973.

Stanwyck, D. J., & Felker, D. W. Intellectual achievement responsibility and anxiety as functions of self-concept of third to sixth grade boys and girls. (ERIC, ED080903) Paper presented at the American Educational Research Association, New York, 1971.

Stevenson, H. W., & Stewart, E. C. A developmental study of racial awareness in young children. *Child Development,* 1958, **29,** 399–409.

Stevenson, H. W., & Stevenson, N. G. Social interaction in an interracial nursery school. *Genetic Psychological Monographs,* 1960, **61,** 37–75.

Strong, D. J., & Feder, D. D. Measurement of the self concept: A critique of the literature. *Journal of Counseling Psychology,* 1961, **8,** 170–178.

Suinn, R. M., & Geiger, J. Stress and the stability of self and other attitudes. *Journal of General Psychology,* 1965, **73,** 177–180.

Sullivan, H. S. Conceptions of modern psychiatry. *Psychiatry* 1940, **3,** 1–117.

Sullivan, H. S. *The meaning of anxiety in psychiatry and in life.* Washington, D.C.: William Alanson White Institute of Psychiatry, 1947.

Sullivan, H. S. *The interpersonal theory of psychiatry.* New York: Norton, 1953.

Survant, A. Building positive self-concepts, *Instructor,* 1972, **81,** 94–95.

Sutherland, R. L. *Color, class and personality.* Washington, D.C.: American Council on Education, 1942.

Swift, M. S. Parent child-rearing attitudes and psychological health of the parent. Unpublished Ph.D. dissertation, Syracuse University, Syracuse, New York, 1966.

Symonds, P. M. *The psychology of parent-child relationships.* New York: Appleton-Century-Crofts, 1939.

Symonds, P. M. *The ego and the self.* New York: Appleton-Century-Crofts, 1951.

Symonds, P. M. What do attitude scales measure: The problem of social desirability. *Journal of Abnormal and Social Psychology,* 1961, **62**, 386–390.

Taylor, J. B. Psychological problems in low income families: A research report, *Bulletin of the Menninger Clinic,* 1965, **29**, 312–325.

Taylor, R. G. Personality traits and discrepant achievement: A review. *Journal of Counseling Psychology,* 1964, **11**, 76–80.

Teigland, J. J. et al. Some concomitants of underachievers at the elementary school level. *Personnel and Guidance Journal,* 1966, **44**, 950–955.

Terman, L. M., & Oden, M. H. *The gifted child grows up. Vol. IV.,* Stanford, Cal.: Stanford University Press, 1947.

Thomas, A. et al. *Behavioral individuality in early childhood.* New York: New York University Press, 1963.

Thorndike, R. L. Pygmalion in the classroom. *The Record* (Teacher's College), 1969, **70**, 805–807.

Tiryakian, E. A. The existential self and the person. In C. Gordon & K. J. Gergen (Eds.), *The self in social interaction.* New York: John Wiley and Sons, 1968.

Tocco, T. S., & Bridges, C. M. Jr., Mother-child self-concept transmission in Florida model follow-through participants. (ERIC, ED047079) Presented at the annual meeting of the American Educational Research Association, New York, February 1971.

Torrance, E. P. *Guiding creative talent.* Englewood Cliffs, N.J.: Prentice-Hall, 1962.

Trent, R. D. The color of the investigator as a variable in experimental research with Negro subjects. *Journal of Social Psychology,* 1954, **40**, 281–287.

Trent, R. D. The relationship between expressed self-acceptance and expressed attitudes toward Negro and white in Negro children. *Journal of Genetic Psychology,* 1957, **91**, 25–31.

Trowbridge, N. T. Self-concept and socio-economic class. *Psychology in the Schools,* 1970, **7**, 305–307.

Trowbridge, N. T. Self-concept and socio-economic status in elementary school children. *American Educational Research Journal,* 1972, **9**, 525–537.

Trowbridge, N. T., & Trowbridge, L. Self-concept and socio-economic status. *Child Study Journal,* 1972, **2**, 123–143.

Tuta, K. M., & Baker, G. P. Self-concept of the disadvantaged child and its modification through compensatory nursery school experience. (ERIC, ED080197) Paper presented at the annual meeting of the American Educational Research Association, New Orleans, La., February 26–March 1, 1973.

Van Der Waals, H. G. Problems of narcissism. *Bulletin of the Menninger Clinic.* 1965, **29,** 293–311.

Van Koughnett, B. C., & Smith, M. E. Enhancing the self-concept in school. *Educational Leadership,* 1969, **27,** 253–255.

Vener, A. M., & Snyder, C. A. The preschool child's awareness and anticipation of adult sex roles. *Sociometry: A Journal of Research in Social Psychology,* 1966, **29,** 159–168.

Vernon, P. A. *Personality assessment: A critical survey.* London: John Wiley and Sons, 1964.

Viney, L. L. Congruence of measures of self-regard. *Psychological Record,* 1966, **16,** 487–493.

Walsh, A. M. *Self-concepts of bright boys with learning difficulties.* New York: Bureau of Publications, Teachers College, Columbia University, 1956.

Ward, S. H., & Braun, J. Self esteem and racial preference in black children. *Journal of Orthopsychiatry,* 1972, **42,** 644–647.

Watson, G. Some personality differences in children related to strict or permissive parental discipline. *Journal of Psychology,* 1957, **44,** 227–249.

Wattenberg, W. W., & Clifford, C. Relation of self-concepts to beginning achievement in reading. *Child Development,* 1964, **35,** 461–467.

Wender, P. H., Pederson, F. H. & Waldrop, M. E. A longitudinal study of early social behavior and cognitive development. *American Journal of Orthopsychiatry,* 1967, **37,** 691–696.

White, R. W. *Ego and reality in psychoanalytic theory: A proposal regarding independent ego energies.* Vol. III. New York: International Universities Press, 1963.

White, W. F., & Bashov, W. L. High self-esteem and identification. *Perceptual and Motor Skills,* 1971, **33,** 1127–1130.

White, W. F., & Richmond, B. O. Perception of self and of peers by economically deprived black and advantaged white fifth graders. *Perceptual and Motor Skills,* 1970, **30,** 533–534.

Whiting, B. B. *Six cultures: Studies of child rearing.* New York: John Wiley and Sons, 1963.

Whiting, J. W. M. Sorcery, sin and the superego: A cross-cultural study of some mechanisms of social control. In M. R. Jones (Ed.), *Nebraska symposium on Motivation.* Lincoln, Neb.: University of Nebraska Press, 1959.

Whiting, J. W. M. Resource mediation and learning by identification. In I. Iscoe & H. W. Stevenson (Eds.), *Personality development in children.* Austin: University of Texas Press, 1960.

Will, J. A. Maternal behavior and sex of infant. (ERIC, ED100518) Paper presented at the annual meeting of the American Psychological Association, New Orleans, La., August 1974.

Williams, D. E. Self-concept and verbal mental ability in Negro preschool children. Unpublished Ph.D. Dissertation, St. John's University, New York, 1968.

Williams, J. E., & Rousseau, C. A. Evaluation and identification responses of Negro preschoolers to the colors black and white. *Perceptual and Motor Skills,* 1971, **33**, 587–599.

Williams, J. H. The relationship of self-concept and reading achievement in first grade children. *Journal of Educational Research,* 1973, **66**, 378–380.

Williams, R. L., & Cole, S. Self-concept and school adjustment. *The Personnel and Guidance Journal,* 1968, **46**, 478–481.

Winn, M. *The fireside book of children's songs.* New York: Simon & Schuster, 1966.

Winnicott, D. W. *Collected papers.* London: Tavistock, 1958.

Wolman, B. (Ed.) *Handbook of child psychoanalysis research: Theory and practice.* New York: Van Nostrand Reinhold Co., 1972.

Wylie, R. C. *The self concept.* Lincoln: University of Nebraska Press, 1961.

Wylie, R. C. Children's estimates of their schoolwork ability as a function of sex, race and socioeconomic level. *Journal of Personality,* 1963, **31**, 204–224.

Wylie, R. C., & Hutchins, E. B. Schoolwork ability estimates and aspirations as a function of socioeconomic level, race and sex. *Psychological Reports,* Monograph Supplement No. 3, 1967, **21**, 781–808.

Yancey, W., Rigsby, L., & McCarthy, J. D. Social position and Self-evaluation: The relative importance of race. *American Journal of Sociology,* 1972, **78**, 338–359.

Yinger, J. M. Research implications of a field view of personality. *American Journal of Sociology,* 1963, **68**, 580–592.

Ziller, R. C. *The social self.* New York: Pergamon Press, 1973.

Zimmerman, I. L., & Allebrand, G. N. Personality characteristics and attitudes toward achievement of good and poor readers. *Journal of Educational Research,* 1965, **59**, 28–30.

Zirkel, P. A. Enhancing the self-concept of disadvantaged students. *California Journal of Educational Research,* 1972, **23**, 125–137.

Zirkel, P. A. Self-concept and the "disadvantage" of ethnic group membership and mixture. *Review of Educational Research*, 1971, **41**, 211–220.

Zirkel, P. A., & Moses, E. Self-concept and ethnic group membership among public school students. *American Educational Research Journal*, 1971, **8**, 253–265.

GENERAL BIBLIOGRAPHY

Backman, C. W., Secord, P. F., & Pierce, J. R. Resistance to change in the self-concept as a function of consensus among significant others. *Sociometry*, 1963, **25**, 102–111.

Beatty, W. H. (Ed.) *Improving educational assessment and An inventory of measures of affective behavior*. Washington, D.C.: Association for Supervision and Curriculum Development, NEA, 1969.

Bowlby, J. *Maternal care and mental health*. New York: Schocken Books, 1966.

Brookover, W. B., & Gottlieb, D. *A sociology of education*. New York: American Book Co., 1964.

Clark, K. *Prejudice and your child*. Boston: Beacon Press, 1963.

Cohen, D. J. *Serving preschool children*. Washington, D.C.: U.S. Department of Health, Education and Welfare, 1974.

Croft, D. J., & Hess, R. D. *An activities handbook for teachers of young children*. (2nd ed.) Boston: Houghton Mifflin, 1975.

Day, B. *Open learning in early childhood*. New York: Macmillan, 1975.

Deutsch, M., Katz, I. & Jensen, A. R. *Social class, race, and psychological development*. New York: Holt, Rinehart and Winston, 1968.

Drager, R. M., & Miller, K. S. Comparative psychological studies of Negroes and whites in the United States. *Psychological Bulletin*, 1960, **57**, 361–402.

Dubin, R., & Dubin, E. Children's social perceptions: A review of research. *Child Development*, 1965, **36**, 809–838.

Erikson, E. H. The concept of identity in race relations. *Daedalus*, 1966, **95**, 145–171.

Erikson, E. H. *Identity and the life cycle*. New York: International Universities Press, 1959.

Frazier, N. & Sadker, M. *Sexism in school and society*. New York: Harper & Row, 1973.

Freud, A. *Normality and pathology in childhood: Assessments of development.* New York: International Universities Press, 1965.

Glasser, W. *Schools without failure.* New York: Harper & Row, 1969.

Gordon, C. & Gergen, K. J. *The self in social interaction.* Vol. 1. New York: John Wiley & Sons, 1968.

Gordon, I. J. *Human development: A transactional perspective.* New York: Harper and Row, 1975.

Grambs, J. D. et al. *Black image: Education copes with color.* Dubuque, Iowa: William C. Brown Co., 1972.

Griffin, L. *Multi-ethnic books for young children: An annotated bibliography for parents and teachers.* Washington, D.C.: National Association for the Education of Young Children, 1970.

Guterman, S. S. (Ed.) *Black psyche. The modal personality patterns of black Americans.* Berkeley, Cal.: The Glendessary Press, 1972.

Hamachek, D. E. (Ed.) *The self in growth, teaching, and learning: Selected readings.* Englewood Cliffs, N.J.: Prentice-Hall, 1965.

Hamachek, D. E. *Encounters with the self.* New York: Holt, Rinehart and Winston, 1971.

Harrison, B. G. *Unlearning the lie: Sexism in school.* New York: Liveright, 1973.

Hartup, W. (Ed.) *The young child: Reviews of research.* Vol. II. Washington, D.C.: National Association for the Education of Young Children, 1972.

Hoffman, L. W. Early childhood experiences and women's achievement motives. *Journal of Social Issues,* 1972, **28,** 129–155.

Jersild, A. T. *In search of self.* New York: Bureau of Publications, Teachers College, Columbia University, 1952.

Jourard, S. M. *The transparent self.* Princeton, N.J.: D. Van Nostrand, 1964.

Keller, S. *The American lower class family.* Albany: New York State Division for Youth, 1967.

Kiester, D. J. *Who am I? The Development of self-concept.* (ERIC, ED082817) Durham, N.C.: Learning Institute of North Carolina, 1973.

Krown, S. *Threes and fours go to school.* Englewood Cliffs, N.J.: Prentice-Hall, 1975.

Kremer, B. *Self-concept development: An abstract bibliography.* (ERIC, ED063015) Washington, D.C.: Office of Education, 1972.

Kvaraceus, W. C. et al. *Negro self-concept: Implications for school and citizenship.* New York: McGraw-Hill, 1965.

LaBenne, W. D., & Greene, B. I. *Educational implications of self-concept theory.* Pacific Palisades, Cal.: Goodyear Publishing Co. 1969.

Leeper, S. H. et al. *Good schools for young children.* (3rd ed.) New York: Macmillan, 1974.

Lewis, H. *Culture, class and poverty.* Washington, D.C.: Health and Welfare Council of the National Capital, 1967.

Lindzey, G., & Hall, C. S. *Theories of personality.* New York: John Wiley & Sons, 1973.

Lowe, C. M. The self concept: Fact or artifact? *Psychological Bulletin.* 1961. **58**, 325–336.

Maccoby, E. E. (Ed.) *The development of sex differences.* London: Tavistock, 1966.

McDevitt, J. B., & Settlage, C. F. *Separation—Individuation: Essays in honor of Margaret S. Mahler.* New York: International Universities Press, 1971.

Minuchin, P. The schooling of tomorrows women. *School Review,* 1972, **80**, 199–208.

Moustakas, C. (Ed.) *The self-explorations in personal growth.* New York: Harper & Row, 1956.

Murphy, L. *The widening world of childhood.* New York: Basic Books, 1962.

Mussen, P. H. (Ed.) *Handbook of research methods in child development.* New York: John Wiley and Sons, 1960.

Mussen, P. H., Conger, J. J. & Kagan, J. *Child development and personality.* New York: Harper & Row, 1969.

National Association for the Advancement of Colored People. *Integrated school books: A descriptive bibliography of 399 pre-school and elementary school texts and story books.* New York: NAACP, 1967.

Parsons, T., & Bales, R. F. *Family, socialization and interaction process.* Glencoe, Ill.: The Free Press, 1955.

Pavenstedt, E. *The drifters: Children of disorganized lower class families.* Boston: Little, Brown, 1967.

Peairs, L., & Peairs, R. H. *What every child needs.* New York: Harper & Row, 1974.

Rabban, M. Sex role identification in young children in two diverse social groups. *Genetic Psychology Monographs,* 1950, **42**, 81–158.

Rausher, S. R., & Young, T. (Eds.) *Sexism: Teachers and young children.* New York: Early Childhood Education Council of New York City, 1974.

Rotter, J. B. *Social learning and clinical psychology.* Englewood Cliffs, N.J.: Prentice-Hall, 1954.

Samuels, S. C. Sex bias—where does it begin, how can it end? *Illinois School Research,* 1975, **12**, 29–36.

Sherif, M., & Cantril, H. *The psychology of ego-involvements.* New York: John Wiley and Sons, 1947.

Silverstein, B., & Krate, R. *Children of the dark ghetto: A developmental psychology.* New York: Praeger Publishers, 1975.

Stacey, J., Bereaud, S. & Daniels, J. *And Jill came tumbling after: Sexism in American education.* New York: Dell Books, 1974.

Stern, C., & Luckenbill, M. *The study of self-concept in young children: An annotated bibliography.* (ERIC, ED076247) Washington, D.C.: Office of Economic Opportunity, Research No. OED-CC-9938, 1972.

Thomas, J. B. *Self-concept in psychology and education: A review of research.* New York: Humanities Press, 1973.

Todd, V. E., & Hefferman, H. *The years before school: Guiding preschool children.* (2nd ed.) New York: Macmillan, 1970.

Torrance, E. P. *Rewarding creative behavior: Experiment in classroom creativity.* Englewood Cliffs, N.J.: Prentice-Hall, 1965.

Trager, H. G., & Radke-Yarrow, M. *They learn what they live.* New York: Harper & Row, 1952.

Warden, S. S. *The leftouts: Disadvantaged children in heterogeneous schools.* New York: Holt, Rinehart and Winston, 1968.

White, D. *Multi-ethnic books for Head Start children, Part I: Black and integrated literature.* Urbana, Ill.: ERIC Clearinghouse on Early Childhood Education, National Laboratory on Early Childhood Education, 1969.

Whiting, J. W. M., & Child, I. L. *Child training and personality: A cross-cultural study.* New Haven: Yale University Press, 1953.

Yamamoto, K. *The child and his image: Self-concept in the early years.* Boston: Houghton Mifflin, 1972.

Yarrow, M. R., Campbell, J. D., & Burton, R. V. *Child rearing: An inquiry into research and methods.* San Francisco: Jessey-Bass, 1968.

SUBJECT INDEX

AUTHOR INDEX

Abraham, K.; 123
Adams, E. B.; 92, 116
Adkins, D. C.; 199
Adler, A.; 48, 63, 95
Ainsworth, L.; 195, 196
Akert, R. U.; 34, 78, 176
Alford, G.; 195, 196
Allebrand, G. N.; 104, 105
Allen, V. L.; 162, 163
Allport, G. W.; 45, 62, 146
Almy, M.; 82, 180
Alroy, P.; 232
Alves, G. J.; 103, 104
Ames, L. B.; 257
Ames, R. E.; 35
Anderson, J. G.; 164
Armstrong, J. G.; 107
Asher, S. R.; 162, 163
Aspy, D. N.; 95
Atkinson, J. W.; 103
Ausuble, D. P.; 91, 159

Ausuble, P.; 159
Auttomen, R. G.; 102
Axelrad, S.; 69

Bacon, M. K.; 127
Bahlke, S.; 109
Baker, G. P.; 166
Bandura, A.; 86, 120, 121
Barry, H.; 127
Bashow, W. L.; 113
Baughman, E. E.; 153, 155
Baumrind, D.; 89, 113, 133
Bayer, L. A.; 126
Bayley, N.; 126
Behrens, M. L.; 88
Benedek, T.; 70
Berg, R. C.; 199
Berger, E. M.; 95
Bernstein, J.; 112, 220, 233
Bernstein, M. E.; 236
Biber, H.; 140

305